Praise for *Higher Love*

"As someone who's never tripped on anything but carpets and stairs, I was SPELLBOUND by *Higher Love*. Think *Eat Pray Love* on acid; insight woven with irreverence, wit with wisdom, devastating heartbreak with laugh-out-loud humor. There's a long and esteemed tradition of men writing about drug use and their attendant spiritual experiences. Why no women? Science, branches of the military, and government are embracing the potential of psychedelics to save and transform lives; *Higher Love* has life-changing potential. If what exists in this genre is all Walt Whitman, Anne Friedman is Emily Dickinson."

Linda Sivertsen, Bestselling Author and Host of the *Beautiful Writers Podcast*

"*Higher Love* is a self-aware memoir that catalogs multiple personal struggles and follows a dedicated pursuit of self-transformation… The text is variously funny, self-critical, wry, cheesy, and reflective of longing. It cracks jokes about difficult moments in the past, but it also becomes serious at the right moments… *Higher Love* is an empathetic memoir that catalogs instances of self-love, discovery, and healing influenced by a healthy dose of recreational drugs."

Clarion Review

"A memoir that'll have you traveling, tripping, and seeing yourself in the passenger seat of a meaningful story of discovery."
"A mind-expanding journey to self-love through self-discovery."

Independent Book Review

"reminds readers of the transformative power of self-love"
"movingly explores romantic loss, construction of identity, and family dynamics"

BlueInk*

"This riveting book by Anne Friedman almost made me miss an appointment because I was so enthralled reading it in the waiting room of my Dr.'s office that I didn't hear my name being called! Whether you want a soulful exploration of a spiritual journey, a gentle intro-

duction to the transformative powers of plant medicines, or simply an engrossing story that takes you around the world and beyond, this is it. I loved every word."
Lynne Twist, Best-Selling Author, Featured Guest on Oprah's Super Soul Sunday, and Founder of The Pachamama Alliance

"Takeaway: Kaleidoscopic roller-coaster ride toward loving oneself."
"heartrending debut, probing one woman's search for worth and meaning in her life"
BookLife

"A probing, often surprising memoir about the search for self."
Kirkus Review

"Everything in this book, from start to finish, spoke to me on a personal level and invited me to look deeper into myself, ask harder questions, and accept gentler answers."
Iris, a Spun Yarn reader in her 30's from Michigan

Leave your review on **Goodreads.com**

Copyright © 2024 by Anne Kiehl Friedman

All rights reserved.

No portion of this book may be reproduced in any form without written permission from the publisher or author, except as permitted by U.S. copyright law.

This book is designed to provide information and entertainment, NOT to render any type of psychological, legal, medical, or any other professional advice. Psychedelic science is constantly evolving and one person's anecdotal experience should NOT be taken as fact or recommendation. The content is the sole expression and opinion of the author who is NOT a doctor or medical professional. Neither the publisher nor the author shall be liable for any physical, psychological, emotional, financial, or commercial damages. The author and publisher assume no responsibility or liability for any errors or omissions in the content of this book. The information contained is provided on an "as is" basis with no guarantees of completeness, accuracy, usefulness, or timeliness. A resources section has been included to assist readers in seeking out trustworthy guidance from experts. You are responsible for your own choices, actions, and results. Be exquisitely careful with any tool or substance as powerful as psychedelics.

This work reflects the real experiences of the author as accurately as her memory allows. Some names and characteristics have been changed, some events have been compressed, and occasionally, dialogue consistent with the character or nature of the person speaking has been supplemented. All persons within are actual individuals; there are no composite characters.

Book Cover by Marianne Wellman

First edition 2024

A Note on Psychedelic Safety
Don't Do What I Did

I'm a writer. Not a doctor, scientist, or health practitioner of any kind. I wrote this book hoping that sharing my experiences might help others find similar healing. Though my experiences with psychedelics have netted out in the positive column, I've had some really bad experiences that could have been much worse without good luck and good therapy.

For your safety and well-being, do **not** use my choices as a guide or example to be followed. Different bodies process substances differently, different substances have different potencies, different sources of the same substances have different potencies… If I've learned anything about psychedelics, it's that there's no predicting the experience or outcome. I've taken small doses and had huge epiphanies, taken large doses and felt stone sober, taken the exact same amount of the exact same substance at a different time of year and had completely opposite experiences. There's still so much we don't know—about contraindications, risks, lasting adverse effects, etc. With something as powerful and unpredictable as psychedelic substances, the only appropriate approach is: extreme reverence. Better to stay away than to be reckless.

Finally, please be exquisitely gentle with yourself in any quest for healing. You deserve gentleness.

Contents

Dedication	IX
Title Page	XI
Prologue	1
1. Better Man	3
2. Somebody That I Used To Know	11
3. Choux Pastry Heart	17
4. Habits	23
5. Take It All	31
6. Magic	35
7. Castles	45
8. What A Feeling	67
9. No Roots	73
10. Bleeker & 6th	77
11. Butterfly	91
12. Bailando	97
13. Can't Stop The Feeling!	105
14. Rock the Casbah	113
15. Open Arms	121
16. The Few Things	125
17. Consequences	127

18. Love's Divine	131
19. Joy To The World	135
20. Annie	147
21. White Horse	155
22. Harvester of Sorrow	159
23. Thank U, Next	171
24. Can't Help Falling In Love	175
25. SUPERBLOOM	193
26. Sweet Child O' Mine	205
27. Umbrella	211
28. Don't Hurt Yourself	217
Epilogue	233
Resources	237
Risk Awareness and Harm Reduction	239
Acknowledgements	241
About the author	243

This book is dedicated to the balcony section:
Phyllis, Howie, Jerry, Sissy, Teddy, and all the benevolent ancestors whose guidance and wisdom nourish us today.

Higher Love
a psychedelic travel memoir of heartbreak and healing
Anne Kiehl Friedman

Boldspark

Prologue
At Last

Big Island, Hawaii
September 2018
Substances ingested: an unquantified but potent amount of LSD

Warm water lapped at my ribs as I arched my body to absorb more moonlight. It felt warm, recharging, palpable like the sun. Though it had been hours since consuming the LSD, a shimmering euphoria still accompanied every sensation. Moving my fingers in the water, I noticed they left streaks like bioluminescent algae. But bioluminescent algae doesn't live in chlorinated hot tubs. As magical as it all felt, I was still in touch with reality.

In reality, over the brown hum of the jacuzzi pump, I listened transfixed to the deep voice listing all the reasons I was "infinitely and acutely loveable."

"I'll begin with the physical: I love the way my hands can grab your hips. I like being able to grab ahold of you."

I felt hands gripping my hips, inching more of my naked body above the water line.

"I love that you're substantial. That you're strong, and powerful, and opinionated."

I gasped. I had never even *thought* someone could love me for that. I had always believed the best I could hope for was someone loving me despite it. Relief washed over me, decades of pain dissolving into unexpected tears. I relaxed into the cradle of the strong hands supporting me.

"I love the shape of your body."

Which shape? The semi-circles of dimpled cellulite on my thighs? The distended bell curve of my belly? Impossible. But I didn't say anything. I didn't want to interrupt and risk being right.

As if overhearing my thoughts, the voice insisted:

"I love *every* shape of your body. *You* are your body, and your body is you; they're not separate. How could I not love every inch of it when I love you?"

Despite my best efforts to argue, I couldn't. The people I love, I don't love in spite of or as separate from their bodies. I don't even think about their bodies most of the time.

The voice returned, louder than my thoughts, and said, "I want you to eat and be fully alive. I don't want you at half-strength; I want the you-est you I can get."

There was no verbal hesitation, no sign of a lie or omission.

I finally relaxed my vigilance. Stopped being aware of my stomach. Took a full, deep breath and allowed myself to enjoy being held by someone who loved me. Happy tears, tears of joy and love and release slid down the sides of my face and pooled in my ears, feeling cool compared to the heat of the water.

I had never known I could be loved like this. Truly seen and fully accepted. All of the "flaws" I'd tried so hard to hide or change were held like treasures under the moonlight.

Was this really happening?

It was.

Finally.

I was falling in love with someone who knew the real me and loved her without reservation, manipulation, or ulterior motives. This time, I knew it was forever.

Chapter 1
Better Man

Washington, DC
March 2011
Substances ingested: strawberry mimosas and a toke or two

Society sets up getting married and having kids as the two most important things a woman can do with her life, and I wanted them at least as much as I was told I should. Nearing thirty, having had boyfriends but never really being *in love*, going to friends' weddings practically every weekend, constantly alone, dodging calls because I didn't want to hear another pregnancy announcement… I didn't know what was wrong with me. Why everyone else seemed to slide so easily into a loving union and I was forced to learn to sunscreen my own back.

If I were *good enough*, I thought that would put me beyond criticism, keep me safe and get me loved. Not consciously, but intractably. Consciously, I knew "perfect" was a capitalistic, patriarchal lie to keep women spending billions of dollars to prop up the global economy on their insecurity. But even seeing behind the rhetorical veil, I still wanted nothing more than the insulation, security, and self-worth I thought came with being chosen. Because little girls are taught to want to be chosen. I hadn't been chosen yet, so I needed to work on being more perfect.

Walking down Connecticut Avenue on one of those rare, perfect spring days in DC, when all the crocuses are blooming before summer's humidity hits, I knew this would be my last date for a while. Not because David2828 looked especially promising on his profile or that he'd wowed me in the chats we exchanged trying to set up this brunch, but because I was thoroughly burnt out from the searing mediocrity—and occasional horrors—of online dating. I was only going out with David because I'd already agreed to it and didn't want to flake. My ambivalence slowed my departure and I was running twenty minutes late. I'd apologized via text but still felt bad about it when I opened the door to Kramer's, a bookstore and restaurant in Dupont Circle that was my go-to for first dates. Even if the company sucked, the strawberry mimosas would make it tolerable. I basically stopped drinking after being diagnosed with chronic Lyme Disease after college, so these occasional cocktails were a rare treat for me.

Flinging the door open, I heard "David, your table is ready," announced as I almost collided with a man perusing books at the entrance. He was my height, or a little shorter, but solid like a brick wall, wearing jeans and a loose flannel. Our eyes met momentarily—his blue and even more intensely so set against his tan. To my automatic question on first impressions of first dates, *Can I see myself ever wanting to have sex with him?* I thought, *Yeah, maybe.*

"Oh, are you David?" I asked as we both moved toward the hostess stand.

"Yeah, Anne?" He asked, pronouncing my name the way it's spelled.

"Yeah, but it's actually pronounced 'Annie.'"

"I like that," he said, but the way he smiled made me think he liked more than my name. I hadn't worn any makeup because I wasn't expecting much from this date, and it was 11:23 a.m. on a Sunday, the most unsexy time ever that can still, acceptably, be suggested for a date. I was wearing a button-down shirt dress I bought at Goodwill and my favorite pair of Steve Madden boots, legs shaved below the knee. I felt myself flush under his gaze, self-conscious that I hadn't tried harder, and tentatively excited that he didn't seem to want more.

"What did you pick out?" I asked after we were seated, gesturing at the bag in his hand.

"Another copy of a favorite. Have you read *The History of Love* by Nicole Krauss?"

"No, is it good?" I asked out of habit, liking the cover and him for choosing a book by a woman author.

"Here, I guess it was for you." He said, sliding his recently purchased copy across the table. "I only shop at independent bookstores and I try to buy something every time I come in." I was smitten before the bread basket arrived.

We ate, talking for hours until we couldn't justify keeping the table any longer.

"Do you want a ride home? I know you walked." He asked, putting his hand lightly against the small of my back as we exited the restaurant's patio.

"It's such a beautiful day; I'd really like to walk. But I'd also like to keep talking." I said, wanting to make it clear that my desire to walk was really to walk, not to get away from him.

"How about I drive you home and we walk around there?"

"Great."

He opened the door to the passenger seat of his silver Range Rover and offered his hand to help me climb in. I gave him directions—there were only two turns—back to the home of a family friend where I was living for the summer. It was a giant, purple Victorian with eight bedrooms and a million windows.

"Which is your room?" He asked on our second loop strolling around the neighborhood.

"That one," I said, pointing to a window on the third floor overlooking the garden.

"I can just see you," he said, "leaning out the window, smoking a cigarette."

"I don't smoke... cigarettes," I said, surprised but excited that he had taken a romantic tone when talking about smoking and a little fearful of how he'd react to my confession.

"Pot?"

"Yeah." My vice of choice was medically legal but not nearly as socially acceptable as wine, caffeine, exercise, or starvation—society's sanctioned addictions. I'd started smoking cannabis regularly right after college when it was still called "weed" and because of the aforementioned Lyme Disease. By now it was a habit. He was a successful business owner with a fancy car and a (rented) house in the suburbs; I didn't know what he'd think.

"Oh, I roll a *beautiful* joint. Truly a work of art. Come over. I'll make you dinner and roll one for you."

"Haha, sure. Threaten me with a good time." I said, relieved by his easy acceptance and genuinely tempted to sample his craft.

"No, I meant now." Two hours of brunch, sitting and chatting, then two hours of strolling meant that it was nearly four p.m. "Do you have anything you have to do today? Get in the car and I'll make you whatever you want for dinner. I really can cook."

Our time already felt so natural together, and I *didn't* have anything else I needed to do.

"You don't need to cook," I said, scared of being too much work and fearful of eating in front of him. I was the skinniest I'd been in a while from limiting myself to one meal a day, and I'd already eaten brunch. But the butterflies of infatuation were making me a pleasant type of nauseous, and I trusted that to curb my appetite. I'd eat like a bird in front of him and he'd like me even more. "On second thought, okay. Let's go."

He took me to his immaculately decorated, three-bedroom rental home in the Maryland suburb, Bethesda. Painted white, sandwiched between equally charming houses that had kids' toys forgotten in the yard, his had a screened-in porch and a dining room table for six.

The other dudes I'd dated had roommates, mattresses on the floor, and the haunting scent of mildew on their sheets.

David was different. He struck me as a *man*. He knew what he wanted and went after it, built things with his hands, drove a stick shift like he was born knowing how. He opened doors and reached for the check. He had all the symbols society taught me to look for and want. Sipping a glass of wine, sitting in one of his matching dining chairs watching him chop shallots for the trout cassoulet he was preparing, made me feel grown-up. I wasn't an aimless 27-year-old doing my best impression of adulthood anymore. He treated me like I was special, and I felt special because chose me.

Over the evening, I learned his family was Jewish and historically prominent. His grandfather was a builder who made a lot of money in real estate (enough to buy an NFL team) but lost the bulk to a combination of betrayal, lousy luck, and generous giving. He would be honored with the Humanitarian Award by some nonprofit next month, and without hesitation, David invited me to be his date.

Coming from money was usually something I tried to hide because I saw it as a personal moral failing, but David's background made me feel comfortable sharing.

My dad's side of the family was Jewish and historically prominent, too, because Levi Strauss was an ancestor far back and off to the side of my dad's family tree. He'd lived generations upon generations ago, but that legacy meant I was born with a lot of privilege and even more guilt.

Perversely, being born with a trust fund (small by comparison with the 1% or anyone who flies private, but massive by comparison with the billions who suffer food insecurity and worse) had always made me feel worthless. I grew up in a very politically active household. Discussions of how the tax code is rigged against low-wage earners and how laws against abortion only apply to those who can't afford a plane ticket to Japan were commonplace dinnertime conversations. My parents saw it as their responsibility to make me aware of injustice, so I would grow up to do something about it.

From as early as I can remember, I knew I didn't do anything to deserve having more than I needed when others didn't have enough. I thought if I were *really* a good person, I would give it all away. But I didn't. I remember crying the night before my 12th birthday because I was getting so old and hadn't done anything meaningful to end homelessness. Money became a source of shame for me. It was proof that I was a bad person, that I hadn't worked for what I had, that if the world were fair, I wouldn't even exist. Anything I achieved, I drew a straight line back to the lucky accident of the zip code of my birth.

Love would be the only exception. Soulmates don't choose each other based on a résumé. If someone *loved* me, it wouldn't be because I had fancy people signing my recommendation letters. If someone—someone good with lots of options—chose me as his life partner, finally, I'd know I was valuable and worth loving. Someone wanting to marry and make babies with me was the one thing I thought would justify my existence.

Quickly after we started dating, I was spending every night with David. He asked me to move in with him on our fifth date, which sounds more dramatic than it was because all I needed to do was transfer two suitcases from the guest bedroom of my friend's house to the empty dresser in David's extra bedroom. The first morning after he and I had sex, I woke up bleary-eyed and disheveled, self-conscious of my morning breath, and worried that he wouldn't want me now that he'd had me.

"Good morning, little bear," he said as he nuzzled into my neck, giving me sweet kisses all over my face. He rolled three things I hated about myself—my hairiness, my irritability, and my intimidating size—into an endearment that made me feel cute instead. I fell in love with him and the nickname at the same time.

For my 28th birthday, a month and a half after we met, he cooked. He made all my favorite foods, but better than usual: flank steak with chimichurri, pesto pasta with oven-dried chanterelles, an arugula salad with shaved parmesan and extra extra extra virgin olive oil hand-imported from Italy. My family—mom, dad, sister, grandma, aunt, uncle, and two cousins who happened to be in town—joined us for the meal, and they welcomed him with open arms. They had every reason to; I was glowing, and the food was delicious.

My dad—a kind man, mid-sixties, with glasses and a penchant for brightly-colored dress shirts perennially stained by the ballpoint pens he keeps in his front pocket—had accepted anyone I'd ever brought home, so it wasn't a surprise that *they* got along. "Anyone who can cook like that is welcome into the family." My dad, a deeply generous, loving, and oblivious person, saw only the best in everyone he met.

My mom, by contrast, was tough. She spent her childhood being repeatedly abandoned by neglectful parents who racked up nine marriages between the two of them and sent her to fourteen schools—including a boarding school in a different country from both of them--before she'd turned eleven. She learned to fend for herself young and has ever since. As a single 20-something, she built herself a log cabin in the hills of South Carolina and lived there alone, chopping wood and fetching water, through rough winters and multiple burglaries. The second time she was robbed she thought "I only have my recipe cards left," and the third time they stole those, too. She was the one who protected my dad from the dangers of his blind optimism about people, planning, and the future.

"Seems honest," she said about David, which was both high praise and a baseline requirement for her, but she'd need more than that to fall in love with him as I had. After my sister's recent and painful divorce, my mom was even more fiercely protective of us, aware that her daughters, having inherited our dad's naivete, tended to fall for charming narcissists. Her childhood had taught her a shrewdness we lacked.

My sister Alison, four years older than me, was the stereotype of a perfect first child—straight A's throughout school and into Stanford, never got caught sneaking out or getting drunk, and has worked on eradicating modern slavery for most of her professional life. Unlike the rest of my hippie family, she has never smoked pot and barely drinks. From the outset, she didn't particularly like or trust David, and David didn't try to win her over. To be fair, he didn't try to win anyone over. Once, my sister invited us to a house party her friends were hosting and fought with David after he drove us home when she thought he was drunk. He insisted he was fine but Alison had been counting his drinks and had good reason to worry. I felt caught in the middle, but released when he said, "Your sister and I are both adults; we'll deal with it directly."

The first time he met my best friend Adelynn and she jokingly threatened him about never hurting me, he didn't crack a smile or offer any assurances that he wouldn't, just that he was sure I could stand up for myself. He didn't say much for the rest of the night and I felt the effort of ping-ponging between them, trying to stitch a friendship. I wasn't surprised when he said he didn't particularly like her on the drive home afterward. "She's just jealous she's losing you to me; it's okay, friendships like that fade away when you meet your person." She'd been my best friend for a decade and he'd only been in my life for weeks, but I let him assert primacy in my life because I wanted to pair up. Perhaps I should have seen the red flags then: his tendency to be controlling, his unwillingness to accommodate others, his imperiousness... Instead, I just saw those traits as the marks of a *real man*.

We'd been dating for just shy of two months when he flew out to join me in Hawaii for a vacation I'd scheduled before we met. On our third day, we went for a swim in the ocean to a private cove. Small waves crashed into smooth black stones as I lay with my eyes closed, soaking up the sun, David next to me. The rocks shifted as he turned onto his side, facing me, and I opened my eyes when he started talking because he didn't usually sound so earnest. He said, "I know you've worried about being perfect enough to be loved. I want this ring to be a symbol—proof—that you are, and that I will love you forever." There were rainbows on his face and scattered across his chest. I looked down to find the source of the refraction, expecting to find a broken sunglass lens or bottle top, but he was holding a ring. A diamond ring. A *big* diamond ring. I thought he'd found it on the beach and started scanning the ground for other pieces of expensive lost jewelry.

"Anytime you get insecure, I want you to be able to look down at your left hand and know that you are perfect."

The ring was for me. He was proposing to me.

Fixating on that sparkling solitaire that symbolized so much, I didn't think about the fact that he'd been married and divorced before. I didn't think about what he must have said to her when he'd proposed and that it probably wasn't *that* different from what he had just said to me. I did not think about how any relationship predicated upon someone's perfection was fundamentally doomed. I didn't even think about the fact that I barely knew him. I just ate up his declarations of love and perfection like I was starved for them. Because I was.

With his proposal, David told me that I had achieved the impossible. His proposal meant that I had been wrong every time I had felt unlovable for myriad reasons: too fat, too ugly, too stupid, too smart, too tall, too hairy, too messy, too demanding, too needy, too pedantic, too prone to list-making. David wanted me on his arm, for life, because he thought it—I—made him look good. He chose me, and therefore I was worthwhile. I could mold myself around him, filling the gaps, taking up the space around his preferences and idiosyncrasies. It wasn't the feminist, agentic, multifaceted existence I'd fight for anyone else to have, but seeing myself as one-half of a pair of soul mates made me feel like I'd finally found my place.

Stanford University had given me two degrees, but no idea what to do with them. I graduated with one BA in political science and another in sociology, with honors and a few awards, but didn't know what to do when the moving walkway of school, grades, and academic accomplishments ended. Through my twenties, I'd jumped from one ostensibly successful career to another—speechwriting for celebrities, running my own strategic communications consultancy, studying business management as a Ph.D. candidate at Northwestern on the path to a professorship—trying to prove I was worth something. Now I knew I was.

David was very clear about who he wanted me to be and I gravitated toward that certainty. With him, I didn't need to worry about figuring out my future because he would. I didn't need to worry that I'd die old and alone, undesired, undesirable, unloved, unlovable. I didn't need to worry about being the last among my friends to marry, or turning 30 single, or all my eggs drying up before a man chose me. My worst fears weren't going to happen!

The intensity of feelings I couldn't name and had never felt before overwhelmed me and I sobbed. He held me and I kissed him desperately, gratefully. I extended my left hand; he slipped the ring on my finger. We made love on the rocks, our feet in the waves. It was the "happily ever after" of fairytales. When we swam back to the beach, I kept my left hand clenched in the tightest fist I'd ever made, terrified of letting go.

Chapter 2

Somebody That I Used To Know

Washington, DC
May 2012
Substances ingested: all my pride and a million joints

Barely more than a year later, I was sitting on the couch, clutching my knees against my chest in the high-rise apartment building David had chosen despite my mild fear of heights. It was one of the innumerable decisions he'd made without me, including…to end our engagement? He hadn't told me he wanted out, he'd just pulled away. Stopped talking to me slowly over time until he wouldn't even answer my calls. I'd worry my engagement ring around and around my finger, wondering if I even *had* a fiancé anymore. None of the wedding magazines I'd bought to shop for dresses had any advice about what to do when your betrothed disappears on you. Nothing *happened*, at least as far as I knew, he just… stopped loving me?

Eventually, I confronted him and he asked for two months of space to figure his shit out. I still loved him and wanted to be with him, so I agreed. But now it was two months later and shit remained, well, shitty.

He paced in front of me, lit from behind by the lamp in the bedroom, hulking, if that word could be applied to a man who had to stretch to reach 5'10". He'd gained weight in the two months we'd spent apart. The added girth made him look not exactly *older* than his 35 years, but tired. I might have taken some pleasure in this, a little schadenfreude, but I was pretty sure my own weight gain had been even less forgiving.

I tried to squeeze my knees closer to my chest but my belly wouldn't allow it. I imagined my body, doughy and massive, weighing down one side of the couch and making it look like doll furniture. I felt the expanse of the back of my thighs and knew David must also be disgusted at the excessive space I occupied. I wished I could use one of his fancy chef's knives to cut off my gut, saddlebags, and loose flesh on the back of my arms.

David was usually tidy to the point of obsession, proud of the fact that every item he owned was the finest of its type with a specific place to live. But here, now, it looked like he had moved in days ago, not months before when we'd begun our trial separation. Cardboard boxes were stacked behind the door, allowing it to open only halfway and getting bashed every time someone entered the room. A layer of dust had settled on every surface. Not fine dust, not the dust accumulated in a week or two of normal life, but visible drifts of lint and dirt and hair piling up against the baseboards.

He paced in the three square feet of space left empty between mounds of shiny black garbage bags full to bursting. One trash bag had torn, revealing what looked like a few of his very expensive, now rumpled, Brunello Cuccinelli sweaters. Typically, they would be folded carefully, loosely, to prevent pulling or pilling, but I could see that the arm of one of his favorites was caught in the head of a metal hanger.

I'd been chain-smoking joints since he picked me up at the airport, needing a layer of emotional anesthetic to survive what felt like losing a limb. The future I'd envisioned and wedded myself to—wife, mother, kids, grandkids, celebrating our 50th anniversary, dying in side-by-side rocking chairs—was gone.

He was talking but I didn't hear what he was saying because I was staring at the industrial meat slicer occupying his coffee table. The size, shininess, and potential violence of the blade had always scared me, but there was something tempting about it now. Every inch of useable space in his kitchen was covered with non-kitchen belongings and I knew he hadn't been cooking. He used to love cooking. He used to love me, too, I realized, and the thought tasted like my tongue on a blade.

I breathed a mouthful of smoke into my lungs and held it for a moment before letting it out through my nostrils. The marijuana did its job, floating me out of the present and into my memories. I remembered last Thanksgiving when David bragged to his father that he could use the meat slicer to cut the holiday turkey so thinly that it would be translucent.

"Because that's how I like my meat," deadpanned his father, "translucent."

His father was gruff like that, but also sweet and magnanimous. I loved David's family. Losing them might be the worst part of breaking up. I took a hit off the joint held between my thumb and forefinger, noticing that it was about half-smoked and I'd have to roll another soon if I wanted to keep consuming at this rate. The smoke curled into languid rings and out the open door to the balcony.

When my Lyme doctor told me that cannabis had the fewest dangerous side effects of all the medications she could prescribe to deal with my symptoms, I considered it a free pass to indulge. I had definitely taken it beyond the prescribed needs, into the realm of self-medication, but now wasn't the time to kick out the only support keeping this conversation from crushing me.

He stopped pacing, caught me in eye contact and held it, imploringly. There was hope in his voice when he said, "I really think this could be the best thing that ever happened for us."

I squinted. "What do you mean 'this could be the best thing that ever happened for us'?" There was so much not to understand in his statement. First and foremost: "us." He had just told me that he didn't want there to be an "us" anymore. He had just ended our engagement. How could our breakup—the dissolution of "us"—be the best thing that ever happened for "us"?

His speech quickened with excitement. "These friends? Stephanie and Tom? They broke up years ago but they're married now. They say the time they spent apart did it. They swear they wouldn't be married or happy now if they hadn't split up. It could be the same for us."

That word again.

But this time it made a little more sense. It made sense that he seemed emotionally immune to our breakup. In his mind, this wasn't the end. It was the beginning of an ellipsis... Something to be continued later when we weren't so broken.

"You think we're going to get back together?" I asked.

"I—I don't know what's going to happen," he hedged.

"I mean. Of course not; neither of us do. But you think that?" My voice, monotone, echoed from the hollow cavern of my body. "You believe there's a future where we're back together?"

"Yeah," he answered, like it was obvious. He stopped fiddling with the corner of the pocket on his jeans and met my eyes again, but softer this time. "Yes," he repeated, and my heart lifted a little.

Taking another toke, I let it settle into my lungs and calm my mind. "What odds?" I asked, trying to narrow down the range of possibilities.

He'd started pacing again but the question knocked him off his rhythm.

"What do you mean?" He'd stopped in front of the coffee table barely two feet away, looking at me confused.

"What odds?" I pushed myself up, attempting to sit a little taller against the armrest I'd darkened with falling ash. He was a business guy, a contractor who owned his own building firm and ran the enterprise based on what the numbers told him. I wanted him to quantify the chances, in his mind, that we would end up married with kids and a suburban home. The life I thought we dreamt about together.

"What do you think the percentage likelihood is that we'll get back together? 10 percent? 15? It's obviously not a hundred. Do you think it's more or less than 25?" Maybe percentages, statistics, would distract me from the searing pain in my chest.

"Anne." He pronounced my name like everyone who loved me pronounced it: with a hard e made soft, like a diminutive term of endearment.

He repeated it, this time it was a plea. He so clearly wanted me to let him off the hook, to stop asking questions, to be satisfied with his "I don't know" to my inquisition about what had changed, when, and how.

I couldn't do it. "Just tell me," I implored, resenting the weakness in my voice. "I'm not going to hold you to it. It can be a range. I'm just trying to understand. To get inside your head because it doesn't seem like this bothers you at all." My voice faltered, eyes welled up, but I struggled to maintain control because I knew he would be disappointed in me if I cried. He always wanted an elegant, unflappable woman, a woman who would check her manicure and say "your loss" to a fiancé who decided he didn't want her anymore.

Maybe he never wanted to marry me. Maybe he proposed impulsively, in the throes of lust and infatuation, knowing an engagement was easily broken if he decided he didn't want me anymore. Which now he knew he didn't.

The thought made me physically ill. Nauseated. That I could be so wrong, love someone so much, get totally blindsided... I wanted to puke but instead took another toke.

My knees had been drawn up tight for so long that I could no longer feel my feet but I didn't mind. I didn't want to feel anything. My arms were crossed, hands clenched into fists jammed under my armpits. I pushed myself farther back into the corner of the couch, needing to find support somewhere. No matter how much pot I smoked, I would not be able to stand this much longer. I was on the verge of breaking down, sobbing, hyperventilating, vomiting, then sobbing again, cycle on repeat. But first, I needed answers.

"I would guess that we have a 50-94% chance of getting back together," he said. Then, he met my eyes again, "If you let us." He said it like he was reaching out for me. Like he was telling me that he wanted to be with me, to end up with me, but first he had to sort out some issues alone. We could live happily ever after, and it all depended on what I said next.

I wanted to believe it. To play along.

"You know that's not going to happen, right?" I wasn't certain about anything except that I could never go through this again. My pride would never allow me to get back together with someone who dumped me once and without explanation, *especially* after an engagement. But even if I set my ego aside, my heart couldn't handle it. "If we break up now, it's for good. I can't..."

I had no idea how to finish the sentence.

I knew I wasn't supposed to tell him how much this was breaking me. I was stoic. Strong. Elegant.

"I just need time," he was pleading now, but only a little. "Listen. I'm doing the same things to you I did to my ex-wife. I don't know how to stop." He couldn't meet my eyes. He had married his high school girlfriend at twenty-five and was divorced by thirty. She cheated on him but I was starting to think their demise was not so one-sided. His voice grew somber, like he didn't want to admit the next part:

"I destroy everyone I love."

A technicolor image of a cruise ship demolishing a tiny wooden pier burst into my mind. His mom, his ex-wife, his sister, the woman he dated before me who wouldn't stop texting him, the other woman in San Diego who told him to stop contacting her, *me*: we were the pier and he was thousands and thousands of pounds of force. He didn't mean to destroy us, he just didn't know how to stop.

Once, during a trip to Puerto Rico, he pulled the barrette out of my hair because he preferred I wear it down, rubbed my blush and foundation off with his hands because he didn't like it when I wore makeup, and ripped a five-inch hole in the waist of my dress because he didn't like that I was walking away from him and had grabbed hold too tightly. Each time, I'd made excuses for him. I told myself it was a good thing that he liked my hair undone, thought I was prettiest unadorned, wanted my company enough to reach for me and pull me toward him. Plus, the dress was vintage with stitching at least sixty years old, so it wasn't really his fault.

I was making new excuses for him now: he was being unnecessarily cruel to himself, taking on responsibility that wasn't his, sparing me the truth of why he stopped loving me. My mind fell into its well-trodden groove of self-blame. If it was my fault, something wrong with me, I could fix it. I just needed to figure it out.

It was something I did. Something I didn't do. Something I did, but not well enough to satisfy him.

I didn't want to ask him because I knew it would make me look weak, needy, and grasping. I didn't want to ask because I wasn't sure I could handle the answer. But this was my last chance to have his leaving make sense. I forced myself to make eye contact because I needed to see him react.

Slowly and with effort, I asked, "Did I do something wrong?" I made it through that question but faltered on the next: "Something to make you stop loving—?" The admission of it, the spoken words broke me. The tears came heavy and fast. I couldn't look at him. I didn't want him to see that I still loved him so goddamn completely. Snot ran from my nose, down my lip, racing for my chin. I tried to sniff it back up but it was too much and there weren't any tissues. Fuck him for not having tissues. But also, he was right not to love me. How could anyone love someone so messy.

I covered my face with my hands and bent over in shame, holding my breath and wishing I could suck myself into nonexistence. Suddenly I was swept up, off the couch and into his arms, then onto his chest in a tight bundle. I had never been a small girl but somehow, in that minute, I fit like one. He sat on the couch and rocked me.

"Shhh, shhh. Shhh, little bear." It was the first time he'd used my pet name since we separated, and he said it with such tenderness. I sobbed harder. "There's nothing you could have done." I didn't open my eyes but he sounded choked up. "It's me. It's my fault. If I can't make it work with you, I can't make it work with anyone. I'm so sorry. I'm so sorry."

I don't know how long I cried. Long enough to leave his shirt wet with tears and mucus. Long enough to exhaust us both.

Eventually, the tears subsided and I rolled awkwardly off his chest and down onto the carpet. I crawled to what was once my side of the bed on his mattress on the floor. It was almost two in the morning. He followed. He kissed me goodbye. We tried to find each other in the dark, tried to have sex to find some sort of comfort, but I didn't blame him when it didn't work. He'd always told me he'd be more attracted to me if I were at least fifteen pounds skinnier and this only proved he was honest. We gave up and slept—not long, not well—fully clothed, clinging to opposite edges of the mattress.

The next morning we both woke up early. He got up and made coffee, but I pretended to sleep until it would be weird to stay in bed any longer.

When I emerged, he didn't want to talk and I knew there was nothing to say. He didn't love me anymore and I refused to try to convince him. There's no compromise to be made when someone says they don't want to marry you. Even if you succeed in wearing them down, what have you won?

He walked to the balcony where I'd gone to smoke a joint before even brushing my teeth. He said it had been a few days since he'd worked out and wanted to go to CrossFit if that was okay with me. I nodded. "You'll be here when I get back?" he asked, trying to pretend like he didn't want me to go, but not hard enough.

"Yeah," I said. I think we both knew we were lying.

Chapter 3

Choux Pastry Heart

En route, Washington DC to Chicago
May 2012
Substances ingested: copious amounts of cannabis

I waited, one minute, then two, after David left before I booked my flight back to Chicago. Fleeing was my reflex to pain. We'd been long-distance for about six months, since I started my PhD program in Chicago, and it had worked in our favor for the last two months when he'd asked for space to figure out if he still wanted to get married. We'd met and fallen in love in DC a handful of months before I was scheduled to start a doctorate program in Management and Organizations at Kellogg Business School at Northwestern University. The distance had been a strain on us then, but in that moment I was grateful I had somewhere to go that wasn't his. I needed to get away, hoping physical distance would soothe my emotional ache.

The chat feature in my email inbox blinked in the lower left corner of my screen as I was booking my flight.

"You okay? What's going on?"

It was Adelynn, checking in on me via another medium after I'd sent her calls to voicemail and left her texts unread since arriving in DC to confront my imploding relationship. Adelynn was the daughter of a Lutheran minister and had grown up in rural Georgia. She'd been valedictorian of her high school, a mathlete, a National Merit Scholar, and a musical theater nerd. We went to the activities faire together during orientation at Stanford after meeting in our freshman dorm—I was trying to be a more outgoing version of myself and pretended to make the invitation so casual that I wouldn't notice if she said no, We'd been friends ever since checking out all the same extracurriculars: politics, theatre, improv, even salsa dancing, though both of us self-selecting out of that last one after determining we weren't sufficiently coordinated. Seven years after graduation, she'd over-achieved her way into a Presidential Management Fellowship and worked for the State Department writing speeches for Secretary Clinton, like a total fucking badass.

But perhaps because I'd held her in the rawest moments after she found out her father had died unexpectedly, there was no pride between us. Adelynn was one of few people I had told when my engagement moved from fact to question mark. She lived in Columbia Heights, a 15-minute drive from David's apartment where I was shoving the few items I'd unpacked back into a rolling bag.

"No. Not okay," I wrote. "We're done. I'm going back to Chicago."

When?

I zipped my bag and responded, *"Now."*

"How are you getting to the airport?" Then, immediately: *"I'm picking you up."*

"I'll take a cab. I don't wanna talk."

In quick succession, she typed:

"I'm picking you up. I'll be outside by the time you finish packing. You don't have to talk. Love you. Leaving now."

I thought I could probably call her off if I tried hard enough, but I didn't know where I'd find the energy. It was all I could do to keep breathing.

I wanted the note I left for David to be eloquent and articulate, simple and profound, the perfect dignified exit. But I couldn't think. I felt numb, my hands rigid. I crumpled up the first draft because I was embarrassed by the shaky handwriting. I wanted this note to be so perfect it would make him regret his decision. I was striving for cursive reminiscent of my mom's feminine, slender strokes because I thought they would make me look skinnier in his memory. I shoved the crumpled paper into my purse so he wouldn't know that my goodbye note required multiple drafts.

"I'm sorry we couldn't make it work. Sorry I couldn't stay for goodbye."

Only after it was written did I resent the repetition of "sorry." But I was sorry. It was the truest of all the words. I was so, profoundly, sorry.

I was sorry I had left a clump of my hair on his shower wall in the shape of a heart four months before because he complained constantly about my shedding and I thought he'd find it funny.

I was sorry I broke my promise to work out at least five days a week without exception other than serious illness because maybe if I had more self-discipline, we could both respect me.

I was sorry I smoked so much that I hotboxed his apartment and he had to deal with neighbors thinking he or someone he lived with was a druggie.

I was sorry I was inadequate.

I didn't know how to sign it. I decided on a heart and drawing it felt like I was carving it into my own skin. It was a symbolic admission that he still had my love even though he didn't want it. It felt shameful. I wrote my signature slowly. It would be the last time I signed "Little Bear."

***

I struggled to get my bags out the door and into the elevator, even though they weren't heavy. By the time I got outside, Adelynn was waiting in the old green Subaru she'd inherited from her father. As I was walking toward the car, my cell phone rang with a familiar 650 number and I answered out of habit. It was my would-be boss from the job I'd applied for a couple of months prior, before everything with David and my Ph.D. program in Chicago started falling apart. The organization had been stringing me along for months. I answered hoping this would be the final "You got the job. Be here Monday," which would mean my future wouldn't look quite so black-hole-ish.

Instead, the voice on the phone told me I was overqualified. But also underqualified. She said that the "nice to have" skills—skills I had been open about not having (Photoshop, WordPress, SEO)—were now "essential."

I started laughing, maybe cackling. "Okay, great! Thanks." I knew I was supposed to feel resentment, indignation, at least disappointment, but I couldn't muster it. The two pillars around which I'd been building my future—my engagement and my PhD program—had disintegrated. Everything else, including not getting a job I genuinely wanted, felt trivial. It also made a strange kind of sense that everything should fall apart at once. In some ways, I had been expecting it. David had fallen in love with me quickly, less than two months from first date to proposal, so maybe it had been inevitable that once he really knew me, he wouldn't want me anymore. It felt entirely natural that the same thing would happen with this job. My life felt like an exercise in presenting a facade of competence, desirability, lovability. It had always been only a matter of time before he, they, the world recognized me for the fraud I really was.

"Are you okay?" the woman on the phone asked.

"Yeah. Fine. Great. Wonderful!" My voice sounded hysterical, screechy. "Thanks! Have a good weekend." I realized it was Wednesday. "Afternoon, morning... life? Whatever. Bye!"

I hung up, distantly embarrassed and vaguely worried about what I would do next. I was apparently still in shock. Because of my compound privilege of being born wealthy and with generous parents, I didn't need the job to support myself. But also because of my compound privilege, work wasn't about earning money, it was about earning self-worth through sacrifice and contribution.

My dad found his calling in anti-poverty and economic development work. My mom's calling was in reproductive justice and Indigenous rights. My sister's was in anti-slavery and corporate responsibility. My calling was...shopping for pretty dresses? Getting good grades on tests that don't measure anything meaningful? Falling for men who claim to love me then don't?

Yeah, if I needed to write up a few sentences about my life for a high school reunion or an alumni newsletter or something, I could spin it to make it sound good. But spin is not substance. My lifelong fear was becoming a certainty: I was a self-indulgent, unlovable dilettante with no real skills who took up too much space and offered too little value. With every step, my nearly empty bag felt heavier.

When she saw me approaching, Adelynn pushed open the passenger door from the inside. I heaved my bag into the back seat and dropped my purse at my feet. She unbuckled her seatbelt to envelope me in a fierce hug but I didn't want to be comforted. I couldn't tell if it was because I knew I couldn't be or if I felt like I didn't deserve it. I turned up the music when I got in and she didn't try to make conversation as we drove, just reached over and squeezed my knee at the occasional red light.

We got to the airport early and I asked her to park in the cell phone waiting area so I could get high. Adelynn had never gotten high in her life except the one time when we were roommates and I talked her into eating a brownie, just so she could know what it felt like. She got so paranoid that she was paralyzed on her side of our couch for hours. Now, her work mandated random drug testing. She told me it was okay to do it in her car, and I worried about getting her in trouble but not enough to hesitate. I apologized through clouds of smoke. She waved a hand in front of her face and said, honestly, "Do whatever you need to do."

I sucked hard on the joint knowing its induced calm had to sustain me for hours—through security, the flight, the taxi ride home. I would be alone. All alone. Always alone. Forever alone.

I sucked harder, trying to absorb every particle of smoke, trying to store it in my lungs. A few cars down, a man in his sixties, maybe seventies, sat waiting in his own parking spot. He looked stern. Scowling, in fact. We made eye contact and I worried that he had caught me, that he would report us, that Adelynn would fail a drug test and get fired because I could not keep my shit together. My best friend, in the act of doing something kind for me, would lose her job because I was a selfish, irresponsible, horrible person. My self-hatred magnified. I opened the car door and used gravity to slide down onto the curb. Partially hidden in the spiky growth of parking lot weeds, allowing them to jab into soft skin, I took one last, long inhale before crushing the remains of the joint into the mulch. I made sure the man saw me empty-handed as I stood up and got back into the car.

Adelynn drove me to the United terminal in silence. When I got out, she did too.

"You're sure going back to Chicago is the right thing right now?" she asked. "I'm worried about you being alone." I was worried too but never thought about an alternative. "You can stay with me for as long as you want. We can cuddle and drink and watch Netflix and eat ice cream and talk. Or, not talk. Whatever you want."

It was tempting imagining having someone to comfort me, to argue against the mean voices in my head, to make me laugh even when my face felt leaden... It would have felt good but I couldn't let myself say yes. I didn't even consider the possibility. I didn't deserve it. "No. Thank you. I can't. I just—I need—" I didn't know what I needed. I needed to not feel this way: empty, terrified, beaten. I needed my life to have a purpose again. I needed David to change his mind. I needed to throw up. "No, thank you. I love you. I need to go. I just . . . need to go." She squeezed me and I felt like I might crack.

I got through security, grateful that everyone hated TSA screening enough that my misery read like strong opposition to the possibility of a pat-down. I stepped into the scanner and raised my hands above my head.

"Feet farther apart," the TSA agent verbally prodded. I was standing with my bare feet just inside the yellow indicator prints, imagining whatever gross diseases lurked there. When I took the larger stance—open and exposed with my hands over my head—I started to cry.

Chapter 4
Habits

Evanston, Illinois
May 2012
Substances ingested: only pot. lots and lots of pot

I made it home and onto the couch David encouraged me to buy, in the apartment he helped me select, in the suburb he suggested I live. There were a couple bottles of beer, some condiments, and a single desiccated lemon in my fridge. Once a day, I would heat up a frozen burrito or boil water for pasta, only making it through a few bites before leaving the rest to molder on the counter. I had no appetite. I didn't care if I lived through this. And besides, maybe he wouldn't have stopped loving me if I were skinnier.

I quit things. I quit everything I could. I had stopped going to my PhD classes two or three weeks before, but I made my withdrawal formal. I had been serving on the board of a non-profit focused on equity in philanthropy and I quit that too. I quit going outside, answering the phone, and showering.

Guilt over my unearned wealth and privilege used to keep me *doing* things—working, studying, volunteering, trying to be a productive member of society rather than just a Marie Antoinette blithely consuming resources—but now I was too depressed to keep it up. Being able to depend on an inheritance to pay my rent and other necessary expenses meant that there was nothing keeping me from falling deeper and deeper into worthlessness. During the day, I binged entire seasons of *Blue Water High*, a wholesome Australian drama about a high school for elite surfers where every problem is PG and solved in 22 minutes. At night, I watched all the HBO shows I typically avoided because the violence, so gruesome and excessive, used to bother me. I slept at random hours, sometimes losing entire days.

During the days, I obsessed over why he stopped loving me and what the first signs were. At the engagement party his parents threw for us, he had taken a few steps away from me rather than standing by my side when the toasts started. I'd assumed it was discomfort with being the center of attention but was it a physical foreshadowing? Or what about the *multiple* long car rides when we ended up fighting so dramatically that I demanded he pull over and let me out? The time he snuggled up close, looked me deep in the eyes, and said, "I want to shave your face." I thought I was the only one who would ever notice that my peach fuzz was brunette. I got laser hair removal as soon as I knew it bothered him but perhaps it was already too late. There were other clues I missed, I knew it, I just didn't know which ones were meaningful. So, I examined every moment, one by one, from the start of the relationship to the end. Then I did it again.

The things I had devoted my life to—my engagement, my Ph.D. program, my future as a wife and mother—all of those were broken. I had no energy to rebuild. The fact was, I'd been making it up as I went along this whole time, hoping that a "Dr." in front of my name and a husband by my side would make me happy. There was nothing to live for anymore and the feeling was unfortunately familiar.

***

I had my first suicidal ideations at eleven or twelve years old, but they were never serious until I came down with Lyme Disease during my senior year of college.

By the time I was diagnosed with Lyme, I also had an active case of mononucleosis and positive titers for half a dozen other opportunistic diseases: Rocky Mountain Spotted Fever, Valley Fever, HHV-6, Bartonella, Babesia, and Ehrlichiosis. A brain scan showed damage concentrated in my left hemisphere that impaired my ability to write, read, and do math.

The physical pain was transient so I could never "get used to" it or know when to expect it to hit. It was in one joint, then another, hopping from my left ankle to my right wrist then to my neck then back to my ankle, all within a day and always severe enough to make me worry something was seriously wrong. The mental pain was even worse. Mere months before, I had graduated from Stanford with honors. I won an award for undergraduate research. Within eight weeks of commencement, I couldn't hold a simple conversation because my memory and cognition were so impaired. I felt like I'd lost my mind and didn't know if I'd ever get it back.

In the first month of my disease in 2005, I lost twenty pounds due to nausea and fatigue. I loved the way it looked but it scared me that I had no appetite. Pot fixed that. It also eased my rage, terror, and grief about being bedridden and dumb. Stoned, I could eat, sleep, and absorb hours of television. Without it, I wanted to claw my way out of both brain and body. So, I started smoking. A lot. Often, with my parents. If I became addicted, I figured it was the least of my problems.

Before I was diagnosed with Lyme, I knew I was sick but I didn't know what was wrong with me. I saw a bunch of doctors who diagnosed me as depressed and prescribed antidepressants, which I took but which didn't address the underlying disease. The first anti-depressant I tried was an SSRI (selective serotonin reuptake inhibitor) that featured a sad onion hopping around beneath a raincloud in its ads. SSRIs often warn about the increased risk of suicidal ideation in some patients. I was fatigued and achy, nauseated and befuddled, but what scared me the most was that every time I closed my eyes, I fell into a chasm of sorrow so dark and deep I couldn't imagine a reason worth living. I would cry and cry for hours, getting more sleep-deprived and closer to harming myself. After diagnosis, I hit a new suicidal low when I found out that Lyme Disease cases as intense and chronic as mine can cause infertility. The only thing I'd ever been wholly, completely sure that I wanted—a family—might be impossible. It was a mild relief when I found out that depression was a side effect of an active Lyme process, and I started getting treatment for the biological disease as well as its symptoms. The depression lifted when a doctor who listened to me prescribed an effective cocktail of antibiotics, antivirals, and immune-supporting supplements on top of the anti-depressant. As the depression lifted, in a burst of clear thinking, I realized that the chance of infertility is not the same as the guarantee of it, and at worst I could always adopt.

These experiences of wanting to die and then feeling better taught me to hold my depression loosely and rationally. Since my teenage years, I had been collecting strategies to keep myself safe, mainly because I promised my parents I would never, no matter what, kill myself. I had developed a list of rules, but I only wrote them down, formally, after Kate Spade's and Anthony Bourdain's suicides to guide me whenever I knew I was falling into dangerous territory:

1. You don't get to kill yourself without at least TRYING anti-depressants.

2. You don't get to kill yourself without at least ASKING for help.

3. You're not allowed to kill yourself until you at least go for a walk/get some exercise.

4. You're not allowed to kill yourself until you at least take a hot bath or a cold shower.

5. You're not allowed to kill yourself before seeing a therapist.

6. You're not allowed to kill yourself until you've written a letter to everyone you really care about, explaining why you did it and why it's not their fault (in articulate and typo-free prose).

7. You're not allowed to kill yourself until your "estate is in order"—e.g. You can't leave a mess for the people you love. It's not fair to them in general, but it's especially not fair to make them deal with grief and logistics at the same time.

8. You're not allowed to kill yourself until you create a bucket list of everything you have ever, even a little bit, wanted to do in life and then done all of it.

Reviewing the list mentally, I stopped on number eight. Creating a list felt way more doable than reaching out to a friend or finding a therapist.

What did I want to do with my life? Fucking nothing.

But: Mandela spent twenty-seven years in prison going nearly blind from working in the salt mines, and in that time he taught his jailers to read. Wilma Mankiller survived a fatal car crash with her best friend, multiple terminal diagnoses, and persistent death threats to lead the Cherokee Nation into solvency as the first female Chief of a modern Native American Nation. Maya Angelou, MLK, Gandhi—all overcame incredible hardship to turn their suffering into gifts for humanity. Whereas I got dumped by some dude and allowed it to destroy me? Nope. I couldn't be that weak.

Using my pride as a crutch, I made another list, this time in a cloud-based server so I'd never lose it. I needed reasons to live, so I listed whatever I could think of that I'd ever had the slightest desire to do. In my state of crushing depression, nothing appealed to me, so I tried to remember what the Anne of six months ago would have found exciting:

- Write a book

- See the pyramids in real life

- Travel on a diplomatic passport

- Have a threesome

- Live in a foreign country for more than six months

- Become fluent in another language
- Learn to pattern clothes and play the guitar
- Join the Mile High Club
- Hike the Inca Trail
- See the Northern Lights
- Try ayahuasca
- Take an overnight train
- Adopt an English Bull Mastiff and name him Pickles
- Meet Richard Branson

When I started to imagine Sir Richard introducing me to his flamingos on Necker Island, I chastised myself for being frivolous. No one's life would be better off for it. I told myself I should be thinking of ways to make me a better and more loveable person. That list came much more fluidly. Typing quickly, I knew exactly what I needed to do:

- Stop smoking pot
- Cure my Lyme's Disease
- Become a daily meditator
- Eliminate the U-shaped fat bulges on the back of my thighs
- Learn to be naturally tidy

I ran out of ideas but not before I had eighty-seven items in total. It would take me years to complete, if ever. Perfect.

Looking at the list, I thought about David's words, that "This breakup could be the best thing that ever happened to us." I decided, in that moment, that I would *make* it the best thing that ever happened to *me*. I would use it as motivation to fix everything that was wrong with me, make David desperate to have me back, and ensure that the next man who chose me would never change his mind. This way, no matter what happened, I would win the breakup. Even depression couldn't kill my competitive spirit.

The next time Adelynn called, I answered.

"How are you?" she asked.

I took stock of the double-XL sweats I hadn't changed in three days. But now I had a list. I said, "Hanging in."

"How are you keeping yourself busy?" Raised with a Puritanical work ethic, she valued productivity as an absolute good, especially when depressed.

"I'm doing nothing." I had no energy to lie.

"Would it make you feel better to go for a walk?"

"Maybe." Even if it would make me feel better, it wasn't going to happen. I didn't have the energy to do something good for myself.

"Just watching movies and stuff?" Her voice softened to show she wasn't judging.

"Yeah." Then I decided to be more honest. "All I can do is breathe . . . and even that hurts."

"Breathing is all you have to do babe," she said, her voice reassuring. "Just keep breathing and you'll get through this."

She was right. It was factually accurate that if I kept breathing, I wouldn't die, which meant that presumably, eventually, I would get through this. Each and every breath was a successful step toward a future that didn't hurt. All I had to do was keep breathing.

"Thank you, that actually helps." I took in a slow, deep breath. It felt good to breathe but it didn't eliminate the gnawing in my gut. "But what am I supposed to do with my life now?"

"Oh sweetheart." I could hear her rolling her eyes. "Come on. You're one of the strongest, smartest, most capable people I know. So you're not going to marry David. There's so much else out there. Just choose something. You could do anything. And let's be real: you didn't *really* want to be Mrs. Weiner."

I laughed. I couldn't help it. Adelynn always struggled with names. "There is zero way I would've taken his name even if we *had* gotten married. But, for the record," still laughing, "it was 'Pecker.'"

***

A few days later, I convinced myself David never loved me, was cheating on me the whole time, and with someone I knew. It didn't matter that there was no evidence for any of my conclusions; my mind was fixated on generating worst-case scenario after worst-case scenario. I sat on the couch searching the internet for salvation in the middle of the night with *Spartacus: Blood and Sand* playing in the background.

I knew I needed rigorous healing, something intense and external to pull me out of this cycle, but I didn't know what. Rehab? Some sort of wellness spa? A monastery?

I googled "Buddhist monastery" because the austerity appealed to me, then added "volunteer" because I craved the rigid schedule, and "Thailand" because I wanted to go somewhere untainted by memories of David. Travel had always seemed like a good way to make heartbreak productive. I could expand my cultural horizons while presenting the image that I was continuing life unphased, nay, better than ever, with colorful stories from distant places. Beyond that, I'm a better person when I travel. I'm more patient and curious, less attached to how I think things *should* be. Travel allows me to think about what's going on around me rather than within me. And at that point, on that couch, I desperately needed a break from myself.

One of the first results, a monastery outside Bangkok, looked tempting. They enforced a 4 AM wake-up then silent service and meditation all day until mandatory bedtime at sundown. It fit my desire for rigor, but I could imagine no greater hell than remaining silent and alone with my thoughts for weeks. There was also a notice that women were not allowed to touch monks or hand items directly to them because women are considered dirty and impure in the form of Buddhism they practice. That tempered my interest.

The next result confused me: Googling "Buddhist monasteries" and "Thailand" had somehow returned a yoga teacher training immersion retreat in Costa Rica. Still, I was drawn in. Yoga, teacher training, immersion, intensity… it was everything I did and didn't know I was looking for.

I clicked on the ad and was immediately sold. It was exactly what I needed: twelve hours a day of demanding exercise, healthy food, learning about ancient medicines, all with a certification at the end! The credential was the clincher. External validation was an ego cookie I couldn't resist. I researched other yoga teacher immersion trainings in Thailand, Mexico, India, and the US, but none looked as good. Well, that's not true. But the other trainings that did look as good all required proven years of yoga practice, which was a problem because I had only been to maybe two dozen yoga classes in my entire life, and only if I rounded up, significantly. I hardly knew the English nicknames for the poses, much less the Sanskrit ones. I'd done a handful of Bikram classes when I decided the heat would make me skinny, but I didn't know Bikram is hardly even considered yoga amongst many serious practitioners. The application for the program in Costa Rica was the only one that didn't require me to lie outright about my experience. I think it was assumed nobody in her right mind would sign up for something so extreme without having mastered the basics.

Ever since contracting Lyme, most workouts depleted my energy and I'd have to spend days in bed recovering after any serious exertion. But as long as I didn't push myself too hard, yoga made me feel good and want to move my body the next day. I was eager to see how I'd feel after weeks of daily yoga practice.

Also, yoga bodies are the best. In the back row of any yoga class, I would wear baggy clothes and objectify the women in front of me, shopping for my desired form. I'd covet one woman's thighs, another's stomach, a third's pert behind. I noticed with envy all the women whose triceps didn't flap like a grandmother's when they extended into Warrior 2. If I did enough yoga, I would look like them (and if I looked like them, David would love me again). I didn't admit that last part of the fantasy, even to myself.

The same night I found it, I pleaded my way into the sold-out teacher training starting in exactly twelve days. It gave me just enough time to pack up my apartment, send David's stuff back to him, and arrange any necessary visas. Making a plan for leaving the country on a one-way ticket for an undetermined amount of time kept me focused and too busy on my to-do list to second guess. I decided I would go to yoga classes every day for the week and a half leading up to my departure but the first one left me so sore that I didn't go again. I figured I'd wing it. I was a fast learner.

Adelynn was familiar with my propensity to seek geographical solutions to emotional problems, so she wasn't wholly shocked to hear that I was planning to disappear into the jungle for an undetermined amount of time. "You know that you don't have to go away, right? I'll have to work but otherwise I can come there, and we can just hang out. You don't have to be okay for me." I knew she wasn't lying but I didn't believe her.

Chapter 5

Take It All

Montezuma, Costa Rica
June 2012
Substances ingested: none. Nothing. Not even plane food. Only gnawing regret

What the fuck was I thinking?

The plane hadn't even landed in Costa Rica before I knew I'd made a major mistake. I wanted to turn around and go home, except there was no home to go to anymore. So, I stayed. With panic, regret, and resignation assailing me, I forgot one of my carry-on bags on the plane. I realized my mistake almost immediately, but it still somehow took an hour and a half for the airline staff to retrieve my luggage. It was the bag with my computer in it—my lifeline to friends and family, distracting TV, and the opportunity to start working on a book of some sort—so waiting was the only option. On top of the computer was an envelope of cash—about $600 for tips—that I expected to be gone by the time the bag was returned. The cash was replaceable and an acceptable cost of my stupidity, but the computer had years of pictures and documents that I wasn't sure I'd backed up. It was supposed to be automated, but had I checked to see if the Cloud link was working since I'd installed it? My fear of losing my stuff barely beat out my fear of getting left behind at the airport with no way of making it to my intended destination, a ferry ride and seven hours' drive away. The retreat center had sent a shuttle for me and some other participants, but now I was an hour late and counting.

I barely looked at the bag when the attendant returned it to me. He insisted on unzipping it and showing me the contents, and when I saw the envelope of cash sitting visible and untouched on top of a magazine I'd bought at the airport in Chicago, I felt a rush of relief. I thanked him, grabbed the bag, and sprinted to the shuttle meeting point. Of course, we ended up waiting another two-and-a-half hours in the van for a woman whose flight was delayed.

I was the fourth to arrive and already felt like I didn't belong. The other women were all yogis and fitness instructors with visible abs. They chattered energetically from the moment they entered the van and were already a clique, growing in size as each new perky blonde arrived. For the first few hours, I was the only one without a pierced belly button. Among the last arrivals were an Ethiopian woman working at a non-profit in Kenya who wanted to teach yoga to the kids the non-profit served, and a 50-something ski instructor from Maine who looked like she'd know what to do in an avalanche. She came because her knees were hurting from a lifetime of skiing, and she wanted to add some preventative yoga to her repertoire. Even though we had little in common, I liked them; they felt similarly out of place and I sensed maybe we could be friends. The rest seemed like the girls I'd avoided in high school because their bodies, boyfriends, and bubbly personalities intimidated me.

Everyone else seemed so excited to be there and I could not remember how to smile. I couldn't make conversation and I struggled to pretend I was alright. The ferry was my first opportunity to separate from the group. Finding a seat outside at the back of the boat, I noticed it had started to mist, somewhere between a heavy dew and a light rain. I watched the milky teal water churn as we moved farther from land and thought, "Would I make it if I jumped in and tried to swim from here?" My panic rose as the port receded into the distance, my answer turning from maybe to definitely not. I could still make out the lighthouse, striped red and white, but were there crocodiles here? Slowly, but too quickly for my comfort, the only land I could see became jungle. The conservation efforts of the Costa Rican government were evident and effective: wide, green forest dominated the vanishing horizon, but somehow, I still felt trapped and wanted to escape. But I wouldn't quit this program. Just like suicide, quitting was NOT an option. I had to be there. I listed the reasons to myself.

First: yoga. If I didn't find a way to move my body regularly, to maintain strength and flexibility, I would end up like my grandmother—mentally sharp as a filed blade, but physically infirm. I needed to learn how to move my body safely in ways that felt good over the short- and long-term.

Second: I was there to quit smoking pot. I had started smoking when I needed it—weed, cannabis, marijuana, flower, ganja, trees, dope, dank, whatever—to eat and for pain relief. But now, seven years later, I was using it all the time and for everything. It had become a dependence. An addiction. A shameful secret I wanted to negate rather than accept. I didn't want to be an addict. I would use this time to quit smoking pot and return that mantle of shame.

Plus, I ate less, generally very little, when I didn't smoke. I would be skinnier if I stopped. I could also travel more freely if my possible destinations weren't curtailed by where I might get sent to prison for buying, carrying, or consuming weed. So, there were plenty of good reasons to tough out the urge to flee.

I figured I could do it all in Costa Rica: get skinny, learn yoga, quit smoking pot, start a book, eliminate the U-shaped fat bulges on the backs of my thighs, and begin learning a foreign language all at the same time. Easy. I would not come home until I had it all figured out.

There on the ferry, I decided to combat doubt and despair with action. I would start writing now. I slid my carry-on out from beneath my seat and unzipped the bag, looking for my laptop nestled in its new purple travel case beneath the envelope of cash. But it wasn't there. I took out the magazine and shook it as if a laptop could get stuck between the pages. I turned the bag upside-down and watched a chapstick roll away. I rifled through the pile top to bottom, then bottom to top, then again, examining every place my computer could have fallen including pockets way too small for it. It took minutes for the realization to dawn. I could not believe it was gone. That someone had stolen it. On top of all I had lost in the past month.

It started to rain in earnest. I did not move inside.

***

I looked as desperate as I felt by the time we arrived at the retreat center. Palms trees stood sentry at the entrance, dripping warm water from their laden leaves. My hair was somewhere between wet and greasy and my eyes were bloodshot from crying. Dinner was waiting for us, as was our instructor for the next month. Andi. She stood outside the open arched double glass doors, beaming like the hammered metal lights behind her. She was about 5'7" with short brown hair that emphasized her Ashley Judd appearance. Lithe and glowing, she hugged each of us as we walked inside.

I was last. "Oh no," she said instead of hello. "What happened?"

"My computer was stolen."

"That's terrible. Do you want to file a police report?" She went into practicalities, suggesting the staff member who could help. She then returned to me with an empathetic,

"Ugh, that really sucks. I'm sorry." Then, tentatively: "You know, sometimes when I've had stuff stolen, I've found that the Universe is trying to speak to me. Sometimes you're stripped for a reason." She shrugged in a way that reassured me that even she believed this perspective might be meaningless, which made it less threatening to consider.

Usually, I would've been offended or at least turned off by a version of "God has a reason for everything." I found it intellectually lazy and probably cowardly to believe in God, a higher power, or "the Universe" as an intentional being with a plan for everyone. I was an atheist who generally believed that: stuff happens, we react to it, then more stuff happens. Basically, cause and effect rather than mystic, inscrutable forces.

Years ago, when a therapist asked what I thought "the Universe" was trying to tell me by giving me Lyme Disease, I said, "That I was bitten by a tick," and never saw her again. So, I was surprised by my reaction this time. This time, I found it oddly comforting. Maybe I was just desperate for *something* to be happening for a reason and for that reason to be my best interest. Everything with David had felt the opposite of that. I *needed* someone to watch out for me. If it was "the Universe" (whatever the fuck that meant), I would take it. At least she hadn't said anything about Jesus; I probably would've scoffed. "The Universe" was vague enough that I could imagine other substitutes I could get behind: "nature," "energy." Even "the Force," as in *Star Wars*. I could at least allow those ideas to exist as possibilities.

Seated between an aerobics instructor from Los Angeles and the skiing instructor from Maine, with a generous bowl of steaming lentil soup in front of me, I played with the idea:

What if, sometimes, we're stripped for a reason?

I held a spoonful of soup aloft, waiting for it to cool. I considered: I had come to Costa Rica to escape thoughts of David, to be in my body and focused on movement. To be present, *here*. I might not have chosen for it to happen this way, but having no computer forced me into it. I had to be here. No escaping into *Real Housewives*, social-media-fueled fantasies of what or who my ex was doing, not even the fictitious world of writing a novel so that I could feel productive. I finished my soup, tasting it, intently focused on staying present. *Sometimes things are stripped from us for a reason.*

Chapter 6
Magic

Montezuma, Costa Rica
June, 2012
Substances ingested: organic beans, rice, shredded chicken and fresh mango

The retreat center sat in a crevasse atop a ravine of sorts, with the yoga platform extending out over the drop, hanging above the jungle. Wild orchids the color of flames grew up the support poles of the deck, their crimson and saffron throats constantly dewy with ambient humidity. Only two sides of the deck had walls leaving a 270-degree view of dense green and bright blue before us. I'd never seen so many shades of green; there's Mint, Kelly, and Hunter, but what's the name for green so fresh and verdant that it looks like it would snap if you bit into it? My sister once told me that the eye can distinguish more shades of green than any other color—just one of the interesting facts she delivers at relevant and irrelevant times—and there in the jungle I fully appreciated its truth.

I paid waning attention to the lecture Andi was delivering at the front of the platform. This first week, she told us, was focused on the chakra system, starting with the "root chakra," because "*everyone* has root chakra issues." I thought I was an exception, mostly because I didn't know what a chakra—much less a "root" chakra—was. I didn't want to ask and risk revealing that I hadn't done the homework, so I framed the question as wanting to hear it in her words.

She explained that chakras are "energy centers, basically dense bundles of nerves." The seven primary chakras were identified roughly six thousand years ago by Hindu sages and ayurvedic practitioners who spent millennia developing sophisticated and simple methods of tapping into the flow of energy within those bundles of nerves. Today, MRIs and other advanced technology can map energy flows, affirming what those ancient sages discovered.

The locations of the seven chakras map onto the seven densest nerve bundles in the body as identified by MRI. The first chakra, the root chakra, corresponds to the largest bundle of nerve fibers in the body. It is the place where all the nerves from the lower body meet and attach to the spinal cord. This all made sense.

Then, Andi shared sounds that enervated and activated the chakra; she told us it's represented by a red lotus flower with four petals; she helped us practice its Sanskrit name: "Muladhara." She talked about "opening," "closing," "charging," or "spinning," nerve bundles with different vowel sounds. I recited the sounds and names and "facts" like a good student, all the while dismissing it as esoteric bullshit. I could understand nerve bundles, and maybe energy being concentrated in a certain physical location. But the rest I categorized as the sort of quasi-new-age mysticism I'd have to tolerate to achieve correct yogi alignment.

As Andi lectured about the mind-body connection and how movement can unlock emotions, I tuned out, focusing again on the view. Dappled and rippling, moving with invisible currents, the trees and vines formed what seemed like an impenetrable carpet below us. For the first time, I had a real sense of the jungle as one big organism, a living entity, each constituent only an organ of the greater body.

Then the lecture ended, and the movement section began.

I expected that the first few classes, if not the first few days, would ease us into the program, starting slow then ramping up.

And I was right, except that slow and easy was not slow and easy for me. The "warm-up" was more intense than my workouts at their peak. I was sweating before we even started standing poses and quaking by the end of the warm-up. Twenty minutes in, I was cramping up and crapping out of most poses halfway through, finishing them by flopping face-up on my mat because even child's pose was too difficult. Andi had said we should take corpse or child's pose whenever we needed it, but I was sure she didn't think anyone would need it as much as I did. Because of CosmoGirl and Seventeen Magazine and every other piece of media I had consumed uncritically growing up, my lack of fitness felt like a moral failing. The other participants squatted, thrusted, lunged, and balanced, as I lay on my back, tears leaking out of me, luckily disguised by sweat. It wasn't entirely clear to me why I was emotional, but these poses were bringing something up besides simple fatigue.

I wasn't alone in that. At any given time, a handful of us were flat on our backs or curled in child's pose, crying.

"Just let it up and out," Andi said, striding between mats, acknowledging the swelling emotions on the yoga deck. Different poses took down different people but even the fittest—the strongest, most flexible, the ones able to do all the binds, backbends, and balances with physical ease—didn't escape this first session without at least one emotional breakdown.

"Don't try to hold onto it. Let the feelings come up, let them out, then don't grab them back. Up and out. Don't hold on to what you want to let go of," Andi continued.

Harmony, a dance instructor from outside Detroit wearing a skintight white leotard, did the most advanced expression of each pose—foot pointed above her head, full splits, going from wrists to elbows and back to wrists while inverted in a handstand. Even she took child's pose once, gracefully, but the rhythm of the rise and fall of her back made it clear she was crying. We were an archipelago of grief, each mat was an island, connected but separate, going through a common experience but not acknowledging it.

Between cueing different poses and giving general alignment corrections, Andi guided us deeper. She talked about how our bodies take in trillions of bits of information every given second—where we are in relationship to gravity, tastes, smells, distant sounds, potential dangers, the pressure from a mosquito's body on our skin—and how the brain can only process a tiny fraction of that. So, the brain, the mind, filters it out. But it doesn't necessarily go away. That information, especially if it's repeated, painful, or important in some way, gets stored in the body. And sometimes, the only way to release it is through movement. "So, pay attention to what you're feeling in this moment. Not just the burn or the discomfort of lactic acid buildup, but notice what emotions are coming up. Do you feel powerless? Victimized? Angry? Resistant? Let it up and out." She said this while leading the group through deeper and deeper squats, but I just listened not even pretending to leave my high-quality corpse pose. "What patterns do you notice? What do you tell yourself when you're struggling? What does your body tell you?" Years later, reading Bessel van der Kolk's *The Body Keeps The Score*, I was reminded that I first learned the interconnectedness of physical and emotional healing in the jungle that day with Andi.

At her prodding, I noticed that when in physical discomfort, I told myself it was my fault. That I shouldn't have signed up for a yoga teacher immersion training for which I was so ill-prepared, that I should've been doing yoga all my life, that if I weren't so weak and undisciplined I wouldn't be embarrassing myself in a puddle of sweat and failure, that if I'd remembered to put on bug spray I wouldn't be being eaten alive by biting ants... I told myself those things instead of simply allowing something hard to be hard. It was hard for everyone. The class, the emotions it brought up, being in the jungle away from all my most favorite and convenient coping mechanisms...it was all hard. But hard doesn't mean bad or that I had done anything wrong.

It was the beginning of realizing the "mind-body connection" is understated. Prior to landing in Costa Rica and this first yoga class, I would have categorized the mind-body connection as a hierarchy: the mind tells the body what to do, eat, and feel, and the body should respond like a faithful and obedient servant without protestation or pushback. At the time, I didn't know how wrong I was, but there, supine on my mat, I was beginning to feel an inkling.

The class ended and I peeled myself up from the floor, thoroughly wrung out and doubting how I would get through a week of this, much less a month. The physical exertion was demanding, but it was the emotional component—the feelings that the movement and body-centered awareness unlocked in me—that I hadn't bargained for. If this was just the first day, what else was going to come up and would I be able to handle it? It was the first time I was really listening to my body, but it would take months and roughly eight grams of psilocybin-truffles to finally hear what it was saying.

Leaving class, I caught up to Andi to ask her advice on balancing poses.

"I'm really struggling. I can't maintain one-footed poses for more than a couple seconds without falling and that's weird for me because usually my balance is pretty good. What's going on?" I asked.

"Well, how's your balance in the rest of life? Do you feel grounded, rooted?" She asked, as if I understood what those words meant.

Pausing for a moment to consider, the truth came to me faster than I wanted. "No." I said, definitively. "I don't feel grounded or rooted at all. This month, the next 30 days, will be the longest period of time I haven't gotten on a plane in two years. I feel like I've been living my life in the air, between places." A tremor of fear and recognition passed through me. Choosing to be in one place was scary for reasons I wasn't yet ready to face.

Andi just nodded.

***

Later that night, Andi unpacked what happened in our first class. She said that "the root chakra governs our most primal feelings: our sense of security, groundedness, and survival. If we feel threatened in those base ways, we carry that energy in our root chakra." She explained that "everyone has root chakra issues" because life is difficult, wounding, and relentless, resulting in energetic scars that make us doubt our inherent worthiness. Those scars can be accessed through movement, and she said she designed the first class to help us "burn through" some of our first chakra issues.

From the lingering red eyes around the circle and palpable feeling of exhaustion emanating from the group, her design seemed to have worked, During our first "Satsang," the Sanskrit word meaning "gathering together for truth," Andi set the tone for what felt like a combination of group therapy and corporate ice breaker. We went around the circle and, instead of two truths and a lie or alliterative adjectives for our first names, we were given five minutes to share our most intimate root chakra issues.

Andi set the precedent by going deep, sharing that she was given up for adoption multiple times, leading to lifelong feelings of abandonment and self-doubt. I don't think she cried telling her story, but the rest of us did. One by one, each person shared devastating stories of poverty, parental suicide, long-term sexual abuse, or some other specific horror that no one deserves.

Then it was my turn.

Staring at the floor in the center of the circle, trying not to cry, I said, "I'm afraid you'll all hate me because I don't have any of that. I don't have awful stories of trauma or childhood abuse. I have two, loving, married parents, and a stable home, and enough money to provide for any emergency. I'm ashamed of the fact that everyone else had to plan and save and carry out fundraisers to be here and I could do it on a whim."

All of this was true, but I could tell I was skimming the surface of what was coming up for me, what had been brewing since the morning's class and what had been latent in me for decades. Still staring at the ground, fidgeting my hands, holding my breath, it came out in a rush: "I feel like an accident. I didn't do anything to deserve being born into privilege. I didn't do anything to deserve being here, or to have all that I do. I just..." I didn't know how to finish the sentence now that I'd admitted to this fundamental driving fear and guilt. I tried again to explain:

"I feel like I need to earn my space on this planet through good works. That I don't deserve what I have but maybe I can earn a portion of it if I do enough good things for other people. That if I help enough people in significant enough ways, then I'm allowed to relax and enjoy my life. But what is 'enough'?" I could feel myself spiraling down a familiar emotional hole. Nothing is ever enough. Nothing I could ever do is enough. I am not enough.

"So, I guess I do have root chakra issues. I don't feel like I deserve to be here." Feelings I'd spent years suppressing were bubbling, churning, pushing at the lid I was desperately trying to force down. It was a struggle to sit through the rest of the shares. When we adjourned for the night, I was overwhelmed by unprocessed emotions. I decided not to walk back with the other women. Instead, I walked to the edge of the property where it was dark and I could be alone.

I found a wrought iron chair hidden beneath a tree and sat. Despite the cacophony of jungle life, the only thing I could hear was the refrain "You don't deserve to be here." It was my voice, on a loop, accusatory and echoing. The more I tried not to listen, the louder it got. I looked for the girls' flashlights wondering if I could catch up with them if I ran, but there was no one. I was alone. It was what I had wanted but also didn't want.

"You don't deserve to be here," I heard again, the voice of my internal monologue, vicious and inescapable. It was the same voice that called me fat, gross and worthless when clothes fit too tightly. The voice that listed all the reasons men had left me and that told me that the other girls were probably talking shit about me on their walk back.

I opened my journal trying to distract myself from the voice, but all I could think to write was "I don't deserve to be here." I gave up fighting it and let myself sink into the shame and self-pity that told me I didn't deserve to be alive. Tears came, then sobs. I was just beginning to really feel the misery when the sound of laughter behind my back stopped me. Embarrassed that someone had caught me falling apart, I wiped my eyes and straightened my spine before looking behind me.

I expected it to be one of the other girls from the training, or maybe kitchen staff on their way home for the night, but no one was there. I searched the darkness, waiting for bodies to materialize and thereby explain the laughter I'd heard, but none did. Was it howler monkeys? Maybe the way I scooted on the chair made a squeaking sound that I interpreted as laughter. I comforted myself that no one had seen me being pathetic, which meant I could get back to it.

I returned to my hunched posture, bringing my knees up to my chest, ready to sob in earnest.

The moment I started to cry, I heard the laughter again. Closer this time. Louder and much more clearly. Unmistakable.

This time I leapt up from the chair, without embarrassment or taking time to collect myself because I recognized that laugh. It was Jaramie's laugh. I didn't know how she'd found out where I was, or gotten here from Hawaii, but she had an uncanny knack for showing up when I really needed her, like some sort of fairy godmother. Jaramie was like Mary Poppins if Mary Poppins had a smoker's laugh, loved a good dick joke, and refused to wear anything with an unforgiving waistband.

She entered my life when I was around nine years old, a friend of my parents. She became a friend of mine, then a guru of sorts. I learned I could ask her about anything—why my shoulder hurt in a certain position, how to do a cartwheel, what was the meaning of life—and she could answer. She wasn't always right, but she was never *wrong*. Her answers always presented some truth, some interesting new perspective, some insight or paradox that I'd never considered. She'd gained most of her wisdom the hard way, from life experiences in the wildest and most diverse set of situations I'd ever heard. She'd done every drug known to (wo)man, been married to three flamingly different men, had a child in each decade of fertility, gave the first up to adoption and raised the second two, started a vegan restaurant in the 1970s after she'd spent time as the drummer for a touring rock band, plus endless other stories I hadn't heard. She was the first woman I ever heard talk about blow jobs and the only one who made them sound like fun. I was surprised she found me in the middle of the Costa Rican jungle, but she was full of surprises.

I heard her inimitable laugh again, then her voice:

"You were born!"

I searched the darkness, wanting to run and hug her, wondering if she could be hiding behind a bush or cloaked by a shadow. I waited a moment, thinking that she was drawing out the suspense rather long and wishing she'd just reveal herself. The soundscape of the jungle returned to normal.

She wasn't there.

I sat back down on the wrought iron chair, feeling confused, unsettled, and even more alone. I had never expected Jaramie to be there, but the dashed hope left a sour taste.

Just as I was sinking back into the chair and depths of self-pity, I heard it again. Jaramie's laugh, then words. Three of them. Simple. Certain. Imbued with meaning:

"You were born."

It echoed in my head. "You were born" replaced "You don't deserve to be here," louder and truer with each repetition.

Each time I heard it, I understood more.

"You were born." This time the emphasis was on "born." It meant, think of everything that had to go right—millions of years of evolution, billions of cell divisions, infinite instances of chance—to result in my existence. My parents meeting, falling in love, having sex, going on fertility drugs to get *me*—none of it was an accident. The Universe doesn't make mistakes. I was born because I am supposed to exist.

"You were born." This time, the emphasis was on "you." Some unknown omniscient narrator was delivering information straight into my brain with few words but lots of meaning. It said, "You were born" and I knew it meant that I was intended. Everything that made me different, aberrant, and insufficient in my own eyes was intended. Those things I thought I needed to fix were actually *intentional*. Good, unique, special.

With each echo of "You were born," the voice told me there was nothing I needed to do to earn space or joy or the right to be here. I earned the right by being born. *Before* being born. Without *doing* anything at all. The Universe decided long ago that I was the perfect person for this moment and this place. I was given the exact right combination of likes, dislikes, and pet peeves to accomplish that purpose without even trying!

It should have felt weird to have this voice in my head, to believe it, to attribute truth and wisdom to it. Other than intuition, which I would explain as subconscious wisdom forcing its way to consciousness without citing sources, I had no frame of reference for an experience like this. I didn't believe in God, or any form of omniscience, and yet...

I felt it.

I didn't know it at the time, but this was the first of my psychedelic experiences, completely sober.

Sitting in the jungle, feeling the metal of the chair unyielding against my body, seeing stars pop out against the inky sky, tasting salt, I let the words—and the meanings—of "you were born" reverberate in my heart.

Walking back alone and without my flashlight, I trusted my feet and the moon. At each step, Halloween crabs skittered away from me. In daylight, their bodies were dark purple, almost black, with bright orange legs. They burrowed shallow holes into the mounded soil, hiding their bruise-colored bodies but leaving their legs poking out, looking as if the pistils of an exotic flower grew straight out of the ground. At night, they were shades of grey and black and only visible in movement but no less extraordinary to watch. Watching their industriousness, struck by how *busy* they were, I wanted to whisper into each ear—do crabs have ears?—the reassuring words, "You were born!" I wanted to let them know they could rest, that they were loved and seen and appreciated and I would NOT accidentally step on any of them on my way home. It took some tiptoeing, but I kept my promise. When I got home, I turned off the AC and opened the windows. I heard what I assumed were howler monkeys calling in the distance. A gecko clicked at me from the corner of the ceiling. I was born, and for the first time in ages, I felt loved. By all of creation.

***

The weeks flew by, each day filled from waking to sleeping with hours of lecture, movement (asana), and meditation. Sitting still through the rush of emotions that every Asana class stirred up and not doing a thing to change any of them was a new form of torture. Everything I'd used pot to damper in the past was surfacing, especially during meditation, and feeling those waves of rejection, anger, and boredom was the worst. When we were practicing poses, learning how to do adjustments, or receiving instruction on Ayurvedic principles, my brain was engaged and kept the emotions at bay. That's when it was easy to quit smoking pot; I didn't even miss it. But on our days off, when I was alone or bored or hungry or sad, I craved it.

At that point in time, I didn't consider cannabis as the "light psychedelic" the Multidisciplinary Association for Psychedelic Study classifies it as, but even if I had, I doubt it would have changed my feelings much. I thought of psychedelics as "hard" drugs that burned holes in brain tissue and doomed the user to a lifetime of haunting flashbacks. I wanted to wean myself from all substances, "psychedelic" or not, on which I thought I had an unhealthy dependence: pot—first and foremost—but also carbs, refined sugar, and external approval.

I could have indulged all my vices within two blocks, with vendors at the beach hawking nachos, ice cream, ganja, and generous catcalls. But I abstained, proving I could be disciplined if I really wanted it. At least for a month.

Too soon, people started to talk about their departure plans.

I had none.

I had come on a one-way ticket and didn't know where I would go when the retreat was over. I didn't know anything about life on the other side of this adventure. My healing—the continued sense that I belonged, that I was worthy, that who I am was enough—felt so fragile that I didn't want to go back home. I was okay there, in the jungle, away from the emotional IEDs hidden across the landscape of my life back in the States. In Costa Rica, I was lean, healthy, strong, and sober. I worried it wouldn't last back home.

What did "home" even mean? Was it my empty condo in Chicago where I'd never been anything but alone? The house I grew up in with my parents in California where I learned to drive and lost my virginity and would be a child forever no matter how old? Where would I go at the end of this month-long vacation from real life?

The final activity before receiving our certificates was to complete a "global mala": 108 sun salutations, performed as a group, dedicated to the benefit of all beings.

I thought it would kill me. I'd never been able to do a *single* pushup, much less more than 100 of them. Maybe it was doing it with the group, knowing we were all rooting for each other. Maybe it was feeling a kinship with my body I'd never felt before—like we were on the same side—but I did it. This time, with none of the same self-talk that assaulted me the first time I found myself challenged on the yoga mat. I didn't berate myself, or tell myself I was weak or a failure for feeling tired. Instead, I pumped myself up. I told myself what a great job I was doing. I had been born and now I was trying my best at something hard. That's how I got through it.

When we finished, everyone was crying with different mixes of relief, joy, and sadness. My mix was probably sadder than most; I'd come to love this place, these people, and how I felt among them. Andi had introduced me to concepts and insights I knew I'd be reflecting on for years. She had reintroduced me to my body, to stillness, to awareness.

As we celebrated the conclusion of a life-changing month for all of us, a quotation from French poet Anatole France floated into my mind: "All changes, even the most longed for, have their melancholy . . . we must die to one life before we can enter another."

I didn't know what would come next. But here in the jungle, I felt surrounded by the potential for new life. I cried with these women who had ended up being unexpected gifts. We hugged and laughed and stripped down to only our bikini bottoms then did cannonballs into the saltwater pool from the yoga deck. It felt like a baptism.

Chapter 7
Castles

Schiphol, Netherlands
November 2012
Substances ingested: airplane food, cannabis, magic truffles

If there is such a thing as a "typical father-daughter relationship," I've never had it. "I thought of it as getting to raise my best friends," he once said of his parenting philosophy. He traveled a lot when I was young and he took me with him to conferences and other work trips as a way for us to spend quality time together. The first trip he took me on was to New Orleans. I was the only eight-year-old in the room, but I listened well enough to learn how and why asset limitations on welfare kept recipients stuck in a cycle of poverty.

The first time I got my period, when I was 12, he was on a work trip to Australia. My mom told him despite my objections saying to me, "He's your dad and this is an important development in your life. He would want to know. There's nothing to be embarrassed about." When he came home, he gave me my first piece of real jewelry—a Black opal pendant on a gold chain—with a long, heartfelt note telling me how proud he was of the young woman I was growing into. I wasn't thrilled with the whole puberty thing, but when most girls grow away from their dads, I learned mine was a safe place.

When I was 14 or 15, after a boy I liked didn't like me back, I flung myself onto my parents' bed crying about how no one was ever going to love me and that I was going to be alone for the rest of my life. Instead of chuckling at my dramatics, my dad said, "Anne, you're brilliant and beautiful and kind and creative; it's not going to be easy to find your equal." I didn't believe him that the problem was me being too *good*, but I appreciated the perspective.

Most people proclaim my dad to be the nicest man they've ever met, but he was more than that to me. He *was* good. One of my most poignant memories from adolescence—the time you're supposed to think your parents suck—is watching a grown man weep like a child talking about all the good my dad had done for him and the world. The man was 6'5" and built like someone you wouldn't want to mess with in prison, which was where he'd spent ten years after being wrongfully convicted on a felony murder charge. He was able to start a business, provide for his family, gainfully employ himself and a dozen other formerly incarcerated men, all because of an economic development program my dad helped start. The man cried talking about how lucky I was to have my dad as a father, and I cried knowing he was right.

My dad has always believed in—and instilled in me—that there is dignity in hard work, that everyone has something valuable to contribute to society, and that doing so was the best way to a life of fulfillment. He taught me early the responsibility of "Tikkun Olam." Tikkun Olam is the Jewish commandment "to repair the world." Jews believe that God made the Earth a ball of perfect light, that it got broken somewhere along the way, and that it's humanity's job to stitch the light back together. Each person holds the responsibility *and* the requirements to sew justice.

It's a beautiful life purpose and I'm grateful that my financial inheritance always came with strict values to guide me. The main problem is that the work is never done. There is always more darkness, more injustice, more wrongs to be righted. My father won a presidential medal in recognition of his work lifting thousands—if not millions—out of poverty, and yet, reflecting on his professional accomplishments, he once said, "Well, I'm not really sure I've done anything with my life." Looking at my father, it's no mystery who my role model for root chakra issues is. We've always been close, and perhaps in this respect, too close.

Soon after I returned from Costa Rica, my dad invited me to join him at an anti-poverty conference in Amsterdam in November. Given that I had a rule of saying yes to places I'd never been, that I'd started smoking pot again a few weeks after getting back home, and that my dad and I have an enjoyable, established history of going to conferences together, I said yes.

I expected that we'd go to some sessions together, cut out on others, go to dinner, and check out the "coffeeshops" that sold recreational weed and made Amsterdam famous to drug tourists. My parents and I had been getting high together since my early twenties when cannabis became a necessary medication for the debilitating symptoms of my Lyme disease. They had been doing it recreationally since before Woodstock (my mom went, and still has her ticket), but had hidden it from me while I was growing up. I found out when my sister once asked me, "Haven't you ever noticed how mom and dad go outside after a fight with us and they come back nicer?" In hindsight, I wonder if my sense of smell was particularly bad or if it was just a familiar but unnamed aroma I associated with my parents being in a good mood. After I graduated college and when I got sick, they stopped worrying about being bad influences and weed quickly became a new normal in our relationship.

I don't remember the first time my dad and I got high together but I remember it being a lot less weird than I expected it to be. My dad got a little silly, prone to the giggles and bad puns. In other words, he was pretty much the same man I've always known.

***

In November, the taxis lined up outside the airport looked like a funeral procession shrouded in a gray mist. My dad and I arrived exhausted and mildly resentful of one another. There's this thing called the "Abilene Paradox" that I learned about in grad school but only understood for the first time after that flight. The Abilene Paradox explains how a group can arrive at the worst possible decision for everyone. The name of the paradox derives from how that research group—following a series of miscommunications—ended up on a vacation to, of all places, Abilene, Texas.

Because I learned from my dad that it is better to be uncomfortable than to make someone else uncomfortable, neither of us was honest about our seat preferences when checking in—both "compromising" for the sake of the other—meaning that we both ended up in our least-preferred seat. If I'm in a window seat, I can sleep; if my dad can recline his seat, he can sleep. Of course, we didn't realize this until *after* the eleven-hour flight for which I had given him the exit row window seat which didn't recline, and he'd given me a middle seat that did. Silently, kindly, passive-aggressively, we spent the long flight not only restlessly awake but resenting the perceived comfort of the other. The perils of people-pleasing had taken their toll, but at least we were both excited about being in Amsterdam.

Bypassing multiple public transportation options, we got into a taxi. I watched the scenery as my dad dozed. The landscape was green and grey and wet with channels carved out beside the freeway, the water streaming in parallel. The taxi ride was getting long and watching the euros mount on the meter made me anxious. The meter hit twenty-five when we'd barely left the airport and passed fifty when I knew we were still far from our destination. I kept thinking that we should have taken a train, a bus, something more responsible.

When it crossed a hundred euro, I felt nauseated with guilt and shame for spending so frivolously—when we were literally attending a conference *to address poverty*—but it was too late to make a different decision.

Finally, we arrived at a signpost of sorts. Amsterdam to the left, Zandfort to the right. We turned right.

I woke my dad. To the taxi driver, I said, "Where are you taking us?" My guilt and shame morphed into alarm and indignation that this man was clearly trying to take advantage of first-time tourists in Holland.

Like many other Europeans, the driver apologized for his "limited English" in perfect English. He pointed to the piece of paper my dad had given him with our hotel's address. He pointed to where the city would be, and he was one hundred percent correct. The hotel was not in Amsterdam, it was in Zandfort. My father is good at many things, but it was not entirely shocking that he had made a mistake like inviting me to visit Amsterdam for the first time when he was not, in fact, traveling to Amsterdam.

Probably the best thing about my dad was his ability to roll with whatever happens. This was no exception. He barely paused before shifting gears into silver lining mode. "So. What's Zandfort known for?" he asked cheerily.

"It is a famous beach town." The driver paused. "In the summer."

After another fifteen minutes and when the meter reached 143 euros in total, we arrived. My dad checked in to the hotel while I checked out the town. The first thing I learned was that there was some sort of racecar convention taking place, which meant that walking down the beach sounded more like walking the median of a freeway. Undeterred, I, like every other stoner, had heard of Amsterdam "coffeeshops" and was eager to see one for myself.

It took twenty minutes to circumnavigate the entire town on foot. There was one small commercial section featuring a grocery store and wind-surfing shop that was closed for the season. The rest was a sleepy residential town in the beginning of winter.

Because I love seeing what people eat in foreign countries, I wandered into the Albert Heijn, and emerged with a bag of somewhat identifiable foodstuffs: yogurts, juices, breads, and cookies, most in flavors like "spaanse sinnasnappel" or "vertrouwde smaak." I have always loved this part of travel, the way that the most ordinary items can be both familiar and foreign. Not understanding the language, flavors, aesthetics, and marketing strategies of different countries means that simply buying groceries is an adventure.

Most of the shops aside from a news kiosk and a children's clothing boutique were closed, but one beautiful brightly lit shop on the corner had "coffee" written in a loose cursive script across a glowing window that beckoned welcomingly. This "coffeeshop" was not at all what I had imagined when picturing these fabled Dutch drug dens. The patrons were scrupulously groomed, dressed in the kinds of work separates one might find at a Banana Republic or an Ann Taylor. They carried briefcases and purses, not ratty backpacks. Not a single person in the line at the shiny, glass-topped counter looked like he lived in a hostel. No one smelled of patchouli. At tables, a mix of ages and races worked on laptops or sat in pairs for what could have been first-round job interviews. It felt like the kind of coffee shop where they would think your cappuccino was naked if it didn't have a flower, leaf, or pinecone drawn into the foam.

Appreciating the bright, friendly cleanliness of the surroundings, I thought, "My god, this country is so *civilized*!" There was no shame in this coffee shop, no lingering air of guilt and sin, no assumed mutual exclusivity of "good and respectable" people from "people who use drugs." I thought I was glimpsing a European approach to recreational drug use that didn't paint it as a moral and individual failing. I was *so impressed.*

I looked at the menu written on the wall. My Dutch was non-existent, but the universal language of coffee and pastries made it clear that only espresso and bakery items were on offer. Where was the good stuff?

A man in an apron near the counter called out to me with a question. I didn't understand the words, but I knew he was asking if he could help.

"This," I asked, "is a coffeeshop?"

"Coffee?" He repeated.

"Um, no. I want . . . a coffeeshop." At this point I realized that several patrons were turning to look at me.

It took a moment, but when he understood, he shooed me out with a flick of his wrist. "No." Disgust flashed across his face. "Not here," he said. "Not here."

Googling, I learned my error: shops that sell coffee are not "coffeeshops," they are "coffee shops." The space between the words equals the difference between caffeine and cannabis. Coffee shop = coffee, coffeeshop = weed. Confusing the distinction a little, coffeeshops might also serve coffee, but coffee shops never sell weed. It seemed like too a subtle difference, that is until I saw my first coffeeshop.

The coffeeshop was only a few blocks away from our hotel, because nothing could be more than a few blocks away in this town. I found its address on a cannabis-related directory after googling "how to find a coffeeshop near me Zandfort." The site offered customer reviews, locations, and open hours for legal and grey area dispensaries around the world. Basically, Yelp but for marijuana.

Immediately I knew this coffeeshop was no coffee shop. The font for "Yanks," applied in vinyl applique across the front window looked like what an uninspired graphic designer would choose to advertise a strip club. The air outside was tinged with skunk. There was a turnstile at the entrance, reminiscent of a New York subway. I was intimidated. Did I need a ticket? A MetroCard type thing? Was this when I showed ID? I scouted the place, trying to look nonchalant, until somebody called out through the open doors of the entrance.

"English?" The interior of the shop was gloomy, and though I couldn't see who was speaking, I knew they were talking to me.

From the turnstile I shouted my response, "No, American. But yes. English. If you're asking about language. But American English. I mean. . . " I trailed off, realizing I was shouting in the middle of the street, and not saying anything that wasn't completely obvious. "Can I ... just... come in?"

"Yes, yes."

I pushed through the turnstile, extra aware of that very specific sensation of the hard, vaguely slick feel of every turnstile on earth, and entered a small hazy foyer. There were two people behind the counter, a man—slight, and swarthy—and a woman—also slight and swarthy. The man waved me forward a little impatiently. A red wooden bar dominated the room, beginning just a few steps from the entrance. Written on a wall-mounted board behind the bar, just like at the actual coffee shop, were all the offerings, each repeated on a laminated menu resting on the bar. I couldn't tell you much about Mr. Marijuana other than the fact that I was not the first tourist to patronize this shop. The man set down his joint in a teeming ashtray and began to walk me through my options:

I could buy bud, pre-rolls, and/or edibles.

Bud was just the cannabis flower, the part of the plant that contains THC and is consumed to get high. Buying bud would mean I'd need a grinder and rolling papers or a pipe to smoke it. "Pre-rolls" got around that as they were pre-rolled joints, but most were mixed with tobacco. "Pure" joints were more expensive, and there were only three available: Purple Haze (sativa), White OG (indica), and Blueberry Headband (hybrid). The fancy names like "Blueberry Headband" and "Purple Haze" indicate the specific strain of cannabis, named by its original cultivator and propagated by cloning. Strains fall into three categories: sativas, indicas, and hybrids. Sativas generally have an uplifting, creative effect, whereas indicas are better for sleep and relaxation. Hybrids blend the effects of the two.

As for edibles, the coffeeshop offered chocolate muffins labeled "space cakes," the sign read "10 mg THC per serving." From experience, I knew that 10mg was a reasonable but strong dose for me.

I bought one of each of the pure joints and two space cakes, then returned to the hotel to present my dad with our treasures.

"Ooh, let's try the Blueberry Headband first. I like fruit." My dad said.

We got high on a short walk down the wet beach, our privacy afforded by the inclement weather, and passed out early from a combination of the indica and jet lag.

***

Though I'd planned to attend at least some of the conference, it turned out to be a much smaller group on a much more niche issue than I expected, and I felt my attendance would be more like "crashing" than participating. Plus, it would be a shame to come all this way to see Amsterdam without seeing Amsterdam.

I wasn't dressed quite warmly enough for the cold on the train platform, so I put my book away and stuffed my hands snugly in my pockets. A Black man with short dreadlocks wearing acid-washed jeans and black sweatshirt striped with bright red, yellow, and green caught my attention with a nod. I smiled at him politely, and he smiled back, taking a couple steps towards me. "Bist du Deutscher?"

I shook my head, confused "I don't speak... Dutch?" I said, wary of being approached by random people, but more open to a random conversation in a foreign country than in the US. In the US, I expected it to end with being asked for money or out on a date, neither of which feels comfortable with a stranger. I had no idea what would happen here and my curiosity won out.

"Ahhh, American!" He had a Caribbean accent I couldn't place. "Have you ever been to Amsterdam before?"

"No, this is my first time," I said, maintaining a degree of caution.

"Ahhh! Then I am your tour guide!" He told me he was a Rastafarian concert promoter who had worked all over the world, but Amsterdam was his favorite city. Something about his vibe was disarming; he seemed like a nice guy I could have a good conversation with, and I liked the idea of having someone to show me around. I figured if my Spidey-senses started indicating fear or danger, I could make an excuse and get away, but it would be a missed opportunity for adventure if I declined before there was any reason to worry. The train arrived and we boarded together, still talking.

"You must know where all the best coffeeshops are then."

"Ahhh! You smoke? You will love Amsterdam!"

I made up some story of my dad knowing my whereabouts and expecting me at a certain time, but other than that, I let him take me by the hand, literally, and lead me around the city. He showed me out of the station moving so confidently across the many train and tram tracks that I almost had to close my eyes to be able to follow him at speed. It was reminiscent of my trip to Vietnam in 2003, when the traffic laws were so lax that the recommendation was to cross the street maintaining a predictable speed and to close your eyes if keeping them open would cause you to panic or stutter step. The idea: behave predictably and you won't get run over. In Vietnam it was young guys on motorbikes; in Amsterdam it was people of all ages on bicycles and trams; but the sense of being surrounded by motion was the same.

And those bicyclists! They were everywhere, so many of them, and all so effortlessly graceful on two wheels. They sat straight up, arms hanging loosely by their sides, turning 90-degree corners without applying hands to handlebars. It was like being surrounded by Cirque du Soleil performers commuting to work. The ringing of bicycle bells was constant, along with the low tooting of gondola horns as tourists and residents cruised the canals, an occasional swan honking angrily as it fled encroaching motorboats.

Amsterdam is laid out like half-a-wheel with the train station at the center, the major streets forming spokes, with canals like ribbons winding through them in soft arcs. We were barely across the street from the train station before I spotted my first coffeeshop. Just behind three full rows of parked bicycles at the point of a triangular building, there was a giant green marijuana leaf lit up in neon on the glass of what looked like a rundown hotel. The sign read "Voyagers Coffeeshop."

I tugged on my guide's hand (I was embarrassed that I'd forgotten his name but was too embarrassed to ask him to repeat it) and pointed. "There's a coffeeshop."

"Don't go to the coffeeshops on the tourist streets, they overcharge." He said without slowing down.

As we wound our way through crowded streets, I began to put my finger on why the flowing masses of people felt so different than crowds in America: the people were taller, slimmer, and talked more quietly but in a greater diversity of languages. The buildings looked old-school European, but the voices, faces, and cuisines represented countless nationalities. There was delicious-smelling fast food everywhere from all around the world. It was easy to assume that was related to the omnipresence of coffeeshops but might have more to do with the Netherlands being welcoming of refugees. If authenticity can be judged by smell, the scents wafting out of every restaurant suggested there was a grandma behind the stove cooking with recipes and spices packed, lovingly, in suitcases from the motherland.

In certain areas, there seemed to be a coffeeshop on every block. Also, sex shops. Some sex shops looked like Apple stores: spacious and well-lit selling expensive equipment in alternating shades gold, rose gold, and platinum. Others looked like cheap Halloween stores hawking slutty nurse costumes, fishnet thigh highs, and neon "lingerie" like crotchless body stockings that came one-size-fits-all, sold in a plastic bag on a plastic hanger. A whole genre of sex shops looked like the tourist kiosks at airports, except the shot glasses, t-shirts, postcards, and magnets all had genitalia on them.

There were sex shows I mistook for restaurants—an easy mistake, it turned out. Men in suits tended to stand outside both the restaurants and the sex shows, always with menus in their hands, trying to lure you inside. I made the mistake of listening to one, expecting to hear Italian pasta specialties, but instead, "Ping pong ball show starting now." The shows didn't sound sexy. Not even titillating. Just sad and degrading. Why would anyone want to watch a person shoot ping-pong balls out of her vagina? My confusion turned to horror when I reached the man trying to entice viewers into a razor blade show with the same concept. How much does society hate women?

It didn't hit me that we were in the red-light district until I noticed the literal red lights. The increasing frequency of sex shops should have been a tip-off, but I was deliberately ignoring much of what I saw and heard, so that it wouldn't become awkward with my tour guide. The vibe, from the beginning, was very friendly and I didn't want that to change.

I didn't notice the nearly naked women in the windows until we'd walked by a few. Initially, I assumed they were performance artists, like the woman who sat silently in the Metropolitan Museum of Art for 700 hours, except that these women were mostly naked. Amsterdam is known for its museums and its thriving contemporary art scene so maybe these women were an extension of that world. I didn't notice the velvet curtains pulled closed against some of the windows until I saw a man leaving through a door next to one. I only realized what was happening when I noticed how drugged one of the women looked and remembered my sister's warnings about the signs of human trafficking (she used to work in the State Department on their anti-slavery efforts). It made me sad and sick to see, firsthand, that legalization of sex work was not a solution to sex slavery. I had already been feeling uncomfortable with all the sex toys and harnesses and accouterments that made me feel like a naïve virgin in a city of advanced hedonism, but this layer of darkness made me want to leave the district as quickly as possible. This time, I was the one who took my guide's hand and cut a beeline through the meandering crowd to get us out of there.

A few minutes' walk into a more residential neighborhood brought us to his favorite coffeeshop. Immediately I could tell that he was right to have bypassed the first tourist traps. Sandwiched between lovely old townhouses from the 1600s, this coffeeshop had the atmosphere of a used bookstore in a college town. Two men who looked like professors sat at a table in the window, conversing over espresso drinks with lit joints smoldering in the communal ashtray. A young woman occupied a small booth, rolling papers, tobacco, cannabis flower and a grinder spread out in front of her. Her book was open on the table, and she kept her eyes glued to it as her fingers rolled a spliff—a hand-rolled cigarette spiced with cannabis—from muscle memory.

It was a two-story coffeeshop, with equally extensive menus of cannabis *and* espresso options. Again, I bought one of each pure-roll they offered (a sativa and an indica), and a space cake for later. To thank my kind guide for showing me around, I paid for his order. We sat upstairs, sipping Fantas, people-watching the crowds below, smoking and chatting about all the different places he put up concerts, where his favorites were, what called him to be Rastafarian, and more, until the munchies hit.

I'd seen people eating French fries out of paper cones with tiny wooden forks and I asked him where we could get some of that. "Ah, Vlaamse frites! Two blocks!" In Amsterdam, fried sticks of potato are called "Flemish" fries, not "French" fries, and there are takeout windows everywhere. We stood in line and I was grateful for the time to peruse the bewilderingly long list of sauces to choose from. I asked my guide how the locals order.

"Ahh! With mayonnaise!" he said, ordering up a serving with mayonnaise, ketchup, and curry for himself. I decided to try the local way, challenging my mayonnaise revulsion. They red and white paper cone was steaming hot when they handed it to me. I speared a particularly golden fry before tentatively dipping it into the swirls of mayo. I was afraid it was going to taste like curdled egg or biting into a lump of raw animal fat. But the moment it hit my tongue, I let out a little moan. I didn't mean to but I couldn't stop myself. The mayonnaise tasted different here: creamy, smooth, flavorful like an aioli and melty like the most decadent emulsion. Calling it "mayonnaise" felt like slander. These were the best fries of my life.

After a solid three hours of walking the city together, we began to run out of things to talk about and he put up no resistance when I told him I was going to head back to Zandfort to meet my dad. He may have even been relieved. We hugged, exchanged email addresses, and said goodbye. So far, Amsterdam was exceeding all expectations.

***

The next evening after his conference ended, my dad took the train in from Zandfort. I met him at the station to lead him back to the hotel I'd booked after making a cheap bid on "unnamed 4- and 5-star hotels in Amsterdam" on Priceline. Those sorts of gambles don't always work out, but that time it did. Not only was the location convenient and the building historic, but when I checked in, they had upgraded us to a two-room suite at no extra charge.

My grandfather was an architect, and my dad learned an appreciation of building design from him. In that hotel my dad was, in equal parts, enamored of the architecture and very high. He'd eaten part of one of the space cakes on the train and it had definitely kicked in. "Anne. This is so cool! See here? It says the building was first built in 1912 by shipping magnates in the classic Amsterdam School style of architecture." He pressed a button on the bedside console and as the motorized window coverings silently rose, he said: "And look at this. The *windows* go up and down."

As much as I wanted to laugh at his childlike awe, I shared it. There was, in fact, a James Bond element to the atmosphere that was very cool. We would have been in awe even if we weren't high. Which we were. Which was why it took an absurdly long time to figure out how to open the actual windows—not just the blinds—so we could smoke inside.

We got high then hungry and headed out for dinner. On our way to the restaurant, we passed a "Smart Shop." I had seen these before on my wanderings through the city. Each one was a little different, but all seemed to feature happy-looking cartoonish mushrooms in their window displays. I was curious about what the shops held, but also kind of scared to go in. The Smart Shops intimidated me in a way similar to the sex shops dotting the streets. They seemed... advanced. I had experience with smoking pot, but other than that, the only drugs I'd ever done were alcohol, and Ritalin *once* in high school when a super popular girl told me everyone was doing it. The Smart Shops made me feel like a wide-eyed virgin. A drug virgin. Though honestly, I was something of a sex virgin, too, having had few partners, unfortunately few times, everything pretty vanilla.

Oddly and unlike a sex shop, it somehow seemed less weird to go into a Smart Shop with my dad than by myself. "You wanna check it out?" I asked, pointing to the Mario Kart-style mushroom with a big smile painted on it.

"Sure. What is it?" asked my dad, happily stoned and amenable to almost any suggestion.

"A 'smart shop' but I don't know what that means."

We went in, and it was like entering Willy Wonka's gift shop if he specialized in psychedelics instead of chocolate. The shelves were stocked with products I'd never seen before: glass vials filled with opaque tinctures, tubes of lotion and lubricants, metal tins containing "relaxation" drops. Some bottles advertised aphrodisiac qualities, others calming effects, others euphoria and well-being. An expansive selection of bongs, pipes, grinders, and other cannabis paraphernalia filled one wall. One display case advertised seeds of all sorts, mostly different strains of cannabis, but other plants too. The vibe was part candy shop, part bazaar. Locked glass display cases filled with colorful boxes in a variety of gemstone hues gave it the feeling of a jewelry store. That, and the man who stood next to the locked cases, observing the shoppers.

My dad explored the left side of the store while I looked at the right, both of us trying to avoid the awkwardness of catching the other looking at an aphrodisiac for too long. We had assiduously avoided entering the red-light district for obvious reasons, though honestly, I doubted my dad would even notice. Jaramie's nickname for him was Oblivious Newton John and it fit.

Against one wall, a refrigerated case had a poster announcing "Premium Magic Truffles" in Dutch and English. The poster listed the types available for purchase and their properties:

"Psilocybe Tampanensis, better known as the Philosopher's Stone. Dark but insightful. A true journey through your own thoughts and feelings. Ideal for self-discovery."

"Psilocybe Mexicana. Are you ready for a 'fiesta del color'? A nice visual trip to the sunny side of life. Feels like a tropical holiday!"

"Psilocybe Atlantis. A forbidden fruit from the lost world. An extremely visual and full-colour adventure through all dimensions simultaneously. Recommended by experienced travelers."

Each of the truffles was rated for visual, energy, body, and brain effects on a 1-6 "out of this world" scale. Sold in quantities of ten, fifteen, and twenty grams, prices range from around twenty-five dollars to upwards of fifty.

I called my dad over. "They have magic mushrooms." I pointed to the poster on the case. "Look."

"That says 'truffles.' Are they the same thing?"

I told him yes, which I knew from a little tourist booklet somebody had left behind on the train that I read on my way back to Zandfort that first night. "Well," I said, clarifying. "I mean. Technically no. But yes. Mushrooms are the above-ground fruit of underground truffles. Truffles are below-ground mushrooms. Technically, mushrooms are illegal here, but truffles aren't. I don't know why." (From here on, I use "truffles" and "mushrooms" interchangeably, even though they have important differences in terms of recommended dosage and legality).

"Would you like help?" asked the store attendant who'd come to stand beside this locked case.

"Yes," I said, feeling curious and nerdy at the same time. "Yes, please. My dad and I were thinking about doing truffles. What would you recommend? Are they safe?"

"Very safe. Yes. Just don't take too much, eat them on an empty stomach, don't mix drugs, and eat something sweet if you want to come down. We have some truffles that you probably shouldn't try your first time." He gestured to the first four of the six listed. "These four are all very gentle for beginners."

"Okay. Sounds good." My dad and I turned back to the list. I read the descriptions again, torn between Tampanensis and Atlantis. "How much is a beginner's dose?"

"Eight-and-a-half grams."

"I'll take ten grams of the Philosopher's Stone."

My dad wanted intense visuals, so he chose Mexicana. The store attendant put two small plastic boxes into a paper bag along with a safety pamphlet and stapled the top shut.

We'd recently eaten lunch and it was getting late so we decided to wait and try the truffles first thing the next morning. We had Indonesian food for dinner, then returned to the hotel where I did some light internet research on "magic" truffles.

The historic and religious use of psychedelics dates back to the origin of our species. The earliest evidence, found in Northern Australia, consists of murals depicting psilocybin-containing mushrooms on rock walls dated to around 10,000 B.C.E. Psychedelic mushrooms, truffles, and cacti existed in religious mythology and ceremony of the Aztecs, Maya, Toltecs, and even early Christians.

Psilocybin is the primary psychoactive component of the mushrooms and has a structure very similar to serotonin. Because of this similarity, psilocybin binds to the brain's serotonin receptors and thereby creates higher levels of circulating serotonin, almost like a super-intense antidepressant. In some ways, it was actually the discovery of LSD that led to the development of pharmaceutical antidepressants because no other drug had shown such potency at such a small dose before, and that led to the discovery of neurotransmitters, including serotonin and dopamine. SSRI anti-depressants (Selective Serotonin Reuptake Inhibitors) and micro-dosed psychedelics might be functionally the same thing: serotonin reuptake inhibitors?

***

I woke up first, around six, eager to get started. I'd never tried a hallucinogen before, and I was ready to see some shit!

My dad had emails to check, then seemed absorbed in what was either reading or maybe napping with the *Economist*, so I warned him I was going to start without him.

I took my box out of the paper bag and opened it to find a vacuum-sealed pouch holding what looked like the insides of five or six acorns. I tore it with my teeth and the smell hit me. It was a cross between decomposing wood and slightly sweaty feet. Not bad necessarily, just earthy. They were tan, green, black, and intriguing if not exactly appetizing.

I put one bundle the size of a raisin in my mouth and began to chew diligently. The texture was unremarkable—like a raw soaked almond, or an undercooked potato. It was the aftertaste that made me gag. Bitter and acidic, it lingered on the back of my throat and the divots in my teeth long after I swallowed. Tiny fragments hid in the crevasses of my mouth, each triggering immediate revulsion when my tongue found it. Nevertheless, I chewed each bite at least a dozen times because I had read the instruction manual that came with our truffle purchase, and it said they work best if you masticate the cell walls. I'm a good student when it comes to doing drugs: I do all the reading and follow all the rules.

It took at least twenty, maybe thirty minutes to choke down the recommended starter dose. I fired off a text to Adelynn saying "FYI, doing magic mushrooms with my dad in Amsterdam. Will let you know how it goes!!" then sat at the desk in our adjoining hotel room and waited.

***

Some minutes later, after rousing himself, my dad walked in. "What?" he said, looking down to check that he hadn't spilled something on his shirt or that his fly wasn't accidentally undone.

"What what?" I said, beaming at him with unbridled joy and appreciation.

"You're smiling."

"Yes," I said.

"What's going on?"

"Nothing." I smiled even bigger. There wasn't anything going on. I wasn't thinking about anything in particular, just experiencing how lovely it was to be alive. I stretched my arms and wiggled my fingers, delighting in really *feeling* my fingers. I flicked them like I was getting water off and it tickled all through the top of my head. Maybe something was going on. Grinning, I said, "You should catch up."

He opened his container, threw about a third of its contents in his mouth, chewed, and then did that again twice in short order.

"You don't have a problem with the taste?" I was shocked.

"No. What's wrong with the taste? Just a little umami-y. Should we call your ooh-mam-my-y?" Turned out he had been getting high in the other room.

I laughed. It felt good. A warm buzzing in my cheeks made it easier to smile vigorously than to make any other facial expression. Joy was effortless.

"Want to go out?" I asked my dad, grooving in my desk chair, fully unable to sit still.

"Do you want . . . " he started to say, before trailing off into giggles.

"I don't . . . I want . . . I . . . " I dissolved into giggles too, which triggered his giggles, which re-triggered my giggles, and we both laughed until our cheeks hurt.

After some time, I recovered myself and my train of thought. Holding onto my belly, aching from laughter, I said, "Seriously, Dad. What do you want to do? I'm happy with whatever!" I said it honestly. I was completely thrilled to stay in the hotel room and do nothing because nothing had ever been so much fun, but I was suddenly afraid that if my dad wanted to go out—to a museum or for a walk in Vondelpark—that he wouldn't say so. I learned my self-denying, people-pleasing ways from him.

"I could . . . " he trailed off once again.

After a suspenseful wait for him to complete his thought, happily, I yelled, "WHAT DO YOU WANT TO DO?"

"Anything!" He laughed. "As long as it doesn't require finishing a sentence!"

"Okay let's go for a walk!" We collected jackets, wallets, room keys, and decided we'd head toward the center of the city. It took probably an hour to leave the hotel room successfully, fits of giggles incapacitating one or the other then both of us each time we tried to speak. Walking through the lobby, we put on our best impressions of normal, serious people, not talking and trying to avoid eye contact.

We started out walking arm-in-arm like we owned the city, awed by the experience of being alive . . . until we hit a crosswalk. Encountering traffic, passersby, bicycles, trams, even fast walkers, was too much. At any loud sound or fast movement, we cowered together like poor twin Simbas in the middle of the wildebeest stampede. Cars and bikes and sleek trams came out of nowhere and seemingly from every direction. Did they drive on the wrong side of the road here?

There was simply too much to watch for, too much stimulation in general. Being out in public meant spending energy trying to look normal rather than enjoying the experience. I asked if we could return to the hotel and my dad agreed, his relief plain.

When we got back, we retired to our separate but connected rooms. I checked the clock and was shocked to find it had somehow been hours, at least six, since we took the truffles. Because the pamphlet said their effects lasted about three to five hours, I was expecting to "sober up" imminently. I wanted to focus on and enjoy the intensely pleasant sensations coursing through me as long as they lasted.

I laid down on the antique-footed sofa with my legs over the armrest, one arm hanging off the cushion, the other over my head.

I closed my eyes and there, unbidden, I saw David. I saw him as I'd seen him a thousand times before: worn Levi's, blue V-neck American Apparel t-shirt, aura of mild frustration. As I was looking at him, David flattened into a two-dimensional being, a light switch plate with limbs and a face. Then the whole world flattened out into 2D. The earth beneath me became a circle with people dancing and holding hands around it like paper dolls. I saw dozens of people—no one I knew, just random examples of humanity—become 2D versions of themselves. They flattened out and paired up. Happy couples joined together, back-to-back. Together, each pair created a 3D being with eyes, arms, legs, heads on both sides of the body. So functional! They danced around with all four feet on the floor, perfect peripheral vision, the ability to grab and move in any direction. All of them were delighted by their partnership, moving smoothly, spinning and twirling like champion square dancers performing their favorite choreography.

I watched them, vicariously joyful in their blissful partnerships.

Then, David again. The man who had shattered my heart six months before was partnered with me, but he was bent over and grunting, carrying me like a backpack, my legs kicking uselessly at the sky. He took heavy steps while I flailed. Watching him struggle, it became clear that he didn't know how to operate any differently—this was how he did love. He had to feel in control. Partnership—the act of trusting, depending, working with and relying on someone else—made him feel too vulnerable. So, he packed me up, put me on his back and kept moving, regardless of my protestations.

I felt overwhelming grief at the vision. I felt so sad, but on *his behalf*. This was his understanding of relationships. He felt like he had to do everything by himself. There was no partnership, only burden

Lying on that couch with my eyes closed, I saw things clearly for the first time. Our breakup, I understood, was not about my inadequacy. David and I had never been the right partners for each other. If he was going to spend his life with his partner on his back, he was right to choose someone wispy, substance-less, someone who wouldn't mind being carried like a backpack. That would never be me and I didn't want it to be. There was nothing wrong with wanting to have my feet on the ground. I could see on my flat face that I hated being pressure someone else's shoulders. I wanted a partnership where I carried my own weight, where my contributions were essential to the functioning of our pair. I wanted a partner who wanted to dance *with* me rather than pick me up so he could choose the steps.

Ever since our relationship hit the skids, I had assumed the problem was me. But now, seeing our relationship in 2D from a removed, omniscient perspective, I finally understood that it wasn't my fault. The reasons David didn't want to be with me weren't about my deficiency. They weren't about me at all. When it came to relationships, David was a backpacker and I was not a backpack. We were fundamentally incompatible. No one to blame, just facts.

This series of revelations washed over me slowly and quickly at the same time. Each vision was layered with nuanced conclusions. I realized I was feeling *compassion* toward David. I had loved him almost since the moment we met, but I had never felt such compassion toward him before. I had always seen him as an authority. I needed his approval too much to feel empathy for him. Now, floating a thousand miles above a flat earth, I saw him from a new perspective, not from below but from within. I saw what he felt like inside: rigid, precarious, heavy, lonely. I was sad for him, and it felt like a release. But time was stretchy and strange on that couch and the vision changed too quickly for me to get more from it.

Like a quick cut in a movie, the scene playing behind my eyes changed. All the paper doll people disappeared, and I saw myself, larger than life, in 3D again and realistic as fuck, floating somewhere between the space above my head and the very top of the Universe. I was twenty feet tall and dressed as I was laying on the couch: black cotton maxi-dress with warm wool knee socks that David had approved back when I'd purchased them. I didn't have time to investigate the rest of my appearance before a thick blue velvet ribbon sprung from the center of my forehead, unspooling itself rapidly. Another one sprung from my heart, unspooling itself equally fast. Then a third from right below my belly, three-inches wide, velvet, the color of midnight, just like the others.

I watched them grow and unfurl themselves, gaining meters by the millisecond. They sped up even faster, racing over the ocean between Amsterdam and DC at the speed of light. I saw David again. Back to 3D, denim clad. He stood on a map in the center of DC, indifferent, his hand casually outstretched like he was ready to receive the bill from a waiter who had provided disappointing service. The ribbons growing from my body slowed. They hovered above his hand, then tied themselves into a dainty bow and dropped into his palm.

David barely acknowledged the extraordinary gift.

Watching him snub me, I understood—finally—that our relationship had been defined, from the beginning, by me giving him power over me that he never should have had. I had allowed him to determine my self-worth. When he told me he'd be more attracted if I were fifteen pounds lighter, I absorbed that shame. When he judged me for wearing clothes made of non-natural fabric, I stopped wearing them. When he proposed, I felt saved because I didn't have to do the hard, messy work of figuring out what I wanted from life because he would decide for me.

The realization hit me that even from Amsterdam, even as I claimed to be "moving on," I was still living in David's world, letting him rule mine. I was still *thinking* about him, imagining his responses before I made decisions: the dress, the socks, the shoes I was wearing I chose because he'd liked them. Thousands of miles away and months after breaking up, I was still dressing for him. The lyrics from a Yuna song about how she decorates her life just "in case" her lover shows up.

Just *in case* he shows up.

I was decorating myself, my life, for David's re-entrance. The ribbons from my head, chest, and womb were the power I was still letting him have over my thoughts, my heart, my sexuality. I still thought of myself as his and continued giving him all my power. And worse, he wasn't even asking for it. He didn't even value it. He was just standing there with an indifferent smirk like it didn't even matter. He watched me tie myself into knots and bows for him.

I saw this—my contortions and his disdain—and was enraged. Fuck that.

No seriously: FUCK THAT.

At that thought, a giant pair of scissors appeared in the hands of my larger-than-life self. They were the kind you'd see at a ribbon-cutting ceremony, except pointed at the end like a stiletto and perilously sharp. I knew *exactly* what to do with them. In a fury of rage and pride, I caught the ribbon flowing from my forehead with the open V of the scissors. I relished the momentary resistance and then the sound of shearing as I sliced through it. I was done letting David own my thoughts.

I sliced through the ribbon coming from my heart. He didn't want my love; I was done giving it to him.

I sliced the ribbon unfurling from my lower belly. I was done thinking, feeling, allowing him to own my sexuality.

I did it quickly, slicing each ribbon with precision and resolution.

Immediately they sprouted anew. It became a race. As fast as I could cut them, they regrew. By the time I finished severing the third one, the first two had already raced over the ocean and landed in his hand. Eyes still closed, still flopped haphazardly on the couch, I was sweating from the mental exertion. My cutting became frantic, but I would not quit. If I could do 108 sun salutations in real life, I could keep cutting imaginary cords forever.

I knew that for as long as these threads connected me to him, as long as I allowed him to puppet me from afar, I would never move on. No one else could access my head, my heart, my sex, as long as I was giving it to him. So, I cut. Frenetically, then studiously. I was in this *for the long haul*. They kept growing, I kept cutting. I was patient; voracious; committed.

I realized that the faster I cut, the faster they grew, so I slowed down. I slowed my breath, and my cutting, counting each ribbon as I sliced it. I counted to ten, then twenty, then fifty. The cutting became vaguely meditative, peaceful. Contentedly, I lost track after eighty. I had the strange sense that if I kept counting, they'd keep growing.

I stopped counting and eventually, I had long moments, full breaths of time before the next ribbon sprouted and I had to cut again. Sometimes they tried to trick me by growing stealthily—in a darker color or making a head-feint in the direction of Asia—but I caught every one. Each time I sliced through a ribbon, I reminded myself that I would not send energy his way anymore.

My power was mine to keep. I wanted it back.

Finally, moments turned into minutes and no ribbons regrew.

Minutes turned into more minutes.

I watched, casually vigilant, almost daring them to try again, until everything disappeared into sleep. I woke, hours and hours later, feeling peaceful and rested in a way that seemed vaguely spiritual. I realized it was morning, the beginning of a new day.

✳✳✳

My dad, coming in from the other room, noticed a difference in me. "You look particularly radiant this morning," he said. He meant it but a glance in the mirror told me he'd be the only one to think it. Rumpled pajamas, blotchy skin, and an imprint from the cording on the couch embedded in my face, I was hardly "radiant," but even I noticed a light in my eyes.

"I feel really good," I said. I wasn't ready to share the contents of my visions or their effects on me yet. I was afraid that if I said the words out loud or looked at the experience too closely, all the good feelings would disappear. I was afraid I'd sound crazy, even just to myself, and it would make me doubt what I was feeling. I didn't want to let go of the sense of well-being nor the revelations about David, so I asked, "Wanna take the train to the airport?"

We hit up a coffeeshop on our way to the station. I was talking excitedly, joint in hand, brimming with ideas for marketing a friend's new jewelry business, when my dad interrupted me.

"Why did you never go to business school?" he asked.

The warm and fuzzy post-psychedelic cocoon wasn't enough to protect me from a pang of frustration. "I went to business school. Did you miss the last year?"

"No, I know. I meant an MBA program. When we talked about it, before the PhD, you said you wanted an MBA. I always thought you'd be good in business."

I told him the reasons I'd used to convince myself out of it: It was too expensive and frivolous. I was too old at twenty-nine. It wouldn't be worth the return on investment because blah blah blah...

I heard myself talking. I sounded justified, rational. These were all "good" reasons, and my dad accepted them. But I heard another voice too. It was a version of my own, but it sounded older, calmer, wiser than my normal internal monologue. It argued against each point as I made it:

To the notion that it was too expensive, and that I didn't need it, the voice said, "So what? You can afford it. And it seems like you *want* to."

I'd told my dad I was too old, that the average age at graduation for MBA students in 2012 was twenty-six and I would be thirty-one by the time I matriculated. But the voice pointed out the irrelevance of those facts: "How old would you be in two years if you don't go?"

To the argument that it wasn't worth the investment because business school was all about building networks and I had a pretty good one already, it said, "Bullshit. You can always know more good people."

I changed the topic with my dad so I could stop the debate in my head. But even after we arrived at the airport and boarded the flight I couldn't get his question and my unsatisfying answers, out of my head. Why *hadn't* I gone for an MBA? What happened? I remembered deciding that I would apply to MBA programs; I did my research on schools but then applied to earn a PhD instead. What had *happened*?

Sitting on that plane, looking down on the clouds from my window seat, I tried to reconstruct my decision-making. As soon as I discovered that I could earn a doctoral degree from a business school, I stopped pursuing the MBA and became focused on getting into a PhD program. PhD program applications are more difficult, they accept fewer students, and the degree comes with the title "Doctor." Plus, in a Ph.D. program, they pay you rather than the other way around. I was seduced by the prestige, difficulty, and social validation. I did it because I told myself it was the better, smarter, more practical decision.

But that was a mistake and a lie. The truth was I couldn't allow myself to do something so big, expensive, and time-consuming just because I *wanted* to. The realization hit me so heavily it felt like turbulence pressing me into the airplane seat: I didn't value my joy. I didn't know *how* to value my joy. I valued self-sacrifice and martyrdom. I didn't think my time was well spent unless I was working, doing something that made me miserable.

This thought pattern was so entrenched that it was hard to see. I had always accepted it as morally right, a fact of life, the sign of a "good person." This belief came from my dad's family. It was reinforced every holiday and gathering where enjoyment was never allowed without guilt-inducing recognition of others less fortunate. Every Thanksgiving, when we'd go around the table saying what we were grateful for, it was traditional for some elder member of the family to spend their time recounting a shortlist of the worst atrocities currently afflicting humanity, making the next person sound like a real asshole if they didn't also recognize those suffering. The problem was not recognition of suffering or feeling solidarity with those oppressed—that was important. The problem was that I learned feeling joy, gratitude, or pleasure should be replaced, immediately, by a focus on grief and suffering. Nauseated from the internal turbulence, I realized in that moment: I didn't know how to be happy. I didn't know how to allow myself enjoyment without dismissing it as frivolous. I felt like, as long as there were people suffering, I should suffer in solidarity.

Except, I didn't want to do that anymore. Something had changed since yesterday. I no longer wanted to be miserable. I didn't want to reflexively self-sacrifice. I was born. I deserved to be here. I deserved to enjoy my life. I needed to learn how. There on the plane, in seat 25A, I decided to apply to MBA programs, just for *fun*.

We were somewhere over the Atlantic and I was frustrated that we had no Wi-Fi, meaning I couldn't start researching MBA programs immediately. It was the first thing I did after we got home. I googled MBA rankings, domestically and internationally, then eliminated options based on location and language requirements, coming up with a top ten list based on what I thought I'd *enjoy* most. I applied to two schools: Kellogg, where I'd been in the Ph.D. program and enviously watched the MBA students do all the fun things we weren't allowed to do; and ESADE in Spain. If I was looking for fun, where could be better than Barcelona?

Chapter 8

What A Feeling

Big Island, Hawaii
December 2012
Substances ingested: apple-bananas, passion-orange-guava juice, and plenty of pot

My family owns a home in Hawaii. My mom oversaw the plans and construction and now we rent it out most of the year, but mid-December through mid-January it's ours. Being unemployed, unmarried, childless, and otherwise completely unencumbered of responsibilities, in the winter of 2012 I arrived about a week before the rest of my family. I parked myself at the affectionately nicknamed "shack," a shingled, 600-square-foot cottage on the peak overlooking Wailea Bay. It had been a true shack when we bought the property—shoddy foundation, rats in the walls, rusted metal roof—but Hawaii waterfront building restrictions meant that if we'd torn it down completely, we wouldn't be allowed to rebuild.

In the winter, waves often pounded the rocks kicking up spray that made the deck feel like the prow of a ship, but it was serene now. Perfectly sized for one person, it was my favorite place to stay when I was alone in Hawaii. I'd rotate from the bed to the beach to the deck to the sofa and back to bed, creating an idyllic island routine of reading, tanning, and fish tacos.

Soon upon arrival, I reached out to Fairy Godmother Jaramie for a visit. In one of her previous lives, Jaramie worked as a rolfer, and then as a Judith Astin Method bodyworker. Over the years her touch had softened from the grimace-inducing intensity of traditional rolfing into a gentle pressure that felt more like a combination of Reiki and Swedish massage. Her massages were excellent, but the real treat was ninety uninterrupted minutes to get her unique perspective on life in general and whatever specific thing was vexing me at the moment.

Wearing a bikini top and shorts I lay on her portable massage table. A light breeze blew through the open doors of the shack. Jaramie rubbed my stomach, hands moving in a clockwise motion while bright green geckos zipped across the plaster ceiling, sometimes clicking at each other and us as if to indicate disapproval or maybe just get our attention.

Jaramie took a sip from her glass jar of alkaline lemon water.

"It feels," she gestured to my abdomen, "like you're hanging on to some old emotion."

"I am!" I was suddenly indignant at myself. The peace and comfort I'd experienced in Amsterdam had become harder to grasp. I felt like I was leaking energy back to David again. I knew he was incapable of the partnership I wanted; I knew I didn't want to give him my power. But I was backsliding. To Jaramie I said, "I keep imagining things that aren't real or won't happen, or I dwell on things that have already happened. Like, I don't want David back, but I keep thinking about what things he could do that would make me consider it. Or I dream about him making fun of me with his next girlfriend or wife or fiancée or whoever. It's like my mind is running a constant search for whatever will hurt me the most. What the fuck?"

"Oh, that is exactly what it's doing." Jaramie returned matter-of-factly to rubbing my stomach.

I gave her a look that asked for clarification.

She stopped rubbing my stomach to explain, "Souls can't feel, only bodies can feel. Souls incarnate for the opportunity to *feel*." She paused, giving me a moment to process and raise objections. I could have come up with some, or at least some follow-up questions, but I wanted to hear more first. She continued, "Getting a human body for a ride on Earth is like the most intense roller coaster you can ever take. Human souls are thrill seekers. They *want* to feel."

Okay, I guess that made a degree of internally consistent sense, but I didn't see how it related to my reflexive self-torture with thoughts about David. Jaramie concluded her explanation: "Our minds manufacture whatever stories will get us to *feel* the most intensely." At least she was right about that. The stories I was telling myself were never neutral; they were the stories that made me feel *the worst*. It made sense based on her theory why I'd do that. But was there a way out?

As if reading my mind, Jaramie offered, "When you're stuck in the worst of it, when you want a break from intense emotions," she paused to tap my chest above my heart for emphasis, "remember that, at any given time, there are thousands of souls clamoring for a body simply for the opportunity to *feel* whatever you are feeling at that moment."

Similarly to when her voice appeared out of the darkness in Costa Rica, I felt truth in her words. I let the parts of her speech go by that didn't make sense or didn't resonate, but the idea that bodies are wired to feel—physically and emotionally—resonated strongly. In my body that was made to feel, her words *felt* true. If I was honest with myself, there on the massage table with Jaramie, I could admit that something about me was enjoying, or was at least attached to, the pain I continued to recreate for myself. If I wasn't getting *something* from it, I'd stop doing it. The truths I experienced in Amsterdam were as true as ever—that our breakup wasn't a reflection of my inadequacy, that David wasn't my forever, and that even if he came back a relationship with him would never be fulfilling—but those truths didn't make me feel as much as the wounds I could inflict upon myself by slicing my heart open with imagined mistakes that, justifiably, drove him away.

Jaramie was right. My soul was a junkie for emotional intensity and only knew how to feel the negative. I was doing this to myself. I was doing it because *it hurt*, not because it was true.

I wanted to stop but I didn't know how. The pattern was too ingrained.

I thought about it for a moment then had a realization: "You have access to ayahuasca, don't you?"

"Of course," she said.

"Would it be too much... I mean, could you..." I was a little scared that I didn't know what I was asking. Whether this was a simple favor or a Herculean request. "My 30th birthday is coming up in April."

"I know when your birthday is: 'The Day of Physical Substance,'" She smiled, quoting the headline of the April 25th entry in the astrology Birthday Book. I hated that even the planets seemed to be calling me fat but I didn't allow it to distract me from my purpose.

"I've wanted to try ayahuasca for years. Even more so now that I know what mushrooms can do. Could I . . . or could you..." I trailed off again, scared I was asking for something inappropriate.

"Get you set up with a ceremony and a shaman?"[1] she asked.

"Yeah, I mean, I guess that's the request?" I didn't know what I was asking, but I trusted that she did.

I'd first heard about ayahuasca in 2008 or so, from an ethnobotanist friend-of-a-friend, who extolled the virtues in incredible terms: it dissolved your ego! You saw God and became one with the Universe! All your cravings and addictions were miraculously cured!

I knew enough to be skeptical of such extraordinary claims, but what's more American than hoping for a drug that painlessly cures you of all ills? I turned to the internet for some quick information. I scrolled the list of web addresses, looking for a familiar and credible source. I found an article on cnn.com, that reported on a study with twenty-seven "healthy normal" participants, meaning they were not afflicted with terminal diagnoses or severe disease. Twenty-six of the twenty-seven said it helped them feel closer to God and more connected to the rest of humanity. A year later, twenty-five of them reported continued positive benefits from the experience. The enduring nature of the experience—that the benefits lasted at least a full year beyond the trip itself—was the most intriguing part of the article. That drugs are capable of making you feel good, regardless of reality, was not new or interesting, but that a drug-induced experience could create a lasting connection to some form of higher power? I mean, that was enticing.

I was tempted but turned down the ethnobotanist's invitation. It seemed too dangerous, desperate, and likely some sort of hoax or cult. In some ways, my instincts were right on.

In 2008, I couldn't imagine trusting a drug-induced experience as anything more than artificial at best. But after Amsterdam it made more sense. After taking The Philosopher's Stone, I'd felt—briefly—connected to universal wisdom. I wanted that experience again. What other insights might the Universe impart to guide the next step of my journey? Plus,

---

1. I didn't know enough about appropriation of spiritual technologies to be concerned about that at the time. At the time, I didn't know anything about how psychedelic substances have been stolen from Indigenous communities and appropriated (largely) by white people representing commercial interests. I didn't know how ayahuasca, particularly, has been extracted from the Indigenous communities of its origin in the Amazon, and that those communities are under current, constant, deadly threat from industries actively destroying their land. I didn't know about the dangers of ayahuasca retreats—to participants and host countries—everything from sexual assault and fake medicine men, to toxic additives included to heighten the visuals for drug tourists, and more. I didn't know nearly enough to keep myself safe or make responsible decisions. Please do better than I did. Psilocybin is arguably a birthright to all humanity so there is no reason or benefit to pursuing psychedelic substances outside your ancestral traditions, and definitely heightened risk for harm of all different forms, known and unknown.

I wanted to break this pattern of torturing myself to feel something. I wanted to be able to feel and value my joy. If ayahuasca was a miracle cure, I wanted it to cure me.

Jaramie thought about it for a beat, "Let me look into the possibilities."

I knew she'd follow up and get back to me, so I changed the topic of conversation to the pair of needy ferrets she was pet-sitting for her youngest daughter.

Chapter 9
No Roots

Washington, DC
January 2013
Substances ingested: *hyper*-local joints

Upon returning from Costa Rica, I'd been living part-time with my parents in my Bay Area childhood home, and part-time with our family friend Leo in DC. My parents met Leo and his former partner Renate (they were never married but had kids and business together for decades) over forty years ago when my mom was pregnant with my older sister. Leo and Renate had been around all my life and consequently, I'd always thought of their family—two kids, two grandkids, a rescue poodle with severe allergies—as an extension of my own. Leo was brusque, bracingly direct, fiercely smart, and a talented gardener who grew smooth but potent weed. He was always generous with his friends.

Living with my parents as an adult had been mostly pleasant. They had always been respectful of my autonomy and there was enough space in the house that we weren't living on top of each other. After college, I'd lived at home while sick with Lyme, and I think we all enjoyed it as much as it's possible to enjoy being or watching someone you love struggle with being seriously ill. It may have even brought us closer together.

Seven years post-graduation, though, it was difficult to watch the distance growing in my parents' marriage. I enjoyed being with them, but it didn't seem like they enjoyed each other much. When I needed a break, I would head to DC to be with Adelynn and stay with Leo in his giant, purple Victorian house that bustled with extended family.

For months now, with increasing frequency but starting before I tried mushrooms or any other psychedelic substance, I'd been having these... "flashbacks"? Except they weren't flashbacks because I'd never experienced the things I was seeing before. "Visions" is also wrong because that makes them sound clear and like something I was *seeing*. These experiences were short and vague, almost a moment of deja vu. A flash and then gone.

When I closed my eyes, or between blinks, I saw myself like a tree, planted up to my waist in soil, torso emerging from the earth, arms free. When I tried to concentrate on it, figure out what it was or what it was telling me, the image evaporated like a dream. And quickly, too. So, I figured whatever my subconscious was trying to communicate couldn't be *that* important, otherwise it would last. It never did, but it kept coming back.

That morning, I was leaning out the third-floor window at Leo's smoking a joint. I watched him work in his wild but carefully tended suburban garden, moving fallen winter leaves, clomping about in loose rubber boots with a wheelbarrow and a pickaxe. The January air was damp in a way that turned the world a misty grey. It wasn't raining and I was warm enough with the window open, but I could feel the moisture in the air settling into my hair. And making it harder to light my joint.

My attention drifted from the five large elm trees that shielded his property from the street to where a hole in the ground, perhaps two feet in diameter and three or four feet deep, had appeared since I'd last visited this window. A few feet in from the sidewalk, comfortably surrounded by vegetation and dark, healthy, carbon-rich soil, the hole beckoned. I felt magnetically drawn to it. I had the inexplicable urge to run downstairs and jump in it. It was my flashback coming true.

I put down my joint on the windowsill, leaning further to get a better look. The hole was deeper than I initially thought. And wider. It looked comfortable, almost spacious. I wanted to hop inside and shout to Leo, "Fill 'er up!" Something in my animal body called to be buried up to my hips, packed tightly into and against the earth, legs immobilized and indistinguishable from roots.

I longed to be rooted. Ever since Costa Rica when I realized I didn't even know what "rooted" felt like.

I craved it but common sense stepped in. Even from the distance of three floors up, I knew that dirt was. . . dirty. I didn't want dirt against my bare skin. Feeling slightly more stoned and creative, my problem-solving instinct kicked in: I could wear jeans! But then any pair of jeans I chose would get ruined. I could wear cheap leggings instead! But those wouldn't provide any real protection from twigs. Or centipedes. Or pincher bugs.

I imagined shiny, wet, and well-armored insects wiggling against and biting the tenderest flesh of the inside of my thighs and shuddered. Maybe I could line the hole with plastic, buy a bunch of bags of organic soil from Lowe's and fill it with clean dirt? By the time I'd hit upon "plastic" and "clean dirt," I knew I was engaging in absurdities.

I saw that the hole had been dug for a lacy, flame-colored Chinese maple when it got delivered late that morning by three men in a pickup truck. Leo helped the guys widen and deepen the hole. Purposefully, almost delicately, they covered the bottom of the hole in a layer of soft mulch. Cooperatively, carefully, they loosened the fibrous tendrils of the tree's root bundle. Fragments of their conversation carried up to my window: the proper watering it needed to protect the transplant from unnecessary stress, the fertilizer it needed to grow optimally, how to prune and cover the roots with burlap in inclement weather. When they were finished nestling the tree in its nutritious soil, I wanted to *be* that tree.

It was incomprehensible, strange to the point of shocking, to feel so strongly towards a plant. I allowed myself to really investigate the feeling because of its strength. Partly, it felt unfamiliar and disconcerting to want something—badly—without knowing what that thing was. "Hungry" was a feeling I'd always associated with being desirous of food, yet it was the closest verb to identify what I was feeling. I envied that plant. Coveted what it had, the care devoted to it, that people wanted to give it what it needed to grow. I felt myself pondering, while looking out that window and into the days and weeks that followed, what might one call the hunger to be planted.

***

The two MBA programs to which I applied required interviews for acceptance. The ESADE interview took place at the Marriott near Times Square in New York and was conducted by a professional member of the international recruiting team, a petite but effective Dutchman named Johannes Dijkman. The interview was an engaging, exciting process of mutual seduction: Your program promotes socially responsible business? I *love* socially responsible business! You need me to learn Spanish? *I* need me to learn Spanish! The recruiter could have been psychic for the way he managed to hit all the selling points that would be the most convincing to me.

Leaving the interview, I decided ESADE was my first choice which was good because Kellogg rejected me two weeks later.

My ESADE acceptance felt like the very best of gifts, arriving about a month before my thirtieth birthday.

A week or two later, an equally exciting email from Jaramie landed in my inbox:

Subject: *Are you wearing your birthday suit???*

It is a good year for you, I can see that already, just try not to get motion sickness when we go round the bend. Lots of changes and they are all good.

I got in touch with the lovable Know-it-All and she's ready to show-it-all to you :) Be here around the middle of April."

It was Jaramie's coded way of saying that she'd hooked me up. A revealing, hopefully life-changing, ayahuasca ceremony would usher me into my new decade, and I was ecstatic.

Chapter 10
Bleeker & 6th

Big Island, Hawaii
April 2013
Substances ingested: a diet low in tyramine to prepare for an ayahuasca journey

In the weeks leading up to the ceremony, I researched the history, composition, and contraindications for ayahuasca. I had no idea what to expect—not where the ceremony would be, not how many people would participate, not what to wear or how long it would last—so I counteracted my uncertainty with research.

Traditionally, ayahuasca is a brew of two plants that work together to increase then maintain the amount of circulating serotonin in the brain. *Banisteriopsis caapi* (a nondescript green leafy vine) and *Psychotria viridis* (another nondescript leafy green plant, but maybe I'm just not attuned to the details) are combined in a complicated and specific brewing process. One plant contains DMT (dimethyltryptamine, found in many plants and some animals) and the other contains beta-carboline alkaloids that slow down the metabolic processing of DMT so the effects last longer. DMT works similarly to psilocybin—they both bind primarily to serotonin receptors to increase circulating serotonin—but without the chemicals of the other plant (beta-carboline alkaloids), the high of DMT would only last around five to thirty minutes. An ayahuasca ceremony can last hours. Imagine the brain as a sink where the faucet produces serotonin. If the sink fills above a certain level it creates a psychedelic experience. Serotonergicpsychedelics (eg: DMT) turn the faucet on high and (beta-carboline alkaloids) partially plug the drain.

That's the basic neuroscience, but it was the mysticism surrounding ayahuasca that built up my hopes and expectations. Successful preparation requires many steps over many days, including harvesting the right plants at the right time of day. Some say this process came to a shaman in a dream as a gift from the spirit Universe and I can almost believe it. It makes more sense to me that somebody acted out what they experienced in a dream than that ancient peoples had the nutritional reserves and tolerance for risk to brew every combination of plants into complex concoctions and consume them for shits and giggles. A dream makes more sense than trial and error when considering the nearly infinite biodiversity of the Amazon rainforest where ayahuasca originated.

More than the science or the history, in my research I found myself devouring testimonials from other first-time users. Though the personal experiences varied from euphoric to hellish, there was a common thread of agreement that, "The Grandmother gives you what you need, not what you want." Most accounts mentioned some degree of nausea and vomiting, but one woman's graphic recounting of her experience gripped me:

"...overwhelming misery. ... A scathing pain rises in my chest—the most excruciating pain I've ever felt... Legions of demons sail out of my body..."

I was horrified by the experience and ravenous for it at the same time. It was another example of me craving misery as if it's a good thing, but I didn't see that at the time.

Reading further from the same account:

"I'm made to see that what is being purged now is a deeply rooted belief that I don't deserve to be alive, that no one can love me and I will always need to justify my existence."

Yes. Me. I wanted that. Desperately. Costa Rica helped to uncover that feeling but it didn't dislodge it completely. I wanted it gone and for good. The woman's description continued:

"I feel a pressure in my chest that could break all my ribs. I grab my bucket, vomit out what appears to be a stream of fire."

According to her account, she vomited a *snake* into her bucket. A real, live, writhing, corporeal SNAKE.

Oh my god I wanted to puke snakes. Whatever it required—the more harrowing the better—I wanted to be purged of my beliefs that I didn't deserve to be alive, that no one could love me, that I would always need to justify my existence. I wanted it all to be *gone*. I wanted to be purified and resurrected and cleansed, and the more dramatic the purging, the more I'd believe it. No pain, no gain, right?

On top of all that, what I couldn't even admit to myself was that I wanted ayahuasca to show me God. Ever since the first articles I read about it said that the *majority* of people who held no religious or spiritual beliefs before trying it had experiences of transcendence on ayahuasca, I'd wanted that for myself. I was God-curious. It felt like a great thing to be able to believe in; the comfort and connection of faith would be really nice, but I just couldn't get there on my own.

My dad was ethnically Jewish but not particularly religious, which was good because my mom had been practically allergic to religion of any sort while I was growing up. I learned—early—that the Catholic church is the world's largest untaxed landholder, that Catholic women are the most likely to have abortions, and that churches were responsible for harboring pedophiles. "Religion" and "hypocrisy" were used roughly synonymously in my childhood home.

From my parents, I learned a primarily materialist worldview—we're born, we die, nothing comes before or after—but always found that unsatisfying. What is "nothing"? How can something come from nothing? What's the fucking point of all this—life, struggle, doing the right thing, any of it? My experience hearing "you were born" in Costa Rica cracked the door to reconsideration of some version of spirituality. I wanted ayahuasca to show me something I could believe in, connect to, and find faith in. Humanity wasn't cutting it for me.

***

The day of the ceremony I woke up before dawn with vivid but illusory memories from my dreams. I held a fading emotional snapshot of myself as an ancient Samurai warrior, strapping on armor before a determinative battle. I could feel the weight of metal and leather and expectation, details so granular and visceral that I wondered, passingly, if it was a vision from a past life. When I tried to remember the specifics, they faded even faster. I teased myself for thinking about reincarnation and considered the much more likely explanations that my subconscious dredged up images from a copy of *Shogun*, the 700-page historical epic of feudal Japan that my college boyfriend's father gave me and therefore I felt like I had to read. I ended up enjoying it, but damn, that gift felt like homework.

I brushed my teeth, and the samurai visions were replaced with lyrics from the song "Bleeker & 6th" by Jesse Ruben. It's a narrative love song about two people who fall in love on a street corner in New York City. I had always hoped it was secretly about me. Ruben introduces the female lead by singing that she's outspoken and thinks that she's broken. At the end of the song, she's seen, loved, and appreciated by the song's male lead.

The line about her thinking that she needs to be fixed played at full volume on repeat in my brain as I washed dishes in the sink, typed out text messages, and got dressed in preparation for the ceremony.

***

Noon sun blaring overhead, Jaramie and her boyfriend picked me up in their biodiesel Mercedes. Jaramie's boyfriend Gary was driving—he would be participating in the ayahuasca ceremony with me, and Jaramie would play the role of "sitter" for the group. She was not partaking of ayahuasca but would be present in case anyone needed help, guidance, or a calming presence. Jaramie was in the passenger seat and I was in the back seat, having slid over behind Gary so Jaramie and I could make eye contact as we talked on the long drive into the jungle. Much of the Big Island is made up of the dry, dark-brown lava—cooled centuries before—that now looks like burnt brownies. Solitary but tenacious patches of grass fight to grow on nonexistent soil only to get picked off by the wild goats that graze the empty miles of the two-lane road that is also the island's main highway. As the fields shaded toward a lighter brown and began allowing more generous patches of grasses, I regaled Jaramie and Gary with the manifold ways I'd prepared for the ceremony.

Jaramie just laughed. "I've never gotten sick off it. All my experiences with the Grandmother have been pleasant and gentle. Like a good grandma. *Your* grandma. My grandma was a tyrant."

Perhaps I was over-prepared. Was I over-prepared? I didn't feel prepared for the intensity of what I hoped was to come. Either way, terrifying or blissful, I was ready for the ride of my life.

Jaramie told us stories of her tyrant grandma as we climbed in altitude. From two thousand feet up looking down, the lava at sea level appeared almost extra-terrestrial, the terrain of a rocky planet too hot for inhabitation. In Waimea, large hills clothed in luscious grasses rose up from flat fields looking like gigantic silicon breasts—perfectly round and perky, as if constructed rather than organically grown.

As we moved up and up, the hillside became rainforest. The pale grasses became ferns silvered with dewdrops collected from the ambient moisture. Spears of flame ginger erupted giant magenta swirls out of chartreuse stalks, dotting the increasingly green landscape with regular pops of contrasting color. The smell of Kahili ginger—as if mango blossom and honeysuckle had a baby—scented the car even through closed windows. Orange amaryllis grew tall and wild in the ditches by the side of the road.

The large house at the end of the 90-minute drive was a stunning construction of teak which, as we found out from the owner who greeted us, was built without a single nail. On this wetter side of the island, dragonflies the size of small birds buzzed through the ventilation gaps at the top of each wall. Birdcalls provided a soundtrack of high joyful notes.

We were the first to arrive and our hosts – a man and a woman in their late seventies with nearly a hundred years of psychedelic guiding experience between them – made me feel welcomed into a safe space. The woman had guided Jaramie on many of her psychedelic journeys and the trust between them was obvious. The two hosts, who we'll call Shah Jahan and Mumtaz Mahal, struck me as familiar, not because we'd ever met but because they looked like so many of my parents' hippie friends. The man had a long white beard and long white hair tied into a ponytail with a multicolored cord. The woman's grey hair was shorn to her scalp in a way that made her look regal and ageless. She wore drapey layers of washable linen, and an amulet necklace with a carving of a goddess in the dark stone.

After a little more about the house and some small talk, they showed us to the circle of chairs where we would be "journeying." I scoped the site, doing my best to act casual, but really evaluating my chosen seat based on comfort and location. In my effort to create a setting conducive to revelation, I determined where I would need to stand for the rest of the pre-ceremony chit-chat such that when they asked us to take our seats, it would be only natural for me to end up in the armchair that appeared to have the best combination of padding and view. I killed it at musical chairs growing up; I was ready for this. I hung out within a few feet of my chosen chair mostly listening as more people filtered in, while Jaramie and Gary caught up with their friends.

The first new journeyers I met were a couple who had flown in for the ceremony and were staying at the house. They were packing a series of ayahuasca journeys into a week's vacation. The man was wearing all white including his socks, which had a separate compartment for each toe. His tunic revealed an excessive amount of chest hair through an entirely too deep V-neck. I'd guess he was in his early twenties, though his hairline made him look older. He greeted me with "namaste," his hands in prayer against his chest. He looked like an actor sent by central casting to fit the bill for "fake spiritualist/snake oil salesman." Everything in my body revolted against him and I had to suppress my urge to sneer.

His fiancé was in her forties. Or fifties? Maybe late thirties? I couldn't tell. She was pale, hollow, frail, and clutching. She wore cargo jeans at least two sizes too big that she kept pulling up, trying to hang the waistband off her hipbone like a limp hula-hoop. She had no butt to hold them up so she kept having to hike them up again and again. With undue harshness and fierce judgment, I thought, "Can you not buy pants that fit? You're not a fucking teenager!" She seemed so pathetic, weak, and *old*.

The two were constantly in contact and conversation, whispering, grasping, glancing. Their codependency was so obvious, so immediate, that I was repulsed. I couldn't stop looking at them, judging them, condemning them. Who was this woman? Wasn't she embarrassed to be so old and to find an equal in someone so young? What happened to her to make her okay with being so pathetic? Trying to will it away at the same time it ate me alive, I found myself consumed by disgust toward these strangers I'd only just met.

I worried they'd sit next to me but tried to pretend I wasn't worried about anything at all. I was here to meet God and I didn't think he/she/it would grant an audience to someone being so petty.

Other journeyers began to trickle in. I worried I'd take a similar dislike to them, so I pretended to be on my phone, even though there was no cell reception or internet, to avoid interacting with other potential weirdos.

By the appointed start time there were about twenty of us, mostly everyone else in the fifty- to seventy-year-old age range. The group as a whole had a collection-of-misfits feel, as if none of us had ever worked a real, regular job with expectations of conformity or professionalism. A few too many of the participants seemed like they would be particularly easy picking for a charismatic cult leader or wacko peddler of conspiracy theories. It wasn't "the dregs" of society, but this was not a collection of individuals who screamed society's definition of success. I had already developed a strong conviction that I didn't belong there. Or worse, that I might.

The host couple clinked whatever the Indian version of castanets are, suggesting that those of us who were journeying needed to take our seats in the large oval of chairs. They asked couples who had chosen seats next to each other to separate so each participant could have a distinct experience without feeling the need to care for their partner. I was seated, in my perfect chair, next to a grey-haired couple that parted easily. With a smile and a squeeze on the knee, the man stayed seated and the woman stood, leaving the seat next to me open. The codependent couple turned inward, whispering loudly, oblivious or not caring that they were delaying the entire group. The grey-haired, fluid-moving woman stood expectantly in front of the codependent man-child displaying excessive chest hair. Slowly, reluctantly, with much clutching and backward glances, he got up. He crossed the oval to sit, of course, next to me.

Fuck.

The hosts tried to continue the proceedings, but the fiancés were still stage whispering to each other. I found myself leaning away from him and the energy shooting back and forth across the circle between them. It was clear his female half was not okay with their distance and this distraction was going to continue until they were re-enmeshed. I couldn't pull my attention away from them, especially sitting so close.

I really wanted this ceremony that I'd been looking forward to for months to be peaceful and revelatory. I figured the only way to salvage the situation was to switch seats with the emaciated woman so at least I'd have a few meters of personal space.

"I'm totally fine either way," I said, even though I wasn't. As they traded panicked glances, I went on, "But let's decide now because I don't want to switch after it starts. Plus, the whole room is waiting for us." Finally, the woman was in my seat, held by the lovely pillows I'd wanted, and I was in hers, with bamboo caning digging into my butt bones. Why had I volunteered my comfort for hers? I thought, let this be a lesson to me. In consolation to myself, I hurriedly gathered a few pillows from the couch to pad my chair and it ended up being fine.

The ceremony started with the hosts leading us in a non-denominational, non-sectarian, interfaith prayer asking for blessing, protection, and guidance from our benevolent ancestors and spirit guides. They told us to resist any stomach upset by sitting tall and breathing deeply. But if we couldn't, there was a "security bucket" and roll of toilet paper by each of our chairs. They then provided silence for us to offer our own prayers.

Directing my prayer to "the Ayahuasca Gods" whom I couldn't imagine and didn't believe in more than say, Tinkerbell or Santa Claus, I said that I was up for anything except nudity. I wanted to be fixed, purged of all that was wrong with me and made loveable. I wanted to feel a connection with something greater than me, and to keep my clothes on while doing it. I was ready to puke snakes, but the idea of being some fat chick in her underwear talking to a caterpillar with her gelatinous rolls of flesh on full display was a non-starter. Nobody had seen me naked since my last night with David and I was afraid it would push someone over the edge if they were already feeling nauseated.

At the end of the moment of silence, they chimed their castanets, and proceeded around the circle with a small pitcher of reddish-brown, molasses-textured liquid, pouring an ounce or so into each of our double shot glasses. We waited until everyone was served, then toasted together and swallowed. The taste wasn't bad but the moment it hit my stomach a violent wave of nausea overtook me. Calling up everything I'd learned about meditation in Costa Rica, I took full, deep breaths, sat up straight, and concentrated on anything other than the rapid accumulation of saliva in my mouth. I was deliberately ignoring the security bucket at the foot of my chair because I was afraid that if I puked too soon, it wouldn't work, and I wouldn't get fixed. I was also afraid that if I hurled, it would start some sort of horrific group vomiting scene where we'd all end up curled over our buckets, triggering and retriggering each other with the sounds and smell of retching. I tried to think about anything other than that. A small red bird flew in through one of the open vents and I watched it, curiously, until it found its way out.

The hosts had turned on wordless music and seemed to be in deep meditation. Once the nausea passed its acute phase, I looked around the circle, trying to figure out what I was supposed to be feeling by the expressions on other people's faces. The hallucinogenic effects were supposed to take roughly a half hour to kick in, and our hosts had told us that at the one-hour mark, they would offer a "booster" shot for anyone not feeling the effects as fully as they'd like. After maybe a quarter hour, I was the only one with my eyes open, still looking around at the others. I was also the only one who looked like she could've been doing her taxes, if necessary. Time stretched and I started contemplating taking the booster. I was afraid I'd vomit it directly into my bucket, but I wanted a more intense experience, to have visions and realizations, to suffer and emerge, like a phoenix.

I took the booster when it was offered and barely kept it down. I hoped fresh air would quell my intense nausea, so I let myself out the glass sliding doors and onto the lanai. There was a pune, the Hawaiian version of a daybed, covered in mismatched pillows where I could lie down, but I chose to stay sitting up to keep down the bile. I practiced yoga breathing and was surprised when I tasted eucalyptus on the wind. I didn't know eucalyptus grew in the tropics. Seeking its source, I was surprised to notice a copse of the pale, papery-trunked trees about thirty feet away, at the edge of the property. Another hour passed as I daydreamed about the eucalyptus of my California childhood, watching iridescent beetles of different sizes float in on currents of wind and land on the siding of the house before opening their wings and flying away again.

Every few minutes, I asked myself if I was high yet. I tested myself with basic math problems: 6 x 7. 42 divided by 3. The fact that I could think through the problems from beginning to end without the numbers taking on colors or flavors or Italian accents told me that I was still, disappointingly, sober. I was thinking about annoying stuff like my parents fighting and the couple inside and how much mosquito bites itch. I didn't feel clear or happy, and definitely not like profound healing was taking place. I never made a conscious choice to move from sitting up to lying down, but as the nausea attenuated, my posture relaxed.

I tried to force myself to think enlightened thoughts. The harder I tried, the more resentful and banal my internal monologue became. Had I screwed up? Did I not deserve this experience? Did I break ayahuasca? I closed my eyes, hoping the removal of external stimuli would allow me to take off, but instead, I just fell asleep.

I woke, splayed out on the pune, groggy and depressingly sober. The ceremony was clearly over, people standing and chatting in small groups, or quietly sipping from mugs of herbal tea and miso broth. The music was gone, replaced by their voices, and I prepared myself for human interaction.

I took one last glance at the eucalyptus grove and gasped. There in the trees was a giant, unmistakable face. It was menacing—gaping mouth, dark eyes, sharp teeth. I blinked and it didn't move. I blinked again and it was still there. My panic rose until I realized that this face was just a trick of light and shadow. Scared as I was, I had hoped the face was a hallucination, but it wasn't. There was the shape of a face in the trees, just like there are faces in clouds, accidental spills, and sometimes the burn pattern on toast. The ayahuasca might have heightened my sensitivity and perception, but it wasn't like I was *seeing things*.

I stood up from the daybed in search of the food our hosts and Jaramie had provided. There was vegetarian soup, but I didn't want anything liquid. I decided on a piece of cornbread but recoiled when I saw it was blue. My hope rekindled—maybe the ayahuasca had finally kicked in! I stared at the cornbread, marveled at it really, waiting for it to tell me something about the nature of my identity when Jaramie interrupted my thoughts. "I made that," She said. "Doesn't blue corn make it a pretty color?"

Not. Seeing. Anything.

Goddamnit.

She asked how I was feeling, and I admitted, "I'm not feeling much of anything really."

"Really? I got a vicarious high from all the energy in the room. I didn't even take anything! Well, if we didn't get you high, the least we can do is get you stoned." She extracted a joint from her purse the size of Cheech and Chong movie prop, and we went outside to smoke it. The scent wafted inside and namaste boy came out with his fiancée in tow. He asked if he could "partake in the sacrament of cannabis." I hadn't realized it was possible to find *everything* annoying about a person with whom I, apparently, shared interests. Not only did I not want to share with him because I wanted to smoke it all myself, but the way he asked—almost piously—made me want to stomp on his disproportionately tiny, bobble-head-like throat.

We passed the joint—rotund to the point it might have been more accurately described as a blunt—and on about the third or fourth toke, I took off. I went from fantasizing about violence toward my peer to feeling incredible warmth and compassion. And not just for him but for every being on the planet. I felt connected to the wind and the trees and all the people around me whom the Universe picked to slot in my path.

My brain, which usually felt overheated and generally irked, felt smooth and lubricated and nimble. I was cracking jokes with Jaramie and Namaste-boy, then calling attention to exquisite details of our natural environment. I felt surrounded by loving family instead of near strangers. I couldn't tell if it was the pot, the ayahuasca, the setting, or the combination of all three, but it was the best high of my life. I was happy, curious, funny. No longer nauseated, I felt engaged with those around me, euphoric even. It was awesome. Amazing. Blissful. Occasionally I felt sick and like I was about to pass out, but back to breathing techniques and I was fine again.

By then, the woman of the couple had joined her fiancé on the wicker lounge across from where I stood. Their hands were clasped, tightly, and I felt myself sneer against my will, entirely counter to all the good feelings that had been flooding me. What made me hate her? Why was I having such a strong reaction?

Then it came to me: I was scared I would become her. I hated the idea that I might be needy, neurotic, hollow, or codependent. I was scared that I was going to end up alone and lonely, desperate enough to cling to anyone who would have me. I suddenly saw that on my bad days, I had her eyes. I felt like she was a part of me, a part of me that I hated and rejected. But I didn't need to push her away, not now in real life, and not in my internal world. She, and the version of her-in-me, needed to be *loved*, not judged and shamed.

"The world wants to be looked on in love." I heard the words in my head as if someone had sung them. It was a quotation from somewhere, but I couldn't remember the source. Oh! It's on a piece of jewelry. I have a necklace with those words. It was a gift. The quote made more sense than ever before and seemed to be bubbling up from my body, from somewhere deeper than intellectual understanding.

"The world wants to be looked on in love."

Love looks on with soft eyes. Like the way you look at a puppy or a small child. Love means forgiving mistakes, errors, imperfections. Loving *because* not *in spite* of. The world wanted to be looked on in love. This frail-seeming woman was a beautiful, wounded, fragile animal in need of love. Her partner cared for her, and their woundedness allowed a deep and meaningful bond because they looked on each other with love. I was now beaming love at them. I radiated love from the center of my chest like a Care Bear. I smiled like I'd just grasped a foundational secret of the Universe that made the world at least 36% more beautiful everywhere I looked. Nothing was unlovely.

The world wants—no, *deserves*—to be looked on in love. I was in love with the world and everything in it.

The chiming of delicate bells called us back to our chairs for a wrap-up session and this time I was thrilled to be in the couple's company. I was seated across the circle from them, and it was the perfect vantage point from which to beam love in their direction. I felt it emanating from me like the golden glow of sunset light suffusing the room. The woman shared with the group that she was hospitalized as a child and kept in isolation for months at a time. It taught her she was unlovable, easily abandoned, and weak. Of course codependency felt secure to her. I felt compassion flowing through me. I closed my eyes and wished that her healing—and mine—would continue.

There in the wrap-up circle, I started to feel more of what I had expected from ayahuasca. I felt connected—the distance or differences between me and everyone else in the circle seemed small and unimportant compared to our shared humanity. I felt like I belonged and that there was nowhere I wouldn't belong. I felt patient, like everything would unfold in due course and there was no reason for me to rush or worry. I felt unattached to outcome or perception, like my sense of "good" or "pleasant" was as arbitrary and value neutral as my sense of "left" versus "right." I felt inspired, like if we had to take that test of creativity where you have to list as many uses for a brick as possible in a minute, that I could come up with fifty-plus. I decided to test myself: paperweight, window-breaker, boring protagonist of a novel, a quiet pet that doesn't poop, risers to add extra inches beneath a headboard, a prop for *The Three Little Pigs* live action film, a doorstop, an example of red…They weren't particularly great ideas, but I felt like I could keep going forever. Except that I didn't want to because it pulled me away from presence.

I felt *present*—able to notice and appreciate exactly what was happening right that moment instead of pulled into the past or future. I noticed the sparkling indigo dragonfly that had slipped through the screen door and was now trying to escape through the screened skylight. I trusted that it would find its way out after fatigue set in and forced it down to where we could help it out. *This* was why I smoked pot.

Most of the time when I wasn't high or focused on something specific that required all my attention, my mind would drift to what I had done wrong in the past and what I needed to do in the future to prevent more fuckups. Not now. Now, I floated from one beautiful noticing to the next, extending love in every direction and feeling at peace with the world.

Since I'd gotten sick with Lyme and started using cannabis to manage my symptoms, I'd carried around an Atlas-worthy load of shame about it. I never fully understood why. I guess I thought I was supposed to. Those early-90s DARE commercials—Drug Abuse Resistance

Education—that likened smoking pot to frying my brain like an egg in a cast iron skillet had stuck with me. I had fully internalized that needing drugs to manage life equaled addiction, and addiction obviously equaled shame. Thinking of myself as "an addict" was the gateway thought to destroying my self-esteem with a bunch of other labels: "degenerate," "fuck up," and "worthless louse."

By most measures, I wasn't addicted. Smoking didn't get in the way of my daily life; I wasn't hurting family or friends because of my usage; I couldn't point to a single major way it negatively impacted me or anyone else. Still, I felt like an addict. I didn't think of anyone else who used drugs as worthless, much less as a "louse," but somehow, on me, the judgment seemed wholly deserved. Even when I had quit smoking pot for extended periods, when I was 100% sober 100% of the time, the shame stayed with me. It was almost as if the shame predated and created the addiction, as if I needed a hook on which to hang my shame and calling myself fat was no longer enough.

A shrink once asked what I got from smoking pot. "You wouldn't do it if you didn't get something from it," he'd said. I gave him what I thought was a thorough and understandable answer: it helped with my appetite, pain, and nausea from Lyme Disease—all the reasons I thought would sound defensible to a doctor. I didn't think I was allowed to say I *enjoyed* the experience. Surely admitting enjoyment would add to my shame. I didn't tell him that getting high allowed me to quiet my mind while accessing inner peace and bodily wisdom. I didn't say that it allowed me to drop my viciously judgmental censors so my muses could play. I didn't say it offered me insight and perspective that was inaccessible when my overly active brain was fully in control. I was so stuck in my drugs-are-bad-and-you're-a-horrible-worthless-drug-addict narrative that I couldn't allow a more nuanced view. I think I *wanted* drug use to make me a bad person so I would have a reason to feel so shitty about myself.

Sitting in that circle as others recounted their ayahuasca experiences and revelations, I found myself wondering: What if my smoking pot was no better or worse than dealing with stress by drinking, or exercising, or eating carbs? Everyone has vices, preferences, weaknesses, coping mechanisms. Most fundamentally, I think I was asking: What if I am not broken?

The collective wisdom on the internet was that ayahuasca gives you the experience you need, not the experience you want. I wanted intensity and transformation. I wanted an all-powerful entity to fix what was broken and make me perfect. I wanted to come out lovable.

Instead, I came out the same as I went in.

In all my preparation and reading, it had never once occurred to me that I would entirely fail to respond to ayahuasca. I felt a surge of disappointment, envy, and resentment but just as I felt those emotions peak, they dissolved into understanding. I remembered Jaramie's counsel, that the Grandmother *gives you what you need* regardless of what you want.

Curled in my chair, trying to be quiet as others spoke, I started to giggle from the sheer obviousness of the message. Not to mention my density in not receiving it. And then, as if playing out of a stereo, I heard the lyric I'd been humming all morning, about a woman being deceived into thinking she was broken.

That was me! I didn't need to be fixed! I'd been deceived, or rather, I'd deceived myself! There was nothing that made me unlovable, therefore there was nothing the Grandmother needed to give or take away to make me lovable. The only thing I needed to change was my perspective: I needed to look on myself with love.

Shifting in my chair a bit, I lifted my chest and beamed love at myself.

It wasn't what I expected from the experience, but it was just what I needed. After my Philosopher's Stone experience in Amsterdam, I had assumed that all psychedelics would speak to me in the same way—with metaphors and visions and strength. Ayahuasca taught me sometimes wisdom speaks with silence.

Chapter 11

Butterfly

Big Island, Hawaii
April 2013
Substances ingested: loads of tropical fruit, fish tacos, and plenty of pot

In the following days I had a lasting sense of warmth toward the world, as if I'd become marginally but meaningfully better at looking on it with love. Even toward myself; I still *thought* I was a bad person for smoking pot, but more out of habit than conviction. I retained the idea that maybe cannabis use was simply one detail about me, like needing a certain amount of protein at each meal to stay energized, or preferring darker tones to pastels. What if, just for debate's sake, smoking pot actually made me a better person? I couldn't defend that argument with any convincing evidence, but as the question took shape in my mind, my self-imposed shame seemed to lessen. Catching up on each other's lives over the phone, Adelynn listened to my recent experience and the questions taking shape. Then said, "I really don't know why you're so hung up on this. You never talk about me being a bad person because I like to drink wine. But I'm glad it was a relief to you."

On my last day in Hawaii, I made my way to my favorite beach. Large, fallen kiawe trees separated the white-sand beach into crescents, and I chose an empty one. I watched the waves lap regularly, one occasionally making a break for the high-tide line but falling back upon the steeper slope of the shoreline. I shared my patch of sun with a small flock of plumed Franklins that pecked haphazardly at the sand. Perhaps forty feet away, on the far side of a fallen tree, a young father kicked a soccer ball with a boy who looked to be maybe seven or eight. A bit closer, only about twenty feet away, two kids buried a third in sand, turning him into a mermaid from the neck down.

Feeling vaguely meditative as I lay there on my stomach, I perused the books on my Kindle and chose *Wheels of Life: A User's Guide to the Chakra System*. It had been Costa Rica required reading, but I'd only skimmed it then. Each chapter started with a guided meditation, and I was hoping one would help me recapture some of the bliss and contentment that had already begun to slip away after the ayahuasca ceremony.

> *You are about to go on a journey... You have been provided a vehicle in which to take this journey. It is your body. One of the challenges on this journey is to keep your vehicle nourished, happy, and in good repair... So, we begin our journey by exploring our vehicle. Take a moment to feel your body...*

I closed my eyes and focused my attention on the pressure of the sand against my stomach and elbows where I leaned into them. I felt my toes, tickled by grains of sand sliding between them. I felt the sun on my back and the top of my head, my hair soaking up heat like a velvety solar panel. I then tuned in to a jittery sensation in my feet, belly, and throat, a mild kind of agitation that had no distinct start or end point, no specific cause or cure. As soon as I began to recognize this sensation—a deep churning blade in my stomach that hummed "you are not okay" as it spun–I was distracted from it by the now familiar flashing vision of myself planted like a tree. It was frustrating, this ephemeral demand that I couldn't satisfy, so I pushed it away out of habit. I tried to focus on the next passage in the meditation, digging my toes deeper into the sand, but the urge to feel myself rooted didn't dissipate. I wanted to feel connected to the earth as if I'd grown from it rather than been placed upon its surface. I wanted to feel organic, plugged in, immovable. As frustration mounted, I silently yelled at myself to be less annoying. Stop wanting!

Suddenly my self-recrimination was interrupted by an image: the kids playing in the sand, burying each other in holes with mounded sand.

I sat up on my knees and began digging furiously like a cartoon dog. I used my hands like shovels, trying to form a hole but the sugary-soft sand slid back as quickly as I tried to pile it aside. I tried digging with my feet but only succeeded in kicking sand up and into my own face. I tried leaning forward to push the sand away with a breaststroke motion but digging like a dog was marginally more effective, so I dug and dug. I worked hard, sweating for every inch of sand I cleared. I envisioned a hole just like the one I'd seen in Leo's yard, maybe four feet in diameter and three feet deep. All too quickly I understood that wasn't going to happen. Not without tools. And hours of time. I didn't have a shovel and the sun was setting. Disappointment rose.

But the desire was too strong to abandon. I didn't need a hole! What I needed was the weight, security, and immobility of being rooted—not necessarily the underground part—and I could achieve the same effect by mounding sand on top of myself! Somehow, I knew what I was supposed to do and trusted the feeling, even though I didn't know where that *supposed to* was coming from. Somehow and with equal certainty, I knew I was supposed to stay there until I got the message it was okay to move.

I dug a shallow trough maybe four or five inches deep, about as wide as my hips, and as long as my legs. I dropped myself in with my legs extending down the slope toward the ocean. I wiggled a bit deeper to ensure there were no pockets of air between me and the sand.

Starting at my soles, I packed sand up underneath my arches then heaved more on top. Methodically, I worked my way up, packing sand under, around, and over my ankles, calves, knees, lower thighs, upper thighs, hips, and lower back. Already it was so satisfying to have my literal trunk—chest, shoulders, and head—free and open to the air, my lower body one with the beach. The weight of the sand soothed me as I melted into the ground. I tuned in further to the sensations in my body, and I couldn't tell the difference between skin and sand. I couldn't tell where my self started or if it ended.

But as my lower body dissolved into the earth, the rest of me started to panic. Stuck facing the ocean, I felt vulnerable to attack from behind, scared someone would creep up and shiv me in the kidneys or slit my throat before I called for help. Suddenly the boy and dad playing soccer seemed dangerously close, close enough for me to imagine the black-and-white leather smashing into my head, breaking my nose, blood streaming down my face and into the sand mounded over my legs. My breathing quickened. When a wave crashed slightly higher than normal, right at the high tide line, I worried it was the beginning of a tsunami and I hoped to die immediately rather than survive the initial impact only to drown at sea. Even the sweet Franklins became menacing as I noticed the sharpness of their beaks. Fact: if I stayed still long enough, they would peck me to death.

I felt myself beginning to hyperventilate. The rapid expansion and contraction of my belly caused cracks in the sand piled around my waist. I tried, frantically, futilely, to keep them from growing. The panic mounted—I wanted to get up and run, sprint, go away, far, then farther—but I knew, somehow, I wasn't supposed to leave yet, that the experience was unfinished. Breathing raggedly, I felt myself sweating, but not from the sun. I tried shaking my hands above my head and at my shoulders to release the energy but the panic only grew. I felt frozen, powerless, and trapped. Attacked, defenseless, small, and vulnerable. I tried to name all the different awful feelings as they arose, but too quickly I was awash in them. Desperately, I wanted to escape to somewhere safe.

A whisper in the back of my mind, a quiet rational thought, reminded me I *was* safe. There was nowhere safer than exactly where I was; the threat, the perceived danger, the irrational fear—they were all internal.

Rationally, I knew I could get up if I wanted to. The birds weren't going to swarm me, the ocean wasn't going to swallow me, the soccer ball wasn't going to hit me. There was a part of me—a consciousness that witnessed my emotions but was unmoved by them—that watched my panic with detachment and reassured me there was something to be gained by sitting still until it passed. It was the part of myself I had first touched in Costa Rica, the part that has access to wisdom and belonging, a reality unclouded by ego. Together, this consciousness and my rational brain convinced me to stay seated.

I let the panic rise without trying to change or escape it. I watched myself make up wild, nearly impossible scenarios, each one more extreme and devastating than the one before it, a constant one-upmanship of possible catastrophes. I felt the dread in my belly, filling the cavity of my chest, and I realized this feeling was acutely familiar. Daily even, just at lower levels. It had risen in me thousands of times: when someone seemed disappointed with me, when I learned I might not be able to bear children, literally *every* time I'm stuck in traffic. The panic was extreme and completely mundane at the same time. I was walking through life worrying about the worst that could happen, some days with more conviction than others, and I realized that this was that same internal monologue, just louder.

My legs started to tingle and I heard myself worry that if I didn't stand up *right now* I'd cause irreparable nerve damage and never be able to walk again. The panic told me I *needed* to move my legs. Or better yet: buy a ticket to East Asia! The panic wanted me to run, but not toward anything. It wanted me to keep running so I'd never stop to look at what I was running from.

I decided, instead, to stay still and pay attention.

I was scared of staying still. I feared being stuck in one place—literally, metaphorically, and energetically. That was why I'd been on a plane every month for the past three years.

I was afraid that if I didn't go to the people who loved me, wherever they were and whenever they wanted me, they would stop loving me.

Acknowledging these deep-seated fears caused new waves of panic, fear, and aversion. Every instinct told me to run, to go distract myself with a joint and a sandwich over an episode of Real Housewives. The intensity of emotions demanded I do something with them, to let them "up and out" as Andi would say. I did jazz hands, then faster, then jumping jacks with just my upper body trying to dispel the energy.

I felt tingling currents running from my toes to my hips and back again, through the veins, bones, and capillaries. My legs seemed to vibrate and then go still all at once, as if they'd been painlessly cut off from the rest of my body. I had no legs—only roots. My immovable trunk was rooted into the Universe.

I wondered if there was any history of ayahuasca taking four days to kick in.

In my mind's eye, I watched my spine grow into the ground, plunging down toward the center of the earth. I felt my vertebrae expand to absorb my entire upper body, creating one energetic cord. Down it shot, into the sand, through the soil and sediment, into a pool of golden, molten lava, glowing just like the sun. I felt the sun on my face, my shoulders, my arms, my trunk. The sun—above and below—was the source of life and I was plugged into it.

This was the feeling of being rooted that I had been craving.

I let the sun feed me, nourish me, recharge me from both directions. Electricity flowed through my trunk, warm and intensifying. I felt overcome by the gift of being alive, moved to tears by the sacredness of it, awed by the sensation of simply *existing*. Both suddenly and subtly, sensation focused and began to grow deep at the root of my trunk where it built—without physical stimulation or intention—toward a climax. Totally unexpected, I felt an orgasm radiate from the base of my spine through my body, out to the top of my head and down my legs. Feeling in my lower body returned, cleansed of the jittery sensation that I realized I had always, always felt. Never had I been so calm, so *grounded*. I felt…fully charged.

It was weird and wonderful to sit on the beach and experience what felt like an echo, like a shadow of a psychedelic trip that never actually happened. I didn't understand if this was a delayed psychedelic phenomenon directly related to the ayahuasca I had ingested, but I also didn't care. It didn't feel induced by my recent drug use, but it felt enabled by it. I felt open to the experience, to being carried away by it, whereas my rational mind would typically resist with questions about logic.

I hadn't guessed the signal to move again would be so… explosive, but I wasn't complaining. I felt a little sheepish having climaxed in public, but I had been quiet. The birds didn't seem scandalized in the least. No one had noticed.

I thanked the Universe for my happy ending, laughing, before treating myself to a sunset swim that felt like cuddling after sex.

Chapter 12
Bailando

Barcelona, Spain
August 2013
Substances ingested: tapas! At 10 PM

I was preparing to leave the US for ESADE. Through Facebook, a classmate introduced herself and we decided to live together after a couple of emails and one easy conversation. She was a friendly, boring-in-the-best-way, former dancer from North Carolina. Deepti was fluent in Spanish, whereas all I knew of the language was what I could remember from sixth grade. I could introduce myself, say I was fine, name colors, and ask where the library is, but other than that, I was dependent on her fluency. It helped, immediately, as she negotiated our contract with the landlord after I found the place online.

We rented a three-bedroom apartment, expecting guests, in Barcelona's Eixample neighborhood and I felt awkward living in a place whose name I couldn't really pronounce. The x's in Catalan sound a lot like "shh" but I know that my ear, not to mention my tongue, missed some of the subtleties. Eixample is the "Expansion District," built on the border of the Old City over the past two hundred years. We lived three blocks from the best shopping in all of Barcelona on Passeig de Gracia, and another three blocks from Gaudi's masterpiece, Casa Batllo.

Deepti and I moved in a week before orientation, and I fell in love the first time I opened the door to our new apartment. It had three balconies, two chandeliers, a washer *and* dryer (a fact I only fully appreciated after learning that they are exceptionally rare in apartments there). We were three levels up, on the "second" floor since the ground floor counts as zero in Spain, giving us beautiful views off all our balconies. Perhaps my favorite part was the door to our apartment itself. It was heavy, and evocative of an earlier, sturdier, pre-Ikea era.

On the Juliet balcony in the living room, Deepti immediately lit up a menthol cigarette and I had a momentary fantasy about smoking a joint on the smaller balcony in my room that overlooked a terra-cotta, white plaster, fern-filled courtyard. Ayahuasca had lessened my shame about smoking pot, but I still thought I'd be a better person if I didn't use it as a crutch. In thinking about the MBA program, I had decided that it was a habit I could leave at home. I'd be busy, intellectually challenged, and in entirely new surroundings; I figured it was a perfect time to quit for all but rare and recreational reasons.

Something had changed for me in Costa Rica, Amsterdam, and then again in Hawaii. In Costa Rica, I recognized the fears that kept me 30,000 feet in the air—never grounded, always chasing love—and felt the alternative to that existence when I heard Jaramie's voice tell me "You were born." In Amsterdam, I learned what was holding me back from moving on with David, and cut those ties. In Hawaii, some combination of ayahuasca and my where-did-that-come-from orgasm seemed to have cured my perpetual restlessness. I didn't feel the need to run anymore.

I felt settled in Barcelona. Not only had my internal landscape shifted, Barcelona made it easy: siesta, red wine, late-night dinners, history, and culture—all right on the beach. Moving there felt like running *toward* a life I had been too afraid to want, much less seek out: a life that maximized joy, pleasure, work/life balance, and sensual delights

To kick off the year, ESADE had arranged a casual pre-orientation gathering and I found myself deliberating what outfit would simultaneously convey "I'm smart, take me seriously" *and* "I'm effortlessly, obviously desirable" in case there were single, attractive men in my class. I chose an above-the-knee beige shift dress that bordered on too short if I crossed my legs, and a wrap sweater that made the dress look longer than it was.

There was one man—tall, dark, handsome—who immediately caught my attention, but he mentioned a pregnant wife within the first few sentences, so he was off the table. The other man who caught my attention did so based less on looks than on the verbal résumé he offered after talking for a bit. Stanford graduate (a few years ahead of me), former engineer turned professional hip hop dancer, now retired with a plan to start a career in renewable energy. Amongst all the finance and econ majors, consultants, and bankers, I felt like a misfit drawn to another misfit. I wanted to know more, but he emitted an aloof vibe that was equally off-putting and alluring. I moved away after our brief chat and decided I'd let him approach me.

The gathering happened to fall on the final night of the Festival de Gracia—a week-long block party during which the streets of the Gracia neighborhood compete to out-decorate each other with elaborate themes. The festival ends in a *correfoc*, which translates directly to "fire run." I googled it, of course. According to Culture Trip, "People dressed as devils and other monstrous creatures arm themselves with pitchforks and set off fireworks in the crowd. If it sounds like a health and safety nightmare, it's usually relatively safe, as those who come to watch the *correfoc* usually come prepared with clothing to protect themselves from any eventual burns."

Despite the 90-degree weather, hoping to avoid the *"eventual burns,"* I covered myself from the neck down in a dark denim duster that is likely what a blacksmith would wear if she had to choose something from my closet. I threw a wrap for my hair, sunglasses for my eyes, and a pair of gloves in my purse, just in case.

Roommate Deepti wore tiny cotton shorts and a tank top.

Between the two of us, I was the one who stood out from the rest of the crowd as locals milled about in their skimpiest summer attire. We sat on the stoop of a closed leather shop, sipping Estrella Dams from paper bags as the temperature began to recede slowly from triple digits. I was training myself to think like a local—in Celsius—but still struggled to reconcile 40-degree weather with stifling heat. I had pulled my hair into a ponytail, tired of its weight against my neck. I was perversely proud of its ability to withstand humidity and still look great. Even as sweat gathered in every fold of flesh, my hair looked shiny, coiffed, and luscious.

The hotter I got, the more I resented having followed the instructions to wear protective clothing. Until I the devils came. I heard them before I saw them, a cacophony of drums, fireworks, whistles, screams, laughter, children's squeals, all muddied as if the soundtrack from a war movie were overlaid on a playground. The sound seemed to come from everywhere. Deepti and I stood as the trickle of people on the street in front of us became thicker, starting to flow from our right. Over the heads of the crowd amassing down the street, red-gold sparks rose into the night. About half a block away, horned figures in black and red wielded spinning metal contraptions that spit embers in every direction. They danced and taunted the crowd, jabbing at the air with their sparking weapons, clearing the way as a giant fire-breathing dragon came heaving around the corner. The dragon itself looked murderous. It shot fireworks from its mouth as it wove up the narrow street toward us, matchheads of flame landing on any reveler who dared get close.

It was aggressively unsafe. It was how I imagined a "flash bang" grenade might feel from the inside, except this scenario included *many* children. In fact, little children seemed everywhere—in strollers, in parents' arms, all of them tiny targets for flaming embers—though none of them seemed to be getting hurt. The spectacle was intoxicating and mind-boggling, looser and freer and more fun than any Fourth of July, though my thoroughly American mind couldn't help imagining how many lawsuits would crop up back home. At all the joy and camaraderie, I couldn't help wondering if we Americans weren't all just a little too careful.

Deepti and I allowed the dragon and its entourage of devils to pass, falling into step a safe distance behind, close enough to feel the percussive snare of the drums, but far enough away to not become human kindling. Swallowed up into a crowd that felt joyous and excessive, brave and reckless, I found myself drawn further and further into the drums, the horns and the guitars. I danced, stomping my feet, feeling so damn lucky to be in that place at that moment with these people.

Elated, Deepti and I pushed closer, wanting to be closer to the drums, feeling daring but insulated from danger by a thick layer of drunken merrymakers.

Suddenly, the dragon changed direction.

How had it not occurred to me that it could do that? Blinding red-gold sparks shot straight toward us, brighter as the spectacle wound around to reverse its course, the dragon and its devils darting closer to us. Deepti and I pressed back against what felt like a wall of people, the crowd surging into us. I started to think about human stampedes and what a horrible way that would be to die. Deepti was little—barely over 100 pounds—with exposed skin vulnerable to burning. I worried for her. We pushed against the surge, hoping we could escape onto a side street or alley, but there was no exit.

And still, the dragon drew closer. Once, when I was young, I leaned over a candle at my grandma's and singed the bottom of my braid. Ever since, I'd been scared of my hair catching fire. I moved to cover my head with the wrap but suddenly worried that the polyester would melt to me if it caught a spark. I envisioned myself disfigured, burning, trampled.

The fear was the same as the beach, everything that could possibly go wrong but wouldn't flooded into my brain. I allowed the fear to swell, felt it make me take short, tight breaths, and yet I stayed still. Instead of imagining bodies crushed by thousands of stomping feet, I returned my attention to the kids. They were having the time of their lives! I decided I could be as brave as the toddlers laughing in delight, some even running closer to weave through the dragon's feet. Tears and shouts when one got knocked down or touched by a falling ember, but nothing serious.

"You okay?" I yelled over the noise to Deepti. "Get behind me." She did and I took comfort in my own bravado. As the dragon lumbered close, then closer, I faced him head-on. I held my breath, willing it to turn again. Burning embers landed on my denim sleeves but went out quickly against the dense ply. Embers were surely in my hair, like the hair of all those around me, but I didn't feel them, and they didn't catch. In the noise and heat and brightness, Deepti tucked behind me, I realized I no longer felt scared. I felt...bold. My heart seemed to beat with the drums, tears of joy welling in my eyes. I had the clear sense that here, in this time and place, I could be anyone I wanted to be, and most incredibly: myself.

***

It turned out that my emerging self was a bit of a partier. I went to frat parties in college, a handful of pub crawls, and maybe one or two nightclubs over the course of my lifetime, but I had basically stopped drinking at twenty-two after my Lyme diagnosis. Many of my medications forbade alcohol, and it felt like eons since I'd really "gone out." I hyped Deepti into wearing the faux-leather romper I had convinced her to purchase when we were business suit shopping. It was on sale, and it fit her as if sewn custom for her petite curves. I donned a body-con bandage dress with an exposed zipper that I couldn't believe I'd had the confidence to buy. The new me then doubled down by adding red lipstick. I'd never worn red lips before. I was scared I'd look whorish, or worse, clownish. But, even to my critical eye, I suspected it looked good. Almost even natural.

Every weekend, the ESADE social director (a fellow student) designated a different club for our American-named but thoroughly Basque-feeling TGIF. That week, she'd chosen Carpe Diem in Barceloneta, the beach part of the city that was thick with nightclubs. Women in their shortest, brightest attire toddled on heels as men with their hair slicked back from sweat and product escorted them from one entrance to the next. When we were handed free entrance cards to the club, I mostly credited my roommate's romper but allowed that I wasn't looking bad myself.

As soon as we walked through the doors, we were engulfed: in smoke, the bump of the music, and flashing colored lights. Smoke thinned as we descended successive flights of stairs toward the largest dance floor I'd ever seen. And I could only see a third of it. In large hoops suspended from the ceiling, women danced in glimmery hot pants and bikini tops. One was blowing bubbles over the crowd. People were packed so tightly that they had to hold their cocktails above their heads to navigate the dance floor. It looked like everyone was carrying their own glowing scepter filled with a magical elixir that glowed an unnatural blue. Turns out, tonic water fluoresces under UV light.

At the far side, the ceiling just seemed to end, opening directly onto the beach. I scanned the patio, recognizing the bald, white head of the engineer-turned-dancer-turned-renewable-energy-dude. He was leaning against the slatted wall that served as a sort of barrier between this club and the next, smoking a cigarette, looking aloof as usual. The patio boasted its own bar and after a pair of tequila shots with Deepti and a vodka tonic for pluck, I decided there would be no more waiting for Mr. Aloof to approach.

I drew close, shouting over the music, "You're Tyler?"

"Yeah. What's your name?"

"Anne."

He flicked ash into the planter beside him as I took a sip of my drink. I saw lipstick on the rim of my glass when I lowered it, and it made me worry that I'd gotten it on my teeth.

"You have lipstick on your teeth." He gestured to my mouth.

"Oh, I..." I tried to lick it away, then gave up on being subtle. Rubbing with my middle finger, I said, "is it gone?"

"No, do your lip like Elvis."

"What?"

"Like . . . " He pulled the right corner of his top lip up in an Elvis-ish way.

I mirrored him best I could, both of us fighting laughter, and he said "No, other side." I tried to lift the other side but I didn't have as much control over the right side of my face so I gave up, gritted and bared my teeth like I would to a girlfriend. Without hesitating, he used the inside of his left ring finger to wipe my incisor and there was a comfort in the action that made it clear we were going to be friends. When he asked if I wanted to dance, I was insecure—he was a literal pro and I have two moves—but I said yes and hours disappeared in a haze of booze, sweat and smoke.

Hot, disheveled, and feeling like I'd never had more fun, we ran into roommate Deepti and the three of us tumbled out the back entrance onto the beach. Shoes off, toes in sand, sipping cervezas, eating ham and cheese bocadillos we bought off one of the men roaming the beach, we talked about our hopes for the next two years. Nearby, a small group of clubgoers had stripped down and were playing volleyball in their underwear. It was four in the morning, still probably 80 or 85 degrees, no, I corrected myself, 30 degrees. Deepti taught a rule of thumb: Celsius is roughly Fahrenheit minus twenty, divided in half.

At some point, probably the fifth or sixth time I heard it, I realized that the men roaming the beach were offering more than beers and sandwiches. "Erowina" sounded like a pretty girl's name, and I felt a little dumb when Tyler casually referenced the obvious: they were selling drugs. "Ooh, you think they have pot?" The only thing that could make this night any better was a slight high.

"Um. Yes." Tyler said. It was clear that was a dumb question.

Other than once in high school, when I bought (but never used) two Ecstasy tablets from a dealer friend, I'd never purchased illegal drugs. Even with as much as I smoked, I never had to buy it because I always had friends who grew it and just gave it to me. Sometimes it was a gift in exchange for kindness or hospitality on my part, but usually just out of generosity on theirs.

Tyler seemed to have the most experience with this kind of thing, so we delegated negotiations of the illegal drug purchase to him. In a rapid exchange that took place in a combination of Spanish, English, and Catalan, he secured half a gram for 30 euro, roughly four times what I paid in Amsterdam, but it felt reasonable considering the risk (turned out Spanish cannabis laws are quite lax, but I didn't know this at the time). Plus, it literally couldn't have been more convenient

On that beach I felt drunk and loose in a way I'd never been before. Under my elbows and bare feet, the sand was soft and a little cool. The night air was warm enough to make the contrast pleasant. Tyler and Deepti smoked tobacco he hand-rolled with hemp papers. There wasn't enough pot to roll a full joint with the small nugs we'd bought, so Tyler took the empty can of Coke I'd gotten with my sandwich and used his keys to carve a hole into the center of the concavity I'd formed by squishing the sides together. In college we used a cored apple when we needed an improvised pipe, which I preferred over the metallic fumes of heated aluminum, but that night the slightly illicit feel of something chemical and dangerous worked for me. When Tyler passed me the can and I placed my mouth where his had been, the contact-by-proxy felt intimate. Not sexual, but significant, an invitation into a deeper relationship. But maybe I was reading too much into it.

My makeup had to be either smeared or gone, my hair was down and probably greasy, and the paunch of my belly was blaringly apparent in the stretched-out bandage dress that appeared to have given up of trying to hold me in, but the three of us laughed and talked like old friends.

Like the slow, rolling waves of the ocean in the background, time had a rhythm in Spain that felt different. *I* felt different. At home, I was always rushed, never doing enough, not being "efficient." But efficiency didn't carry the same value in this town. Waiting in line for the club had given me more time to enjoy people-watching. When the electricity had gone out at the restaurant the night before and dinner took two hours, Deepti and I savored our leisurely candlelit meal. Train delays due to labor disputes—frequent there—taught me to respect the power of unions and collective bargaining. When I walked in this city, I didn't listen to music or podcasts or audiobooks, because I didn't want to escape being present. I wanted to listen to the dialects, street performers, even traffic sounds. Here, compared to

San Francisco and DC, there were so few sirens, quieter voices, horns that were more toots than blasts. Here, I walked more slowly, keeping my energy alert in part to communicate to would-be pickpockets that I wasn't an easy mark, but mainly because every stroll in this country reinforced how people moved a little more languorously here. I liked the pace and the Spanish version of myself.

It felt like an honor—when I started wearing less clothing and more red lipstick—to be mistaken for a local by taxi drivers, grocery clerks, and American tourists. I felt cosmopolitan when Spanish tourists from Madrid asked me directions to one of the Gaudi buildings and I knew where to send them. Granted, it was only a few blocks away, but my stock answer in the US was always "Sorry, I'm bad at directions; I can Google it for you," because I didn't trust myself not to get it wrong.

I ran for president of my MBA class and lost, but the biggest sign of internal progress was that I didn't berate myself for it. I was genuinely proud I had been daring enough to try. Maybe it was Barcelona, maybe it was the comfort of being in an explicitly educational environment unencumbered by past versions of myself, maybe it was the flowering aftermath of successive psychedelic trips. Whatever it was allowed me to experiment with new ways of being. And it was fun.

Chapter 13
Can't Stop The Feeling!

Amsterdam, Netherlands
Early December 2013
Substances ingested: copious amounts of marijuana

When my dad was invited to the same conference we'd gone to in the Netherlands at the end of my first semester in Barcelona, we decided to meet in Amsterdam for another long weekend of recreational drug use. Probably because it's so the *opposite* of debauchery or daredevil recklessness, doing drugs with my dad has an aura of safety around it. Neither of us wanted to ruin our brains or careers. Both of us are, relative to the average person, risk-averse.

We both wanted to try mushrooms again, he for the joy and I for the transcendence. I still felt changed—liberated—by the insights provided by the Philosopher's Stone and I wanted more of that feeling. I hadn't expected that first experience to be so revelatory, and although my experience with ayahuasca had been slightly underwhelming, I felt a sneaking confidence that psychedelics opened a channel to wisdom I needed.

In a way impossible to articulate, I *felt* that the wisdom gleaned from experiences was trustworthy. The wisdom I received on psychedelics made more sense—seemed more truthful, less contradictory and incomplete—than what I experienced in normal consensus reality. I wanted more of that wisdom, more of the sense of calm and connection to ultimate truth, more of what felt like joyful exuberance at being alive. At the same time, psilocybin reminded me of the ocean: powerful, immense, containing leagues and leagues of unexplored mysteries... My mom always taught me to be careful around the ocean. I wanted more, to go deeper this time, but *carefully*.

In early December, Amsterdam appeared transformed into a Christmas postcard. The houseboats lining the canals were draped in white twinkle lights that reflected off the water, tossing immaterial glitter across the city. The gas streetlights, first designed by an artist in the 17th century, turned the puddles on the sidewalks into pools of liquid gold. Despite its obvious, almost trenchant beauty, it was *cold*. It couldn't have been much more than five or six degrees Celsius. I walked with my collar turned up around my ears to soften the wind, gloveless hands in my pockets, nose pink, but smiling. Catching a whiff of pot, I felt at home, even though it was only my second visit.

I wove among cyclists, trams, tourists, and inebriated Brits on "hen dos," feeling more like a local each time I managed it without slowing my pace. My dad left it to me to figure out lodging for the weekend and I rolled the dice with another blind booking site. This time, we lost. We ended up at a non-descript chain in the Eastern Docklands with two queen beds in a room barely larger than two queen beds. We could have gotten a second room, or changed hotels to make it more comfortable, but it seemed unnecessary. When I traveled with him as a little kid of course we shared a room, and though our relationship changed as we aged, it never got weird. He snores and spends a long time in the bathroom, and I'm sure it annoys him that my toiletries took up 90% of the sink space within five minutes of arrival, but we adjusted to it quickly.

On our first morning we entered the Smart Shop with purpose, like we were old pros. I knew exactly what I wanted: a stronger dose of Philosopher's Stone. My dad decided to switch it up and try the Philosopher's Stone, too. We bought 25 grams and headed straight back to the hotel room to prepare for travel.

Dad ate his easily and reclined on his bed. It took me longer. I was aiming for around 10 grams but was open to as much as 12.5. After twenty minutes I had choked them down and my dad was snoozing lightly. I thought about waking him—I didn't want him to sleep through his trip—but he was jetlagged, and it was still early so I thought I'd let him sleep until it started to hit.

I tried to read while I waited for the effects to kick in, but I was too restless (maybe too excited). Quietly, I stood up to stretch. Bending my knees, then straightening to reach toward the sky, I allowed myself to fold at the waist and hang limp from my hips. I found myself squatting, then stretching all the way up onto the balls of my feet, then adding a tiny hop.

"Anne, are you...okay?" My dad sounded concerned and I had no idea why. I felt *great*. I was sprinting from one end of the room to the other on my tiptoes, trying to spend as much time in the air as possible because I was playing Floor is Lava with myself. I hopped from foot to foot, trying to hover in between each landing, not wanting either sole to get scorched by imaginary molten goo.

"SorrydidIwakeyou?" I apologized, without slowing my sprints. My body buzzed with energy that needed a way out. It felt like being mildly, *pleasantly*, electrocuted. I didn't want to—couldn't—stop moving, but if my dad was concerned then maybe my behavior would attract the attention of hotel staff. Skipping still felt too loud so I switched back to marching with high knees, my arms looking like I was playing the world's biggest trumpet or leading a parade at triple speed.

"No, no," my dad said. "It's okay. But are you okay?"

"I'm great!" I said as I marched in place, kissing each knee as it came up. I was feeling an intense rush of love and appreciation for my knees. They did so much for me without ever being thanked. I stood on my left leg, flamingo-style, and cradled my right knee in my arms like a swaddled baby, rocking it back and forth cooing my gratitude for its service until my left knee got jealous and I had to switch.

Breathlessly and sincerely curious after remembering that he was there, I asked my dad, "How are you?"

He had relocated beneath the covers and had them pulled up to his chin. "I'm fine but cold."

"Want another blanket?" I asked, sweating profusely. "You can have my comforter."

"No no. I'm fine. We can talk later." My dad snuggled into the blankets and closed his eyes.

I dropped to the floor for pushups. I lowered onto my elbows in a plank. Plank turned into downward dog, my body forming a perfect triangle with the floor. Ever since my first yoga class and all through my teacher training in Costa Rica, I'd been told that downward dog was a resting pose, but I had never understood it before this moment: my legs felt warm, strong, and rooted, heels grounded. My palms blessed the earth and worshiped it at the same time. I was in balance. Relishing the smoothness of synthetic wool, I spread my fingers wide. I felt energy from the center of the earth coursing into my palms, my wrists, up my lengthened arms, into my shoulders, then up my spine. Energy shot out my tailbone like a column of white light, connecting me to the ground and infinity at the same time.

Just like on the beach in Hawaii, the energy wasn't coming from me, it was flowing into me from an infinite source somewhere between the center of the earth and the edge of the universe and maybe everywhere in between. It forced energetic obstacles from my spine like a strong current of water clearing debris from a gutter. With the current came a message: I had been living my life the wrong way. In the wrong direction. From the wrong place. I had been walking around with my head up, allowing my brain to give directions rather than insisting it be a servant to the wisdom and knowledge of my body. I felt the current of energy flowing from an invisible sun into my sacrum, down the column of my spine, and into my heart. Then, lastly, into my head. Instinctively, intuitively, viscerally, I knew that was the order of the flow of wisdom: the sacrum, the heart, the head.

I understood: The brain is a computer, excellent for analysis, sums, strategies, calculations, and intellect. But the questions about what I should do with my life, who I am, what is right for me—those big, existential, important questions—can only be answered by the heart and the soul. I realized in that instant: I'd been using the wrong tools. Letting my brain take the lead in life was like trying to sew with a chainsaw. "Is the sacrum the seat of the soul?" I wondered, neither expecting an answer nor noticing that sometime in the past year or so I'd accepted the idea of souls.

"Sacrum, heart, head," I whispered silently, repeating my new order of operations so I wouldn't forget it when I was sober. I tried to force memory through repetition because I knew it was an important realization. I didn't want it to fly away like so many of the other pretty birds of cosmic wisdom that fluttered by, offering glimpses but no lasting imprint. Repeating it again, "sacred, heart, head," I noticed I made a mistake in my transcription: I was thinking "sacrum" but saying "sacred." But *was* it a mistake? No. The sacred sacrum. The sacrum was sacred. It could not be an accident that those words were so similar. How had I never noticed before? I felt so silly for not realizing it sooner, but also like a *genius* for realizing it at all. "Sacred sacrum, sake-red sake-rummmm," I sang in my head, tickled that I'd finally figured out that clue. Shaking my hair and loosening my neck, stretching the consonants of "sacred" and "sacrum" until they lost their meaning, I bent my elbows and knelt into child's pose.

The moment my forehead connected to the earth I became a radio receiver on the right frequency. Suddenly messages were louder, crisper, and more coherent. I felt plugged in. The first message was, simply, to stay put. Child's pose was another resting pose that had never felt like rest. It hurt my hips and my pride because it was supposed to be easy—*child's pose*—but it wasn't. My pelvis dug into my thighs, my knees hated the pressure, my feet lost circulation, and I fucking *hated* it.

But not this time. This time, I relaxed into it, flowed into the form without discomfort or resistance. Immediately, I found rest. With my forehead pressed to the ground, I felt the place Andi called our "third eye." It felt like a magnet in my skull being drawn to the earth. I felt it connect, and all the anxious spinning in my brain just... stopped. I breathed, my arms extended in front of me, palms toward the sky. Time passed and I stayed. Still. Silent.

Restful. Connected. Minutes passed. Hours? And I recognized for the first time that child's pose is a position of prayer. It is a position of surrender, submission, vulnerability.

Maybe that was the real reason I've always hated it.

"Anne," I heard my dad say. "You have a perfect heart." But Dad was over there sleeping peacefully, and I realized it was a memory of the best compliment I'd ever received. Back when he'd really said it, at the forgotten moment when I'd actually heard it, I hadn't fully believed it was true... but I had hoped. Hearing it again now, I knew it was the truth.

Expansive relief filled me. My heart was perfect. I had a perfect heart. I didn't need to do anything. I didn't need to improve it or change it or force it in any direction. I just had to *listen* to it.

At that moment, inexplicably and not in words, something—my body, the Universe, an instinct, I don't know—told me to do a backbend. A full backbend, only feet and hands touching the floor, my body arched in a half-circle above the ground. Every cell of my body craved it.

Except I couldn't do it. That backbend had a name—Urdhva Dhanurasana, or "full wheel"—and it had remained my white whale throughout Costa Rica and beyond. I tried, for weeks and months, but my arms weren't strong enough and my back didn't bend that way.

But something told me to try again anyway.

I positioned my feet and hands. I energized my legs and arms. My hips, belly, ribs rose. Never had I gone this far. My own strength shocked me. But the real surprise was how easy it felt. Only my hands, feet, and the top of my head were connected with the ground. I just needed to push a bit harder, I could almost—

But the more I thought, the weaker I got. I could *almost* get my head off the ground. But also, not at all. I wanted to force beyond my limitations, but I collapsed instead.

I started to cry. Tears streamed down the sides of my face. I didn't know why I was crying. Waves of pent-up emotion moved through me: sadness, loss, abandonment, loneliness. I didn't understand where they were coming from. "Why?" I asked silently. No one answered. But I saw an image: my shoulders folding toward one another like human origami, my chest sunken, concave. And then it made sense.

When David proposed, I gave him my heart, but then when we broke up, in the division of stuff, someone had to take it. Since it was inarguably mine, I had taken it, but I hadn't really wanted it back. It was a broken, distorted, unlovable thing that I did not want to carry, so I shoved it behind my ribs, as far back as it could go where no one would see it. It had been there, atrophying, ever since.

Doing a backbend had unleashed waves of unprocessed grief. Ever since I connected with my body in Costa Rica, and more since Amsterdam and Hawaii, my body had been more communicative. Or maybe I'd just started to listen.

Now, crumpled into a pile of despair on a dirty beige carpet, I wanted to curl up again, curl up *against* it, to stop this tsunami of loss. But I didn't. I pulled my shoulders back and expanded my chest, even as it was shaken by silent sobs. I let the emotion up and out, as quietly as possible so as not to wake my dad.

Eventually, my tears abated and, lying still, I heard a voice. It sounded like my own, but this voice was more peaceful, more grounded and confident, than I'd ever been. It was the same voice that offered convincing reasons to apply to MBA programs. She sounded like the person Andi referred to in yoga teacher training as our "higher self." In soothing, motherly tones, she said, "Open your heart."

Again, only three words, just like the message "You were born." Just like that, I knew so many layers of truth. It was entirely, wholly, inescapably true: If I ever wanted to love and be loved, I needed to open my heart.

Physically, metaphorically, all of it.

I needed to move through the world with my shoulders back and chest up like someone who deserved to be loved, beaming love at myself and everyone else at the same time.

My body knew what I needed.

What I needed was more backbends, more downward dog, more child's pose.

Utterly exhausted—physically spent from all my exertions—I noticed that the weft of the carpet had imprinted itself on the side of my face from pressure. I didn't remember ever choosing to lie, face down, on a dingy hotel room floor but I didn't mind. I felt like me and that floor had been through a lot together in the past… six hours! Eventually, I climbed up off the ground and into bed. I hadn't noticed the sun going down, but the sky was pitch black now. My body felt delightfully used up and wrung out; my mind full but empty at the same time. I felt a stillness—in my body, mind, spirit—that was unfamiliar, but welcome.

Beginning to fall asleep, I felt a twinge between my left hip and belly button. It was the only tightness left in my body. I began to dig at it with my fingers, exploring the knot. As I poked, a stern but not unfriendly voice in my head said, "Don't release that until you're ready to have babies." In deference to the warning, I laid my hands gently over my abdomen.

***

In the morning over breakfast, my dad and I discussed our respective trips.

"Mine was amazing," I said. "Energetic."

"Yeah," my dad laughed, "I'd think you were gone and start to get worried then your butt would pop up over the edge of the bed."

"Yoga." I smiled, at a loss to explain it more fully. Andi taught us that "yoga" meant union, oneness, "the yoking together of the body and mind, the sacred and mundane." I wrote the words in my notes and got 100% on the final exam. But before that night, I didn't really get it. I had always thought of my mind and body as separate entities, linked maybe, but my body definitely the dumber of the two. Now, I thought, maybe "I," my intellectual self, was the dumb one. My body contained wisdom that I'd spent most of my life aggressively ignoring. Being attuned to that wisdom felt so *different*, this new relationship with my body so revolutionary, that "yoga" seemed the only word full enough to describe it.

Chapter 14

Rock the Casbah

Marrakesh, Morocco
December 21, 2013
Substances Ingested: tagines, pastilla, apricots and almond-argan oil

Still reveling in my lessons from the recent Amsterdam trip, I decided to skip the winter holidays with my family in favor of back-to-back yoga retreats in Essaouira (Morocco) and Fuerteventura (the Canary Islands of Spain). Barcelona's proximity to so many places in Europe and Northern Africa that I'd always wanted to visit gave me a good excuse for breaking with tradition. It was an excuse I wanted; the distance enabled me to deny the growing cracks and increasing animosity in my parents' relationship. I tried to get Adelynn to join me, but Christmas with her family was an unshakeable tradition.

I arrived at the airport in Marrakech two days before the start of my first retreat, hungover from a typically excessive night of business school partying. Through Airbnb I had booked a room at a traditional Moroccan riad—a rectangular mansion with the center cut out and open to the air—inside the walled section of the Old City.

Sitting in a taxi hired and arranged by my Airbnb hosts, I watched the traffic, awed by the diversity and balance of vehicles competing for space on the street. It was a mix of mopeds, cars, brightly decorated horse-drawn carriages, and sometimes wooden carts pulled by weary oxen. Whole families—mothers, fathers, multiple kids, and a babe in arms—traveled on a single moped. Amidst the movement, orange trees bearing globes of bright fruit lined the medians and sidewalks, looking positively regal. The walled city rose up in a sunset-colored clay that gave it the nickname, "The Red City," even though "dusty pink" would have been more accurate.

When my taxi driver suddenly pulled over just outside the gated entrance to the city's walls, unloaded my luggage into a wooden cart attached to a bored-looking donkey, and said, "You go with him now," I was flustered but obedient. The "him" my driver meant was an older man, the same height as the donkey, wearing dusty Wranglers and leather slippers. Though he walked with a limp, he was not slowed by it, and I struggled to keep up with him as he used the donkey's girth to cut a path. Cars were not allowed inside the old city and even a donkey-drawn cart needed an embarrassing berth to get through the metal gate that modern architects of the city added as an opening to Jemaa el-Fna square.

It was unlike anything I'd seen in the thirty-plus countries on five continents I'd visited. The space—as large as a city block—felt busy like New York City or Tokyo, but the people *milled* rather than rushing. It was a vibrant, dynamic playground for the senses, buzzing with colors and smells and music like Jaipur or Sao Paolo, but the souks—maze-like marketplaces filled with stalls—made it feel much more commercial. I sought to take it all in, my ears, tastebuds, even my skin attempted to absorb my surroundings. Awash in it all, I felt... excited.

Before my spontaneous orgasm on the beach, before finding and reinhabiting a connection with my body through yoga and feeling plugged into an infinite source of energy in Amsterdam, all this stimulation would have been too much. I certainly wouldn't have sought it out, much less would I have reveled in it like this: alone.

Snake charmers played bewitching tunes on gourd flutes, entrancing both cobras and tourists. Trained monkeys wearing hats and leashes darted at foot level along with horned lizards and other exotic animals. Tourists paid the leash-holders to pose with the creatures for photo ops. Taking up precious real estate in the open square, permanent cloth-covered stalls offered freshly squeezed pomegranate and orange juice, dried apricots, roasted almonds, candied hazelnuts, Brazil nuts, and dates. So many dates: sliced dates, stuffed dates, raw dates, soaked dates, stewed dates, dates covered in coconut, dates rolled in nuts...

I slowed down for a moment to appreciate all the different preparations, but the man leading the donkey was on a mission. He was moving across the length of the square, headed into the depth of the souk. I caught up, one hand on the wooden cart, so I could follow by touch while consuming with my eyes. The difference between the souk and the square was immediate: the temperature dropped at least five degrees and my pupils dilated in the shade provided by slatted wood and canvas rooves. The passageways narrowed and turned labyrinthine, filled to bursting with tourists (like me) haggling loudly over wares. I had reached shopping nirvana. Shoes, bags, leather goods, not to mention glittering carved metal and intricately woven rugs called to me from a dozen different stalls, all begging me to admire them. I slowed down as much as dared before rushing to keep up with the determined donkey driver. Three minutes' walk out the other end of the souk, and he deposited me at my riad.

The owners of the riad—a married couple in their forties —ushered me from the dust and bustle into their oasis of calm. A fountain occupied the middle of the ground floor, its cool splashing sounds covering outside noise. The wife poured hot mint tea from a gilded pot into a gilded amethyst-colored glass, drawing the pot higher and higher as she poured, creating a froth of bubbles. The tea was delicious but sweeter than I expected, and I politely declined when she offered an igloo of sugar cubes. As with so many people I've met in other parts of the world, her English was excellent, making me feel provincial, or just lazy, for only speaking one language. Other than the two-week Spanish immersion I took before starting classes at ESADE, my skills had not improved at all in Barcelona. Not that it would have helped here, except, the couple did—in fact—speak Spanish as one of their five languages. We made small talk until I felt myself yawning uncontrollably.

In my room on the second floor, with the window open to a light breeze, I slept unusually deeply for a nap. Twice, I was awakened by what my dreaming brain registered as loud and insistent camel noises.

The memory of so many beautiful shoes so close by eventually roused me from bed. A little groggy, I retraced my steps to the souk and was immediately sucked in by a display of footwear so varied and colorful that I gasped. Flat leather shoes with curved elfin toes and tassels, sturdy leather sandals with thick cords that laced up the ankle, soft suede smoking slippers in plastic bags piled in different colors according to size. I hadn't changed much money and didn't want to let myself buy anything, so I tried to look disinterested.

Still, of course, vendors called to me, trying different languages, and I was flattered each time someone's first try was "hola" rather than "hello." I gave a hurried, "Just looking," and hustled away until a flicker of light caught my eye. I don't know how I saw it. It was set back on a high shelf in a stall slightly down a side street. Maybe I felt it before I saw it. Nah, that's silly.

A golden orb, the shape of an ostrich egg but the size of a football, sat on a small pedestal and issued the softest, warmest light through delicate hand-etched whorls that turned metal into lace. Before I even knew I'd moved, I reached out to stroke it. The shop was filled with carved metal light fixtures—wall sconces, chandeliers, and reading lamps—but this one was special.

"Beautiful, yes?" A man, presumably the owner or employee of the shop, materialized behind me. "You can touch."

I'd stopped short out of respect, but now I let my hand fall on the item. The metal was cooler than I expected, even more delicate than it looked. He offered me mint tea, and I turned it down saying, "No thanks, I'm just looking," as I continued caressing the lamp.

"For you, good price. Normal, 800 Dirham. You, only 650 Dirham." I couldn't do the precise math quickly, but he was charging over $100, maybe almost $200. It wasn't cheap. Even if I managed to negotiate him down to half what he was asking—as was the norm in souk pricing—it would still cost more than I knew I should spend. I began to walk away out of habit. I told myself: I didn't *need* it, it was frivolous, and I had already been too self-indulgent by spending so much on a holiday from school when school already felt like a holiday. I told myself I did not deserve the pretty thing.

But even as the thoughts coalesced, I realized this was old thinking, martyrdom that no longer appealed. Self-denial for the sake of self-denial. For the first time, self-denial as habit felt empty and even marginally ridiculous.

Returning to the shop with purpose, I tried to negotiate with the guy but we both knew I wasn't walking away emptyhanded. When we settled on the Dirham equivalent of $120, I didn't let him wrap it up. Instead, I nestled it into my arms like an infant, cradling the lamp against my chest. That is, until I realized that it was safer bubble-wrapped and let him package it for international travel. Probably seeing an easy mark, the vendor asked if he could take me to his cousin's spice stall, pointing a few donkey-lengths away to where a tall, handsome man about my age stood outside what appeared to be an apothecary of magic substances. I said yes.

The man had vibrant blue eyes that looked kind and even paler against the black of his jellaba, the traditional loose-fitting hooded robe worn by Moroccan men over their shirts and pants. He smiled—warmly, genuinely, disarmingly—and offered me his hand to shake, saying his name was Zoubair.

I told him up front that I wasn't buying anything because I didn't want to take up his time and disappoint him, but he smiled and waved a hand motion that I understood to mean he wasn't expecting anything. He poured mint tea, offered me a seat, and began to answer my questions. The small, dried bundles that looked like decorative objects from Pier One were thistle flowers, used as functional and flavorful toothpicks. The black metallic-looking stones were crushed into eyeliner that kept sand and glare out of the eyes while in the desert. Tiny tagine pots held traditional Moroccan lipstick; clay that turned to saturated red pigment when applied with a wet finger.

Off a high shelf, Zoubair lifted an airtight jar the size of his palm. From it, he extracted a small bundle of saffron threads and placed them in my hand to examine. He explained that real saffron—a spice more precious than gold—was made from the dried, inch-long stamens of crocus flowers and came in bundles of *three*, which is how to distinguish it from the dyed corn silk locals tried to pass off to unsuspecting tourists. I listened, fascinated, when I realized I was hearing the same far-away camel sounds I'd heard while napping. Only then did it click that the sound was a human voice—a muezzin—calling Muslims to prayer at a nearby mosque.

Retroactively mortified that I'd confused a human with a dromedary, I covered my face with my hand in the universal gesture of embarrassment. Zoubair asked why. Reluctantly, I shared my mistake, and he laughed without malice or offense. I joined him, our laughter feeling like permission to ask deeper questions: about Islam, calls to prayer, if people responded immediately, how the religion was practiced.

Smiling kindly at my ignorance, he said, "It's like any other religion. Some are devout, some just ignore it. What is it like in America?"

We sat in his shop talking for an hour or more until I felt like I'd overstayed. I purchased a few of my favorites of what he'd shown me: some lipsticks for gifts, and two of each of the hard perfumes—amber musk, jasmine, and rose—that looked like soap and smelled like heaven. When he offered a price, I didn't negotiate. The amount he suggested seemed perfectly reasonable, small compared to the value of the time he'd given me. He asked where I was going and when I said I didn't know, he offered to show me around. After asking a cousin, but not the same one as before, to watch his store, he led me out of his stall.

We spent the rest of the evening and all of the next day together, shopping, talking, and exploring. Our connection wasn't sexual—I was there for yoga, he wore a ring and behaved as if he was married—but there was some sort of platonic chemistry that made us choose each other's company. When I bought two rugs, a leather pouf, and a camel bone mirror from his "cousins," I hoped he got a commission. I wanted his time with me to benefit him but paying him directly felt like it would sully a genuine connection.

During my final hours in Marrakech before heading to the beach for my retreat, Zoubair volunteered to help me ship my packages back to the US. I met him at his shop where two mopeds, loaded with boxes, sat awaiting us. Another cousin, who looked no older than twelve but managed the cumbersome bulk of my purchases with apparent ease, would drive the second moped. When I climbed onto the padded seat of Zoubair's bike, my skirt hiked up to expose my shins, eliciting cat calls from nearby stall owners. Zoubair tugged the hem of my skirt down before I realized what was happening, surprised that it was okay to straddle this man from behind, but my ankles were too sexy for public consumption. I held on lightly, not wanting to cross any lines inadvertently, as we wove our way through obstacles that popped out with varying degrees of suddenness. As we scooted past donkeys, horse buggies, fancy cars, taxis, and motos similarly loaded with humanity and cargo, it occurred to me that there was a decent statistical chance my brains would end up splattered on the pocked and dusty roads. And yet, I didn't care. I was having too much fun. The wind caught my hair, and it billowed out behind me as we drove. I knew it was stupid to be doing this without a helmet, but I hadn't been offered one. Weirdly, I wasn't scared. If these were the last moments of my life, I would die happy. I squeezed my knees in close to avoid grazing doors and side mirrors, but the truth was I didn't feel like I was in any danger. Zoubair's protection felt solid, like a guardian angel.

Zigging and zagging through traffic on the back of that moped, I fell in love with traveling "alone." Never would I have been so open to meeting someone if I'd been with a romantic partner or friend. I never thought I would—or could—enjoy this kind of independence. It had never occurred to me that traveling solo wasn't necessarily being alone.

Gratitude flowed through me. I squeezed Zoubair's waist a little tighter. Sitting tall, smiling, I beamed love in all directions, wondering if I had met this man because I had learned to open my heart.

***

Essaouira sits on the western coast of Morocco, an ancient, walled, fishing village that has been inhabited since prehistoric times. From this land came the original purple dye that was used to distinguish the togas of Roman senators more than 2,000 years ago. The cobalt hues of the small, wooden fishing boats bobbing against each other in the harbor right outside the towering, white, lime-washed walls of the city hinted at this rich legacy. I arrived at midday after a three-hour van ride, during which I daydreamed out the window until an unbelievable sight had me certain I was experiencing my first true hallucinations. We'd been driving fields of trees the van driver said were argan. It was a beautiful, lulling landscape until out of nowhere, I saw dozens of full-grown goats, with rotund bellies, perched on spindly limbs of trees too small to hold them. Sturdy, adult, heavy *goats* just hanging out in a handful of trees along the side of the road. I did a double take, then a triple take, then flipped around to look at the other passengers to see if any of them were reacting to this. But one was asleep, another occupied on her iPod, and the driver didn't seem to be seeing anything out of the ordinary. Worried that I had in fact burned holes into my brain with my recent use of psychedelics and I would no longer be able to distinguish between what was real and not real, I closed my eyes and tried to find a grasp on reality. Then, a woman behind me shrieked.

"Holy shit! There are fucking goats in that tree!" She dropped her iPod and everyone except the driver flung their bodies toward the window.

"They eat the argan nuts. If you want, I pull over. Take pictures." He pulled over and we posed for pictures with goats, taking thumbs-up selfies with the cutest black-and-white one. Beyond relief that my brain was still a working computer with its software intact, I felt an overwhelming sense of wonder. Reality is as awesome as any psychedelic.

The van dropped us outside the walled perimeter of the town, near the beach and the boats. Between the white walls and the turquoise sea was a rocky stretch where striped tents provided shade for the most wild and diverse selection of freshly caught seafood: lobsters, crayfish, monkfish, crabs, prawns, squid, and at least eighteen other ocean dwellers I couldn't name. My stomach growled at the scent coming from the grills. But I had my baggage in tow, so I tabled my desire, promising myself that I'd treat myself to lobster on my last day.

***

The weeklong retreat took place at a hotel within the city's walls, breakfast on the roof and yoga in a nice but nondescript room large enough to accommodate the dozen or so of us. I was not generally a breakfast eater, but in Morocco I was voracious. The only challenge was finding enough room on my plate for traditional Moroccan pancakes topped with almond butter, honey, argan oil and cinnamon; fried eggs; a whole selection of goat cheeses; olives; *and* fresh fruit. Aggressive seagulls helped themselves to all scraps and anything left unguarded.

Before the realizations that had come with opening my heart, learning to look on the world in love, and that traveling alone doesn't have to be lonely, it might have bothered me that I was the only one at the retreat without a partner. But I felt no self-pity. I *loved* wandering on my own.

After our final class the last day, I hot-footed it to the seafood stalls. With only an hour before the shuttle returned us to Marrakesh, I felt rushed and self-conscious as I stood before the bounty. I couldn't eat a whole lobster by myself. It would be wasteful to ask for one. The man taking my order stood with his tongs aloft; his eyes, and the impatient family behind me created altogether too much pressure. I hastily pointed to a pretty, light pink fish about the size of my hand, and four prawns.

The fish was yummy but filled with tiny, dangerous bones that made eating it feel like work. The prawns were sweet, but too mild to stand up to grilling. As I rose from the picnic table I wasn't hungry, but I wasn't sated either. Even before I left the lovely little town, I knew I'd be back. Rolling my luggage to the van, I made a promise to return to Essaouira and eat lobster on the beach with someone I truly loved.

Chapter 15
Open Arms

Canary Islands, Spain
December 2013
Substances ingested: none

The flight to Grand Canaria was short, and from Gran Canaria to Fuerteventura was even shorter. Landing on the volcanic island 100km off the coast of Morocco in the North Atlantic Ocean, the near-tropical landscape made me homesick for family holidays in Hawaii. The plumeria trees, the winds that kicked up out of nowhere and blew gritty dust across vast reaches of open space, the world-renowned surf—it all reminded me of the Kona Coast. Imagining my mom, dad, sister, and niece on the Big Island, I felt alone *and* lonely for the first time this trip. I longed for a family scene from the best of times, and imagined everyone together, playing Cranium, laughing in sincere joy and appreciation of each other, my parents especially. I wanted to talk to them, but the eleven-hour time difference meant that it was three AM there. I decided to call someone else who reminded me of home.

After checking into my new Airbnb—a bright yellow, one-bedroom condo with plastic grass outside—I connected to Skype.

Ben and I met over a decade ago, just before we started college. My sister was graduating from Stanford just as I was starting, and in one of her coolest older-sister moves, she invited me to tag along to a preseason football team party. One of her football player friends introduced me to the incoming freshmen on the team and everyone else disappeared when I saw Ben.

Proportioned like a Greek god, so chiseled that his body could be an anatomical guide to musculature, he moved like someone who knew what to do with *all* his limbs. Visually stunning, it was his smile—warm, kind, sincere—that made him breathtaking. He beamed at full-wattage and felt like a heat lamp. Immediately, I wanted to get close to him.

"Anne, meet Ben," my sister's friend said, as he disappeared from my awareness.

Ben took my hand, held it in both of his, and our eyes met. I couldn't help but start giggling. Legit uncontrollable *giggling*. I'd only experienced a similar feeling once before: when I met Eddie Vedder backstage after a Pearl Jam concert fundraiser for the reproductive rights nonprofit my mom co-founded. Eddie said, "I saw you out there tonight," and I said fucking nothing. Just like that moment, standing in front of Ben the ability to form words escaped me. All I could do was grin and make heart-eyes. Finally, I managed to stammer something, and too soon but probably for my preservation, my sister rounded me up to go. Ever since that August night in 2001, Ben was the most beautiful and charming person I'd ever met in real life, including the man whose proposal I'd accepted.

Twelve years later, Ben was definitely "the one who got away." Each time we had tried dating in the decade between meeting and me getting engaged, something got in the way: his football schedule, my insecurity at being with someone objectively *much* hotter than me, one of us getting back together with an ex... Each time, I told myself various stories about why it hadn't worked, but never admitted the fundamental truth lurking at the edge of my perception: neither of us knew how to be vulnerable—how to let ourselves be cared for—in a relationship. We competed to give the most and receive the least. Of course that was doomed to fail, but I had never been able see the problem, much less know how to fix it.

Though we grew up in almost opposite circumstances—his childhood marked by periods of significant deprivation and racism, mine insulated from those realities—we both learned to take care of those around us and put our needs last. For completely different reasons, we learned that the way to be safe in relationships was to always be of value, to be constantly giving and helpful, and that needing your partner is a great way to get yourself left.

Once, during one of the times I thought our casual dating would turn serious, he got into a car accident that broke his nose. I wanted to rush to his side, thrilling with fantasies of him needing me and me nursing him back to health. But he wouldn't let me in, said he didn't want me to see him weak. I resented him for keeping me at a distance, but I also knew that if the roles had been reversed, I wouldn't have let him see me disfigured. I already felt like I couldn't let him see me without makeup, or if I weren't waxed, plucked, shaved, and shaped. I thought for sure he'd run if he saw the real me.

But now, with the wisdom I'd gained, an open heart, and the sense that I didn't need to constantly deprive myself of what I wanted, I felt like maybe if we tried again, it could be different this time.

Ben answered on the second ring.

"Anne," he said my name like it was a complete sentence, slowly with relish. In just two syllables, I remembered how good it felt to be the subject of his attention. "What's up?" I could hear him smiling. "I'm glad you called."

When he asked what was going on and I'd filled him in on a short history of the last eighteen months or so—engaged, PhD candidate, disengaged, PhD dropout, yoga immersion, MBA, Spain—he said, "Wow. When you blow up your life you really go nuclear." He said it like a compliment, and I could feel his approval.

We talked until my phone started beeping low battery and instead of saying goodbye, I plugged it in, sitting on the floor leaning against the wall where I got the best reception. I asked about his life, film, football, family, and incredibly, he answered. He never used to talk about himself.

We talked about him quitting football, how that felt, and what he was going to do next. We talked about his passion for movies and storytelling, about him maybe going back to school for an MFA. We talked about people we both knew, exes and when we should have known better, giving each other gentle ribbing for past disastrous choices. Occasionally, one of us would say, "well, I should let you go," but neither of us wanted to be let go of. I didn't notice the time passing other than the adjustments I had to make to avoid the sun. We'd started talking when it was bright, full-on overhead, but now it slanted through the shade, umber, and catching particles of dust.

We only got off the phone when I realized I was late for dinner with the new yoga group. Rushing out the door thinking about the *four hours, four minutes and thirty-one seconds* we had spent on the phone, it felt like the beginning of something big. We still had plenty to talk about and I already missed his voice.

The following night, I texted him a picture of the street party that appeared like a flash mob: a Spanish-flavored Britney Spears lookalike, topless backup dancers in ruffled panties, hundreds of drunken teenagers and 20-somethings grinding on each other, all of it over the sound of waves and the smell of seafood. It felt like Barcelona—wild, drunk, and salacious—but more tropical and less familiar. I was happy to be a stranger there. There was something liberating and exciting about being part of a crowd where no one knew me. I felt heady watching a young couple, the woman in tight white jeans with her legs wrapped around the guy's waist, his hands planted firmly on her ass keeping her aloft as they swallowed each other's tongues.

It made me wish Ben were there. Not necessarily to make out with (well yes, that too) but because I wanted to share the experience with him. I wanted him to know what it sounded like, what it felt and smelled like. I wanted him to know what I was seeing and experiencing, what it was like to be in my skin. I wanted to share my life with him. Wait. I wanted to share my *life with him*?

Chapter 16

The Few Things

Barcelona, Spain
April 2014
Substances ingested: love.

"Anne, I love you and I'm in love with you. My love for you is romantic and platonic. I know I could be happy with you long-term, and I want a real chance."

I was back in Barcelona, putting on light, professional makeup to head to class when I got his text. It came without preamble, in response to my somewhat academic discussion of the difference between loving someone and being in love with them, prompted by the recent news that my parents had decided to separate.

I sat down on the closed toilet lid, eyeliner in hand, in happy shock. It had been months of intense, daily, texting and talking—openly, honestly, us both being ourselves—and I knew I was falling but I hadn't known where Ben stood. I didn't know that someone could state it so plainly, without hedging or controlling or asking anything in response. I didn't know it could feel this *good*. He loved me. Without wanting me to change or demanding anything back. He just loved me.

The miracle was, I believed him. He'd known me since I was teenager, through many stages of awkwardness and finding myself. Ben knew me, saw me, and loved me.

I had another couple months in Barcelona before summer break and neither of us wanted to wait that long to see each other. I invited him to come for my birthday at the end of April and he immediately booked tickets for a long weekend.

I met him at the front door of the apartment building and shivered as his arms wrapped around me. He didn't even put down his luggage. I could feel the handles of his weekender bag pressing against my back and I enjoyed the weight of it pushing me into him. He held me tightly, and I felt myself melt, any stubborn doubt or resistance were memories from a past life. I gave him a tour of the apartment that ended in my bedroom and there we stayed. Tender, tentative kisses turned passionate and unrestrained. Though we'd had sex maybe a dozen times before, we had never made love. In so many ways, it felt like the first time. We had both grown into different people, and we were having a lot of fun getting to know each other again for the first time.

The next morning I came out of the shower wrapped in a towel, feeling totally in love and vulnerable because of it. During every past iteration of our relationship, I tried to be nonchalant, feign some degree of indifference so he wouldn't know how much I cared and how much he could hurt me. But this time it was different. I would make it different. This time, I knew better.

I rolled my shoulders back and lifted my chest, consciously opening my heart. I crossed the room to where he was getting dressed and waited, silently but expectantly, for him to finish buttoning his pants.

"What's up?" he asked, his voice husky and attentive, curious about the palpable change in my demeanor.

"Nothing. I was just hoping for a kiss." I said, feeling more exposed by that request than any nudity from the prior night. Hearing me say that, he visibly relaxed. Hands on my hips, he drew me into him. I stretched up, curving against him into the sweetest good-morning-kiss, which deepened until we both emerged somewhat breathless.

Surprised but appreciative, he said, "I didn't know you could be so soft."

Neither did I.

It felt like a new way of being in the world, exciting and terrifying at the same time. I hoped it could last.

Chapter 17

Consequences

Continental US
Summer 2014
Substances ingested: BBQ, beer, and family drama

Growing up, I thought my parents were totally in love. I watched them kiss in the kitchen over dishes, speak in shorthand only they understood, and make each other laugh like best friends. But that was decades ago. Over my teenage years, and even more so in my twenties, they'd grown apart, their patterns ossifying. My mom played the role of vexed, over-burdened wife who had to control everything because her buffoon of a husband couldn't be trusted. And my dad played the role of mincing, underappreciated spouse. Neither was that one-dimensional, but their relationship had become perfunctory, shallow, lacking in any joy or intimacy. I gifted them with a weekend away at a romantic spa for their 35th wedding anniversary, and they fought against going.

I thought they'd find their way back together. I thought they'd be the couple holding hands, dying within hours of each other, making the hospice workers cry with the intensity and endurance of their love.

It hit me like a rockslide when they told me they were separating. It was even worse when they told me they had decided to sell my childhood home because that decision made their separation feel permanent. If they weren't both tied to the same physical location, I knew they wouldn't get back together. I felt deep grief and worry at the thought of my parents *not* together, overwhelming resentment toward them for not trying hard enough, unrelenting sadness at the loss of my home, family, and childhood.

Returning home for the summer felt like a funeral, even though my parents were smiling through it. I accepted I was perhaps being too sensitive. My mom was noticeably happier, and even my dad—who claimed he didn't want the separation—was beginning to imagine possibilities for his future that excited him. For the first time in nearly forty years, my dad was thinking about what *he* wanted.

They decided to throw a party: part birthday party (my dad's 65th and the house's 100th), and part real estate showing. If my parents could be amicable enough to co-host a party, I figured I needed to get onboard with their decision. I invited Ben to join me for the shindig, then for a week in Hawaii with my immediate family, only thinking about how nice it would be show off this gem of a man who didn't want to leave me.

I didn't consider the emotional maelstrom going on inside me, or that a family vacation mid parental divorce was never going to be easy, or that my entire extended family would be at the party and what an insane amount of pressure that would put on any budding relationship. The party was going to be huge—a hundred-and-fifty people or more—a gathering of *all* my aunts, uncles, cousins, nieces, nephews, their spouses, all my parents' friends and colleagues, past and present.

***

At the party, Ben glowed. He was the Boyfriend MVP. He talked sports with the uncle who cared about sports, film with the uncle who cared about art. He charmed my grandmother, making sure her chair was in the shade and that she had a fresh drink in her hand. He won over my cousins, aunts, and all the gay men in attendance by wearing a lightly transparent linen shirt.

At night, in my childhood bed, I asked him versions of the same unfair questions: "So you've known me over ten years and at least a thirty-pound weight range, when was I the hottest? When were you the most attracted to me? How much weight would I have to lose to be your ideal?"

"You know my body responds to yours at any weight," he would say, squeezing me into his chest, perfectly passing my test with exasperating ease. If I pushed, he'd say, "I don't care. I don't think I even really notice—aside from how you feel about it. You're more fun when you feel sexy." Or: "It's your body. It's not mine to have an opinion on. I love it however you like it." Or: "Jesus Christ stop trying to trick me, devil woman!"

But I didn't stop. I couldn't.

***

My tests continued and my softness passed. I turned brittle. In Hawaii, on the family vacation, maybe just to distract from the grief over my broken family, I started picking fights. He broke a wine glass, accidentally knocked it over when trying to shuffle between the coffee table and the couch. He apologized but instead of reassuring him that it was no big deal, I made a vocal point about them being "my mom's *favorite* wine glasses," effectively shaming him in front of my family. Even my six-year-old niece noticed my uncharacteristic lack of charitability. My sister called me out for being a bitch, but Ben didn't.

The bitchier, more nitpicky and aggressive I got; the more Ben took it. His linebacker form shrunk, and once, I noticed him flinch at the sound of my voice. He receded into himself, offered no resistance when I pushed, picked, and poked.

"Why don't you hate me? Why don't you fight back?" I asked, in tears of shame after apologizing for attacking him about something that had probably been nothing.

"Because I define love as complete submission," he said. "I accept everything about you."

But he *shouldn't* accept being treated poorly. I wanted someone to set limits with me, tell me when I was underperforming or hurting them, and hold me accountable. I didn't want to be able to get away with being my worst self; I didn't want his submission. I didn't know if this was a real problem between us or one I was manufacturing because I still couldn't fully allow myself to be loved. I worried we'd end up like my parents. I already saw the seeds of it. Usually I was my mom, being a bitch, and he was my dad, being a doormat, but sometimes we flipped, Ben becoming passive-aggressive while I became the calm, kind, reasonable one. I didn't know if I was creating the dynamic by expecting it, or just recognizing it as it played out in front of me.

I had opened my heart enough to fall in love, but I couldn't sustain it. Loving him and allowing him to love me made me too vulnerable. Watching my parents' forty-year marriage dissolve made me disbelieve that anything could last. So, I destroyed what was there between us, first actively, by trying to push him away, then slowly by disappearing. I'd gained a lot of wisdom from psychedelics, but not enough to know how to deal with this.

Chapter 18

Love's Divine

Istanbul, Turkey
January 2015
Substances ingested: none

I pushed aside thoughts of Ben, and my parents, and what I was going to do after graduation by making myself busy. My time in Europe was rapidly coming to a close and I hadn't been half the places I'd hoped to travel. That's when Turkish Airlines advertised a sale: roundtrip flights to Istanbul for under two hundred bucks. Deepti and I booked tickets that day.

We struggled to settle on an itinerary as we only had four days and there was too much to see. Istanbul alone had thousands of years' worth of cultural and religious sites, but we also wanted to go hot-air ballooning in Cappadocia and visit the salt flats of Pamukkale. Ultimately, we decided to spend most of our time in Istanbul because of how much there was to see, not to mention being the only city in the world that straddles two different continents. Still the largest European city by population, and one of the most visited cities in the world, it boasts numerous significant sites, including the Hagia Sophia, the Blue Mosque, the Hippodrome, Suleymaniye Mosque, Topkapi Palace, and the Basilica Cistern. Deepti and I decided to see them all.

At the airport, instead of queueing up at the official taxi stand or taking the bus, when some random man asked us if we were headed across the bridge to the Asia side of the Bosporus Strait, we answered yes, like polite little girls.

"Great, I will take you. Only twenty-five dollars." Before we could object, he'd grabbed our suitcases and was striding toward the parking lot. Twenty-five dollars seemed reasonable and, perhaps each thinking the other would object if something were wrong, we followed him. He drove fast, but it wasn't until he pulled over on the side of a busy four-lane thoroughfare, tossed our bags from the trunk and demanded more money that I got scared. Giving it to him and finding a marked taxi to take us the rest of the way to our Airbnb seemed like the safest option. I chastised myself for being so naïve while stuffing the bills into his hand. I think I may have even tipped.

By the time we had muscled our baggage through crowded pedestrian streets, ignoring frequent hissing catcalls, my guard was fully up. Istanbul was not Marrakech. There were similarities: souks overflowing with spices piled in mounds outside apothecaries that looked like Zoubair's, rug shops upon rug shops upon rug shops, street food mouthwatering enough to risk street food consequences. But the overall feeling was different. Istanbul felt grittier and harsher than Marrakech.

The mosques were all beautiful, but they quickly ran together in my head. Topkapi Palace was a museum, and the Hippodrome had no hippos at all. I didn't *actually* expect hippos, but I did expect something cooler than … a big town square? I learned: it was named the "Hippodrome" thousands of years ago when it hosted chariot races (in ancient Greek, horse =hippos and course=dromos).

The rest of the sites on our packed itinerary were interesting, aesthetically pleasing, and worthwhile, but the Basilica Cistern left the most lasting impression.

During the sixth century, the Romans of Constantinople had the engineering skills—and exploited the labor of 7,000 enslaved people—to build an underground cathedral that served as a reservoir and water filtration system. It functioned for nearly a thousand years. Now, it is serves as an underwater palace and tourist attraction. The pamphlet told us that the arched stone ceiling was held aloft by 336 marble columns repurposed from distant Roman cities, relocated to Istanbul, and resurrected underground. Deepti and I spoke in hushed tones as we crossed through the haunting space.

It felt like a church and a mausoleum and glass-bottomed boat all at the same time: sacred, eerie, beautiful. The light was ghostly—yellow and dim but bouncing off the water and casting wavy shadows onto the jaundiced columns. Making our way deeper underground, I felt my breath quicken with the fear of becoming trapped or drowning, of the scaffolding giving way and us having to claw and climb over each other to reach the exit stairs. I let the catastrophic scenarios pop up and float away like toxic little bubbles.

My breath hitched when I looked down and saw snakes writhing underwater. The head of Medusa, inverted so the serpents of her hair reached toward the surface, was carved into the base of the pillar. Tradition dictated that images of the gorgon be installed sideways or upside down to thwart her power, but she appeared only more menacing, more disorienting, as if I were the one wrong about gravity. The image stayed with me long after we ascended to ground level.

That night, still slightly unsettled, I convinced Deepti to attend a Whirling Dervish ceremony after seeing a printed advertisement taped to a light post. The advertisement piqued my attention because I grew up thinking a "whirling dervish" was something like the Tasmanian Devil from the cartoons. But also, my psychedelic exploration had kicked off a bit of a spiritual quest, one that led me to reading—and actually *enjoying*—books of poetry, particularly translations of a 13th-century Sufi mystic named Jalāl al-Dīn Muḥammad Rūmī.

Sufism is a sect of Islam that seeks direct experience of the Divine through contemplation and self-surrender. Rumi was known as a "drunken Sufi" because he found transcendence in dance, music, and poetry. Using the combination, he created a method of meditative and devotional movement called sema, still practiced hundreds of years later by modern whirling dervishes called "semazen." His poetry is timeless, always calling me back and offering new layers of meaning. One poem, the first I remember reading and accidentally memorized, replayed itself in my mind:

> "Out beyond ideas of wrongdoing and rightdoing,
> There is a field. I'll meet you there.
> When the soul lies down in that grass,
> The world is too full to talk about."

That there is a place of refuge, solace, and fullness out beyond our "ideas" of "wrongdoing" and "rightdoing"... I think that is what I was seeking with psychedelics. Rumi was the reason I wanted to see the dervishes.

The show started at six PM in the Galata Mevlevi Museum, but we arrived early to get good seats. Two rows of chairs ringed an ornate inner wall that kept audience members to the perimeter of the circular room. I got antsy waiting, squirming in my chair, uncomfortable with the height of the armrests. Impatiently, I watched as the semazen finally entered, walking in a line, serene and with eyes downcast, in heavy black cloaks and tall earth-colored hats. After much elaborate and choreographed bowing, they shed their cloaks as, another pamphlet explained, a symbolic rebirth to Allah and the Truth. Then, in long, flowing white robes, accompanied by a singer, flute-player, kettledrummer and cymbal player, their whirling began.

Slowly, then faster, each man spun from right to left, in spirals around his own heart. His right arm extended up, hand open to receive the beneficence of God, while his left arm reached down, hand open and turned toward the earth as a point of focus. Faster and faster they spun, never frantic or jerky but as if propelled by the same steady forces that cause planets to rotate. I felt myself energetically pulled into the center of the room, resisting the increasing urge to jump out of my seat and join them in their spirals.

As peaceful as if asleep, the dervishes spun in perfect unison, their skirts twirling in hypnotic waves. It could have been boring, soporific, but instead I felt part of an ancient tradition and spiritual technology. I understood why Rumi came up with this dance, this meditation, this prayer; even just in proximity I felt a swelling of love and interconnectedness, the presence of an infinite energy extending across space-time, a calmness reminiscent of my prior psychedelic journeys. There was no reason to be anxious about anything, ever, because something wise and powerful was in control, handling every detail immaculately. All I needed to do was breathe, exist, and be myself. I felt a divine presence, God perhaps. Not a bearded man in the sky with an insatiable need for praise. But a force. A feeling. A reason for deep relaxation and trust.

Rumi wrote that "all loves are a bridge to Divine love." I'd never questioned the existence of love but had always questioned the existence of God. Watching the dervishes, sitting still but feeling deeply moved, I pondered Rumi's words. Love is an interconnecting energy, a force for thriving, and source of support. Love is what makes moms lift cars off babies. Love (or something on that continuum) makes people make babies to begin with, which is what continues the species. Love is usually the source of all the best art, music, movies, books, etc. What if God and Love are the same thing? What if I could use my ability to love—my family, Adelynn, French fries—as a bridge to the Divine? If Rumi was right, maybe God and I could be friends after all?

As the audience finally began to stir, I exchanged blissed-out smiles with the people rising around me, all of us looking a little drugged and happy.

Chapter 19
Joy To The World

Amsterdam, Netherlands
November 2015
Substances ingested: stroopwafels, Gouda, and psychedelic truffles, but separately

I graduated in May, took a job with a startup that failed a few months later, and by the fall of 2015, I found myself evaluating next steps. It had been almost two years since my last psychedelic journey. I felt like I'd integrated what I'd learned and was eager for another dose of wisdom. I had enough airline miles to make a flight to Amsterdam free and chose a relatively inexpensive Airbnb in a part of the city I'd never stayed in before.

I arrived in the evening and went straight to sleep. Well, first I went to a coffeeshop for some Indica, then straight to sleep. The next day I wandered the city, collecting supplies for my journey, and indulging in a bit of shopping at the vintage clothing stores that rival any Brooklyn street. I snagged an enchanting woolen cape for $56 that made me feel like a character from a historical romance novel. I texted Adelynn a picture and she responded with "Love it! Very subtle. For a cape."

More practically, I had purchased my psychedelic truffles (Philosopher's Stone again). On the recommendation of the psychedelic concierge at the Smart Shop, I also got some dark chocolate to intensify visual effects and milk chocolate to dampen them if needed. For snacks, I bought aged gouda, two ripe pears, and four boxes of caramel stroopwafels telling myself I would take at least two boxes home as gifts. The stroopwafels (a specific type of wafer sandwich cookie) pair particularly well with the high-quality cheese—probably no accident as both originated in Gouda, Holland.

Sitting on the brown, pilled couch of the AirBnB, thinking how much better the photographs made the place look, I was glad I'd be spending most of my time in this apartment with my eyes closed. The bathrooms were so small I had to enter sideways. The sound insulation was negligible, and I could hear everything going on inside and outside the apartment building—flushing toilets in a neighboring unit, conversation from the street, the industrial refrigerator of the gourmet market below.

I took a walk for a change of scenery and meditated on my intention for this trip. My previous three experiences with psychedelics—mushrooms twice and ayahuasca once—I had entered without specific intention, but this time I wanted to test what was possible. Maybe if I asked the questions causing me the most strife, I'd get answers and end my suffering. Sitting at a coffeeshop, I journaled possible questions, taking a while to narrow it down to five. More seemed like too many to remember and too much to ask of the entity (maybe) answering. I circled the winners then rewrote them as a list to cement them in my memory:

1) What am I supposed to do with my life?

By now, I had tried and eliminated all my best guesses. Not a business PhD leading to professorship, not starting a social enterprise, not management, not speechwriting, not ghostwriting, not nothing. Of everything I'd tried, doing nothing was the worst. This was only my third week without a job and already I felt useless.

2) Why do I keep choosing behaviors (procrastination, self-punishment, eating carbs, smoking too much pot, whatever) that do not contribute to my health, happiness, or feelings of self-worth?

There were so many ways, big and small, that I failed to act in accordance with what was best for me. I was self-sabotaging, with everything from being lazy about exercise to swearing I'd give up sugar and then downing a sleeve of Oreos twenty minutes later. No matter how many times in how many different ways the Universe told me to give up my shame about smoking pot, I held onto it. I felt like smoking pot *must* be a hindrance, so why did I continue to get high, every goddamn day, when I knew it wasn't in alignment with what I truly wanted?

3) Am I supposed to have a baby?

This seemed important and I was conflicted. Maybe the Universe had a strong and convincing opinion.

4) Do I get a forever love?

I felt like I could relax if I knew. Yes or no. Yes was obviously preferable, but if I knew it wasn't going to happen for me, I would stop trying. The hardest part of the uncertainty was that it kept me hoping, and then being disappointed when a relationship didn't work out. If I simply knew that I was destined to be alone, I'd stop with the dating apps, stop worrying about the size of my thighs, stop investing in my appearance at all. I'd buy a farm or join a commune or maybe just plan to travel for the rest of my life. I needed to know whether I should put energy into looking for partnership or developing a satisfactory Plan B.

5) What am I supposed to eat to be healthy and hot?

For much of my life, really until I got Lyme Disease, "hot" meant skinny and healthy was irrelevant. Before getting sick, all that mattered to me about my body was its proximity to the societal ideals promoted on magazine covers. Now, now that I was trying to befriend my body, health mattered, too. But so, still, did being skinny. As much as I wanted my health and vitality to be my only concern, if feeding myself regular filling meals meant looking overweight or fat, I didn't want it. Where was the achievable middle ground that would have me healthy—not starving or unduly restricting myself—but also unassailable to the criticisms always hurled at fat people?

Armed with my dark chocolate, milk chocolate, and list of questions, I felt like I had a gas pedal, a brake pedal, and a steering wheel. I'd read the informational booklet cover to cover each of the three times I'd received it—one that someone had discarded on the train, and two I'd gotten from the Smart Shop—but it had been years, and consuming information made me feel more in control, so I read the pamphlet again in case I'd forgotten anything important:

- Take your time and ensure a safe and trusted environment.

- Make sure there is someone in the neighborhood who is sober.

I didn't have a trusted neighbor, but my Airbnb was in the residential area on the edge of a strip of restaurants, bars, and grocery stores, so I took solace in the likelihood that all I had to do was run into the street and ask for help if something went drastically wrong. I would surely not be the first dumbass tourist to land in the hospital for irresponsible drug use. At least here I wouldn't be sent to jail.

- If you become anxious, stay calm: the unpleasant feeling always passes.

- Do not resist what comes to mind and relax. It usually helps to think of something fun and to listen to some music.

- Smoking marijuana extends and intensifies the trip

- Do not combine mushrooms and truffles with alcohol. This increases the chance of a bad trip.

- Do not drive after using truffles!

- Take your time, don't use truffles if you don't have the time. Make sure you have nothing important to do the next day. You can be tired after a truffle trip.

- Do not take truffles if you feel anxious, stressed, or depressed. People with a dormant psychosis or schizophrenia should not use truffles.

- Do not take truffles if you use medication.

- Do not take truffles if you are pregnant, breastfeeding, or younger than 18 years.

There were some red flags on this list: I was alone, and nobody knew where I was or what I was doing, but I decided not to dwell on the risks. I'd come all this way specifically to trip, I wasn't going to go home because a pamphlet recommended supervision.

In the late afternoon, after reviewing my list of questions, I settled on the couch to consume my Philosopher's Stone with reverence. I chewed and swallowed slowly; the taste had not improved or dulled in the years since I'd had it last. To keep myself entertained with something suitably wholesome as I waited for wisdom to kick in, I streamed *Planet Earth: Shallow Seas* on my computer.

Before I knew it, I was wide-eyed and slack-jawed in amazement at life on Earth. My face only inches from the screen, I felt like a sea creature myself. A segment on octopuses created a kaleidoscope of emotions toward cephalopods: love, guilt, admiration, fear, curiosity, wonder, aversion, envy, confusion. One blended into the next as I marveled at the magnificence of nature—until, without warning, the octopuses were replaced by snakes. Thousands of them, swarming and writhing like a choreographed nightmare, swimming across the screen with mouths agape, ready to devour prey. I slammed my computer shut and flung it across the couch.

I closed my eyes. Then giggled at my overreaction. I knew I was high when I couldn't stop laughing. The giggling turned to guffaws, and it didn't matter that I couldn't remember what was so funny.

I was then standing—with no memory of rising from the couch—bending my knees as if stretching before a big race. I felt an enormous current of energy course through me. It made me bounce up and down, jumping then squatting, squatting a little lower then jumping up again to land only on my toes. My body craved movement. It needed to be used, appreciated. I dropped to the floor for mountain climbers.

I craved muscle. Strength. I hadn't been using my body enough. I needed to dance. I couldn't *not* dance. The rhythm of life demanded it. I moved to no music, only the rhythms of the Earth. Shaking and grooving, but rooted.

I twirled in slow circles, spinning through lifetimes. I watched as the Big Bang began in darkness, in mystery, then exploded into fireworks against inky black, each pop of color the creation of a new galaxy, constantly birthing and rebirthing. Everywhere, the eternal cyclical mystery of nothingness. Birth, life, death, nothingness then birth again. I was the beginning and the end of the Universe. My hips, my womb, my soul—I was all that ever was. I was creator and created.

Religious and philosophical truths that had once seemed like platitudes or unknowable mysteries now struck me as obvious, undeniable. I understood what the most devout Christian felt toward Jesus, the sense of peace a Buddhist master felt meditating.

All my life, I had felt some combination of being behind and rushed. But now, I saw time as a fungible illusion, a force that stretched and contracted and moved in both directions and three dimensions. I was where I was supposed to be because...because I existed. I *was*. It was impossible to be somewhere I wasn't supposed to be. The Universe wouldn't allow it. I was always where I was supposed to be. Always. Definitionally. Never behind, always in the perfect time and place.

Some distance away, an ambulance drove by and at the sound of its siren, I envisioned a man, hand clutched to his chest. I saw a wife and children panicking. My sense of peace vanished.

I was high now and getting higher.

I felt overly raw, emotional, sensitive to every stimulus. The softness of the synthetic shearling blanket I pulled over myself as I laid down was sudden, full-body ecstasy, but distant shouting voices and car horns pounded like jackhammers in my head.

I needed a buffer. Navigating my phone's vivid bright lights and glaring notifications was torture, but I managed to put on a chakra meditation album full volume, set to repeat, before plugging my phone in and setting it face down against the wall where it wouldn't die or distract me.

The single word—om—for the entire first 30 minutes of the album lulled me back into relaxation and deeper into my mind. I was lying on the bed now, on the covers but under the blanket, eyes open.

Nope, they were closed.

But I saw so much more with them closed.

When they were open, reality intruded: dull curtains bleached by time, Ikea furniture, and worse—Ikea art. A streetlight outside the window flickered maddeningly.

But with my eyes closed, I floated. In and out of my body, in and out of the atmosphere, in and out of a consciousness that encompassed all that ever was and all that ever will be.

Unclear how much time had passed, if I was already beginning to come down without having asked a single question, I started to panic.

Rapidly, I began to ask my questions without waiting for answers. What am I supposed to do with my life? Why do I keep choosing behaviors that do not contribute to my health, happiness, or feelings of self-worth? Am I supposed to have a baby? Do I get a forever love? What am I supposed to eat to be healthy and hot?

Hoping for rapid-fire answers to my barrage of questions, I paused, waiting impatiently, ready to take notes.

All I heard was laughter, distant but in my head, like a memory of a laugh track.

Then a voice. It wasn't one I recognized but she sounded like chamomile and Xanax and sunshine. Lovingly, she said, "Oh sweetheart. Slow down." Then, reassuringly, "You have all the time in the world."

Initially, I was pissed. "No, I don't!" I argued. "This isn't going to last! I'm going to come down, lose touch, and I won't have answers! I won't know what to do and everything will be awful." Then, despairing, "I'll have wasted so much time and money—and this experience!"

The voice offered no response, only an echo of "you have all the time in the world."

Impossible. I dismissed it again, my habitual feelings of being rushed and behind in the race of life were too strong.

But what if life wasn't a race. What if I believed what I'd felt just minutes before—that I was always exactly where I was supposed to be—not behind or ahead or smidge to the right, but *exactly* where I was supposed to be in every possible way. What if I did have all the time in the world?

The words echoed, and each time I heard them, they rang marginally truer. I was flooded with perspectives, and realized they all depended on my definition of "I." This silly little Anne-shell had an expiration date of roughly a hundred years. But the Anne shell was the least of my I's. I was made up of so much more. I was the same stuff as Jesus and the dinosaurs. The phosphorus in my bones came from stars. Death didn't end this version of "I," it only transformed it. I—the particles that composed my body and the form of energy that carried my consciousness—had existed since the beginning of time. I just saw the Big Bang. I was there. It was a different I, but all I had to do to have literally *all the time in the world* was change my "I".

I heard tinkling laughter. The voice sounded proud of me. In affirmation and encouragement, she said, "You can ask anything you want and you will get answers, but it has to be with the spirit of open inquiry not interrogation." This, I understood, she offered as a rule for communication with the Universe on psychedelics, but also a rule for intimate interpersonal relationships. *If* the spirit of the question was genuine curiosity and loving acceptance, questions were welcome. If the questions came from a place of judgment, the desire to be right or win or prove someone else wrong, then it would be better not to ask. Once she knew I'd caught the general applicability of what she was telling me, she continued, "There are no right answers—meaning that if you made a different choice with your life than what you would have if you'd gotten a chance to ask us your questions, it wasn't the wrong choice. There's nothing to be scared of here, but you have to listen."

At "have to" I felt a slight, quick, cramping sensation in my brain that dissipated as swiftly as I noticed it. The cramping was her way of correcting me: she didn't say that I *had* to do something. It was my voice that transformed her meaning. It was *my* voice interpreting all the "have tos" and "shoulds." She existed in the field "beyond ideas of wrongdoing and rightdoing" Rumi. Fucking genius.

I felt appropriately chastened and treasured at the same time. I saw myself through her eyes and felt a swelling of love for this adorable, eager, try-hard. I saw the six-year-old me who thought she was a failure because she wasn't born knowing how to read and because learning how to was hard. I saw the sixteen-year-old student wanting a perfect score on the SATs to prove she was smart enough. I saw the twenty-seven-year-old who supplanted her inner knowing with David's outward show of certainty. How badly I wanted to get it—everything—right, just to be good enough to be loved. I saw myself through the Universe's eyes and I wept with empathy for this poor, sweet girl who tried so hard and so often felt not good enough. How *wrong* she was.

I stopped trying to ask any questions. I took a long moment to hold all the different mes, all the ages I'd been in different versions of suffering, and simply *loved* myself. I held each image of myself in my mind's eye and showered her with all the things I wish I'd heard and known and felt when I was younger.

It was healing, but I was not healed. When it felt right to move on, discarding my predetermined order of importance, I asked: "Am I supposed to have a child?"

"I don't know." She was casual, like I'd just asked what she wanted for dinner. "What do you want to do?"

I didn't appreciate her asking me questions. I wanted clear, actionable guidance on what—lacking a better word—God wanted from me.

"That"—her voice was privy to my internal monologue—"is not how we work."

She'd already told me there was no such thing as right answers. "So, what? I'm supposed to figure this out on my own?" I asked, annoyed.

"Yep."

"But I expected divine guidance."

"And you have it."

"You just said, 'What do you want to do?' That's not guidance. It doesn't tell me what is wanted or expected from me. How am I supposed to know what I'm supposed to do?" I whined.

What do you want to do? The question echoed in my mind, but this time in my voice. She—the voice and presence of Wisdom—was gone. It was my voice now. I hated my voice. I hated my obsessive thoughts. I hated not knowing what to do.

The loop was inescapable: What do you want to do? What do you want to do? The loop sped up, louder and louder until all I heard was, "What do you want to do? **What do you want to do? WHAT DO YOU WANT**..." Just when volume became intolerable, I understood.

There was a reason the Universe was repeating "want" with such force: my *desires* were a built-in compass for what I was "supposed" to do. The echoing stopped. Silence. Peaceful, relaxing silence. The realization continued: I'm *supposed* to do what I *want* to do.

I felt the cramping sensation again at the idea of "want." I'd gotten something wrong in translation. I slowed down and clarification came. What I "wanted" was a passing fancy, ego-driven, not tied to my highest self. I didn't need to focus on "want."

Joy was deeper. Joy did not need to be taught or learned, but rather emerged organically from body, mind, and soul acting in concert. I was supposed to be asking, "What would bring me joy?"

Distant laughter told me I was right. Whenever I was confused or uncertain, I was supposed to ask myself, "What would bring me joy?"

The Universe wanted me to be joyful. I needed to follow the whispered hints and hidden signs in my own body that pointed to joy because joy was where I was supposed to live. It was a spectacular miracle that I was born into a human body, at this time, with these opportunities. Every moment was an opportunity to feel joy, to celebrate and to revel in joy! This was the answer to my question about what I'm supposed to do with my life, too: follow joy.

"But wait." A thought jerked me out of my joy: "Does that mean I'm supposed to have a baby or not?"

Her laughing voice sang my words, "What would bring you joy?"

I didn't know; I thought I could love a little human well. I wanted the opportunity to do so. But I also liked traveling at the drop of a hat. I certainly wouldn't be tripping in Amsterdam right now if I had a baby. Also, and probably more importantly, I didn't want to do it by myself. I didn't want to be a single mom. That sounded too hard for me.

But what if I missed my chance?

I just didn't know.

"'I don't know' is an answer," she said. Having a baby and raising a child was too big a decision to be driven by fear of missing out. "I don't know" *was* an answer. For now. Anything other than a full-bodied "Yes, I am sure," was less than I wanted for a child.

Lying on the thin cotton sheets, blankets in a pile at my feet, I felt peaceful and receptive as a series of realizations washed over me: I had years of fertility left. If it took longer than my biological clock allowed, I could still be a parent. Mothering was about showing up and loving. There would always be someone who needed mothering. I could be a mother at any age, and I could mother thousands if I ended up not having any biological children.

The weight of fear and internal conflict dissolved from my shoulders my chest. I could breathe more freely now.

Feeling like any questions that started with "supposed to" or "should" were moot because I already knew the answer I'd be given ("What would bring you joy?"), I moved to the question that had me genuinely stumped: Why do I keep doing things that make me unhappy? More specifically, I asked what needed to change. Why did I keep picking up habits, thought patterns, and behaviors that no longer served me (assuming they ever did)?

Cryptically, in a voice that sounded like a robot trying to be human, I heard her say, "You will for as long as your hair is long."

"I HAVE TO CUT MY HAIR?" I screamed it loudly, but silently in my head. The commandment was so unwanted that I began trying to distance myself from the Universe, from the from the trip, from being high. I opened my eyes and considered eating the entire bar of sugary milk chocolate. I wanted to slam on the brakes but even more, to erase the last thirty seconds from my memory. I was wailing in my head and whimpering aloud, "Nooooooooo. I would never have done any of this if I'd known I'd have to cut my hair!"

"You don't *have* to do anything," she—the warm, laughing, calming presence of Wisdom—corrected, but I couldn't be pried from my negative spiral.

My hair was the only beautiful thing about me. I was nominated for Best Hair in high school. A Persian girl won, and she deserved it, but she *did* her hair every morning. Whereas I just rolled out of bed, ran my fingers through it, and was good to go. With almost zero effort, tools, or maintenance, I had the hair of shampoo commercials. Glossy and thick, falling straight or in loose waves without so much as a hairbrush, my hair was my pride. Even before adolescence brought blemishes, I hid behind my hair because *everyone* liked it. Boyfriends, hair stylists, random women on the street—everyone told me my how beautiful it was.

And now the Universe was telling me to cut it off.

Knocking lightly on my attention like it was a window, the voice reminded me "You don't have to do anything," but it didn't matter. I knew I didn't "have" to cut it. But I couldn't *not* cut it knowing what I now knew. It changed the way my hair felt, both growing out of my head and my feelings about it. Before this message from the Universe, I thought it was my crowning glory but suddenly it felt like dead weight. I had put my hair up with two elastic bands before tripping because I knew I'd want it off my neck and it was too heavy for just one. At some point, probably during my jumping and mountain climbers, the elastics had fallen out. Now, my hair hung heavy and limp, pulled down by gravity, leaching me of energy. It was history and story—baggage, inherited, in HAIR it is! I thought about all that had happened in the past decade that I didn't want to hold onto, and thought about it being stored in my hair. Mildly hysterical, I thought about searching for scissors and hacking it off in the bathroom sink. But I'd forbade myself from doing anything irreparable or dangerous until I was fully in my right mind again.

As frantic as I was to chop it off, I was still more terrified of having short hair. I knew it would make me look—or rather, reveal—how fat and ugly I was. I felt man-ish enough; I did not want to try dating with the stereotype of a lesbian haircut. That was all I could imagine with short hair. My Victoria's Secret supermodel hair was the only thing Victoria's Secret supermodel about me. I was sure it accounted for roughly 96% of my right-swipes on dating apps. Who in their right mind cuts off their one asset? As a sign that I was maybe sobering up, I decided to go to sleep.

I floated in and out of "sober" thoughts. When my feet got cold, I sought socks and an extra blanket. I couldn't help but think about how many people had had sex on the bed I was trying to cozy into. It disappointed me slightly: no matter how high I got I could never get away from my brain completely.

I remembered another question and asked it: Do I get a forever love?

I heard a man's laugh—*his* laugh, the laugh of my forever love—deep and genuine, throaty with surprise and true humor, pure joy. Yessssss.

Beyond the relief, the sound imparted knowledge: I would embrace, in a partner, what I saw as flaws in myself. I was messy, but I would accept messiness in a partner if he were kind, funny, smart, and loving—which I was. Sure, I was hairy, but I didn't mind hairy men. I didn't even mind hairless men! Bald was no big deal to me; I liked bald. And I would happily accept some extra weight on a guy if it meant he enjoyed what he ate and wasn't neurotic about the gym. In fact, I would *prefer* those qualities. In a partner, I would accept every trait I saw as horrible in myself—as long as he had all the things going for him that I had going for me. I was capable of loving deeply, completely, responsibly. I was kind, funny, smart, and loyal. I wasn't asking more from a relationship than what I brought to it.

I asked the Universe what I needed to do to meet this man.

Again, the familiar, beloved, female voice of the Universe: "Keep asking: What brings me joy? What brings me joy? Use it like a homing beacon. When evaluating decisions, when panicking and anxious, ask: What would bring me joy? It is that simple."

Coming off that message, I felt silly asking my last question. Even now, even flooded with serotonin in this sacred moment in this extraordinary city, I was trying to make myself unhappy. I had decided that my precious and waning time with Wisdom should be spent asking about *food* in the context of being "hot". Gross!

When sober, I wanted rules and deprivation, dicta with moral weight: "good" foods to accept, "bad" foods to reject. When sober, it felt like a really fucking big deal. Now, it felt embarrassing to ask of such penetrating Wisdom, but I didn't want to disappoint my past or future selves by not asking. And I knew my future, sober, self would care.

Sheepishly, I asked, "um, it's probably below your pay grade. But I told younger Anne I'd ask and I'm trying to do right by her… uh, what should—oops, I mean, what would you advise me eating to be healthy and hot?" I tried to swallow the last word a little bit, but I knew she heard me.

"Food is lovely. Food is enjoyable. Stop punishing yourself for eating."

I couldn't believe it. It couldn't be that simple.

"Just do the other things you need to be healthy," Wisdom said. "Use your body to rejoice. Worship. Dance! Have sex. Do yoga. Just enjoy it. Stop judging. You are beautiful and soft and perfect and whole and complete. Don't allow the other voices space." She paused. "Unless you want to. If you want to be unhappy and judgmental, go ahead. It's okay." She meant it. She wouldn't stop loving me if I chose to make myself miserable. It would hurt her to see me suffering but she wouldn't punish me for it.

This was what unconditional love *feels* like. I wanted to live in this space all the time—loved and safe, enough and in awe, euphoric and grounded. I cuddled into the safety and fell asleep.

***

I woke around nine the next morning, my mind clear and enhanced, like my operating system got upgraded overnight. As I checked in with my newfound insights—that joy is a compass, that "I don't know" is an answer, that I have all the time in the world if I want it, that food is lovely, that I would love a partner who brought my balance sheet of characteristics to the table—all felt as valid and valuable as the night before.

Except the part about my hair. I was still shocked and depressed about that. It seemed like too much to ask of me. What could the Universe reward me with that would be worth losing my hair? World peace? An end to genocide? Environmental justice, respect for Indigenous rights, microplastics out of the oceans...? There was no shortage of global issues for which I'd be willing to trade my tresses, but I doubted that was the scale of the reward on offer. I tried to think smaller, dredging for childhood fantasies.

The Universe said I was going to meet my forever love; he could be a prince! I could be royal. The anti-colonialist, anti-elitist, pro-democracy feminist in me might not have loved it, but I grew up when being a "princess" was still fairy tale rather than nightmare.

I paused my packing, retrieved my computer from where I'd tossed it the night before, closed the browser window that immediately opened with a still shot of swarming snakes, and googled "available princes." I did it to reassure myself that there were still eligible, desirable bachelors more holistically appealing than the men on reality TV and dating apps. Deepti had gotten me into watching *The Bachelor* and the show had activated a feeling of scarcity around men. Most of the results to my search for unmarried royalty looked like the product of hundreds of years of inbreeding (probably because they were), but a few seemed acceptable. I didn't actually see myself becoming royalty, or truly even want it, but it was fun to indulge such wild fantasies.

Chapter 20
Annie

Burlingame, California
November 2015
Substances ingested: none

Early on the Tuesday morning before Thanksgiving, I sat on my bed with my laptop open, body and hair wrapped in towels, still wet from showering after my redeye home from Amsterdam. I was set to begin a new job doing strategic communications for an education non-profit in the Bay Area. Though I would get paid well, and could have afforded an apartment regardless, housing costs in San Francisco—and even Oakland where the non-profit was based—were absurdly high. My parents had put our house on the market shortly after moving all our stuff out of it, they'd taken it off again after it didn't sell quickly. The big house—the one I'd lived in—remained empty but there were two cottages on the property, and so I moved into one of them. My dad was in the other and my mom was in Oklahoma.

The first six months of separation had been hard on everyone—my parents, sister, extended family, me. My mom had a new partner, and my dad was starting to date. He was dating men, exclusively, and that came as a surprise when he told me, but the surprise passed quickly. I liked that I wouldn't have to deal with a new woman replacing or competing with my mom in any way. In some ways, his gayness made sense. I could imagine how 40+ years with the same woman could make you want to try something wildly different, especially if you were always bisexual and never really had the chance to explore. And that's where I tried to stop thinking about it because thinking about your parents having sex is gross.

There's no way to end a 40-year marriage painlessly. To give them due credit, my parents managed to stay family even while getting divorced. The end of their marriage and romantic relationship was the end of a phase of life, but it wasn't the end of our family unit or our unity. We would still go on vacations, celebrate special occasions, and participate in text threads *as a family*. Neither their physical nor legal separation changed anything about the decades they spent together raising us, building our branch of the family tree. Watching my parents negotiate their divorce, as friends, healed many of the wounds their separation opened. It wasn't perfect—my dad played the victim and allowed my mom to shoulder more than her fair share of the blame (blame that friends and family members on both sides tended to assign, no matter how unhelpful). Both of them had their passing moments of pique and pettiness, but those moments passed, and they remained friends, steadfast co-captains of Team Kiehl Friedman. They were living their best lives, happily apart and friendlier than ever, so I couldn't help but be proud of them even if I wouldn't have chosen it this way. Turns out, there is a way to end relationships without destroying everyone involved.

With browser tabs open to all Yelp's four-starred hair salons within a fifteen-mile radius, I dug into reviews and scanned for repeated names heaped with praise. My first choices, at fancy salons in San Francisco and Palo Alto were booked for months. Figuring that I was on the verge of hacking it off myself and any professional would do a better job, I called the salon I went to in high school. Never a wait then, no wait now. But because of the Thanksgiving holiday, the soonest they could do was the following Tuesday morning.

That fateful Tuesday, a week later, I decided to walk the hour round-trip to the salon because late November in California is still glorious. The eucalyptus trees were blooming, showering their delicate blush-colored fringe on the sidewalk, and calling my attention to the many different shades of pastel in their trunks that looked painted in watercolor. I walked with my hair down, saying goodbye to the feeling of it brushing my shoulder blades. Then I got warm and swept it into a high ponytail. I got it swinging, creating its own airflow, and making me feel like a high school cheerleader—cute, peppy, young. Even though I wanted it off, I didn't want it *gone*. My hair felt poisonous, but I still saw it as the only beautiful thing about me.

Yoga pants and an oversized sweatshirt with no makeup had seemed like a reasonable choice when getting dressed for an hour of walking, but I regretted all of it the minute I sat in front of the brightly lit mirror. I looked haggard: dark circles under my eyes, skin sallow and blotchy, eyebrows unkempt, chin weak. Elaine, my stylist, a petite and efficient woman with tasteful tattoos peeking out from her blouse, took my hair out of its ponytail and ran her fingers through the waves cascading down my back. Her manner was curt, not particularly talkative or friendly, and I was grateful for her brevity. "You have really healthy hair," she assessed. "Keep it long? Trim half-an-inch for maintenance?"

Meeting her eyes in the mirror so I could stop dissecting all that was wrong with my face, I said, "Thanks. I want it off."

"What do you mean? You've got a lot of hair here," she said, letting it slide through her fingers, skeptical of my commitment and giving me a chance to change my mind.

"I know. But I want to cut off as much as possible without making me look hideous or butch." She was no-nonsense, verging on brusque, but maybe that was because I was stilted, trying to disguise my inner conflict and rising grief.

"Why? You've got such great hair. You're going to donate it?" she guessed.

"Yes," I said. I'd researched donation programs once I decided I was going to cut it off. If I wasn't going to benefit from my gorgeous hair, someone else should.

"Then it needs to be in a ponytail. I wouldn't go any shorter than . . . " She made a low ponytail at the base of my skull. ". . . here. That will leave us some asymmetrical fringe to work with around your face. How does that sound?"

"Sure. Fine. Sounds good." If I sounded rude it was because of impatience. I felt like I'd done my part in getting myself into the chair, said my peace with "I want it off," and now I wanted the Universe to take over through Elaine's hands. I had come to terms with what I figured was the worst-case outcome: I would be ugly for two years until my hair grew back and I could hide behind it again. People survived way worse: Mandela, Gandhi, MLK, Mankiller. After running through my list of names that reminded me not to be a coward, I reassured myself that surely I could manage bad hair for a few years.

I focused on my lap as she chose scissors then confirmed yet again that I was okay with cutting off more than a foot of hair.

"Yes," I said, preparing for her scissors like I was waiting for the guillotine.

"Really?" She asked, *again*, and I wondered if she'd ever been sued for cutting off too much hair.

"Yes. I am absolutely certain," I lied.

When I felt her gnawing at the thickness of the ponytail with the scissors, I realized that I'd expected it to hurt, at least in my heart. Eyes still down, I waited for tears, but they didn't come. Not even as I felt the cool metal of the scissors against the back of my neck as she worked. I kept looking down, even as I felt my ponytail come free in her hand. I felt breath on my neck—like someone was blowing on it—but realized it was just the ambient breeze of a San Mateo salon with the front door open. My neck had never felt so *exposed* before.

I trembled, part from nerves, part from the breeze on my neck. Since the first time a boy kissed me there, my neck had been one of my most pleasurable erogenous zones. The breeze felt vaguely erotic.

Finally, I sensed that she was finished. "It's a big change," she said. "What do you think?"

Slowly, hesitantly, scared at what I would see without my hair softening and obscuring it, I looked up into the mirror and met my own eyes.

I didn't recognize myself. Not immediately.

I was steeled for the familiar sight of my pudgy pie-face and the revulsion it was bound to elicit in me. But the face before me was one I'd never seen. It had angles, cheekbones, structure, held aloft by a long and graceful neck, almost giraffe-like in its elegance, above strong prominent shoulders.

I looked at myself harder, more closely, confused.

Without the distracting mass of hair, I could see my eyes. They were green and gold and chocolate-colored. They were dark and deep set, so alive and tinged with sadness at the same time. My lips were luscious, curved and full, pillowy and tinted a subtle shade of mauve.

My nose? It was cute! Covered in a spray of freckles that spread to my cheeks. It was the perfect size, creating nice relief in my otherwise smooth skin. I didn't want it bigger or smaller or straighter; it was the perfect nose for my face.

Because I'd spent my life hating it for being weak and receding, I was shocked to find that my chin was doll-like, dainty and narrow. In other words: pretty.

Elaine—some kind of blessed sorceress hair magician—had echoed the angle of my jaw in the line of the bob. I looked 1920s retro. I looked . . . French? Definitely not butch at all, but bold and feminine at the same time.

I loved it. I loved it so much! But I loved it tentatively, too, because I didn't trust it. This confidence was too different from the reality I'd lived for decades. I searched for explanations: maybe it was an exceptionally flattering mirror or the lighting had been professionally designed. But no, it was the same mirror and the same lighting that had made me feel so badly about myself just minutes before. The only change was that I had less hair hiding me.

Uncomprehending and processing it in real time, I blurted, "I'm . . . not ugly?" It was sixty-percent statement, forty-percent question.

Elaine shook her head, blunt and reluctant to be drawn into what was clearly something for a therapist. "No," she said, definitively, with a pleasing lack of warmth that made it feel like a factual statement. "You are not ugly."

Realization came in waves.

First, relief: I didn't need to give up on dating, love, or romance for the next two years. Second, confusion: What *other* delusions did I hold about my appearance? I had believed

I was ugly for so long and on such a deep level. It was entirely destabilizing to realize that might not be real. Where else was I wrong?

The third wave was hope: Could I be more than "not ugly?"

***

I had always, I realized in the days following, judged myself against what I was not: A Nordic blonde with ice blue eyes, miles-long legs and visible abs. But if you liked darker hair, full lips, and eyes that really looked into you—I was kinda hot. Cutting off the one thing about me I thought was pretty had revealed what I hadn't been able to see.

I started wearing the red lipstick I'd bought in Barcelona and could not stop looking at my lips. They looked like a Maybelline commercial. I kept finding myself making flirty faces in the mirror and attracting my own attention. I posted a two-second video on Facebook showing off the cut and guys I hadn't spoken to since high school flooded my likes.

I was not ugly!

With the revelation—not an illusion after all—I decided to start dating again. Ben was seeing other people—gorgeous, accomplished, superior people. After a slew of disappointing experiences across all the relevant dating apps—Bumble, Tinder, Hinge, Coffee Meets Bagel, J-Date, Match, and even e-Harmony—I wanted to try something new.

Upscale matchmaking services seemed largely geared toward wealthy men: women were allowed to join databases for free, whereas men had to be clients which cost somewhere between hundreds, thousands, and *hundreds-of-thousands* of dollars. One outfit promised the men of Silicon Valley to find the women of their dreams—I imagined supermodels with weaknesses for coders, Leonardo DiCaprio-castoffs who could be worn as arm candy to make all the kids who teased them in high school feel thoroughly beaten—for a mere *quarter-of-a-million dollars*. Despite the stereotype of the men who used these services and what they wanted, I figured there was likely an exception. Somewhere, there must be a desirable, adult man looking for an adult woman as a full partner, who valued personality and depth over cellulite-free thighs. At least, I hoped.

Realizing that I would move anywhere for love, I took cute new selfies with my neck exposed, cleverly answered boring questions, and submitted applications to services in California, New York, and a few others that worked nationwide. With each click of submission, I felt like I was making myself passively available to fate, without committing myself to the effort and disappointment of *actually dating*. I expected nothing, but I liked being open to possibility.

I also started seeing a therapist. I was pleased with all the self-guided growth from Costa Rica and Amsterdam and Hawaii and Barcelona, and Amsterdam again, but that growth had highlighted a bunch of places in my psyche where I was stuck. I seemed to—compulsively—make myself miserable.

I wanted professional help getting out of my own way but didn't want to go through the hassle and expense of trying to find someone good. It felt like another type of dating, except more expensive and even harder to judge whether the relationship was likely to work upon first meeting. Thankfully, a very smart male friend of mine recommended the psychoanalyst who had helped him through his divorce. The shrink's resume was bulletproof: faculty at Stanford, first in his medical school class, multiple teaching awards, and best of all, he had a Golden Retriever named Zoe that he'd trained as a therapy dog who came to every session. Done.

On hot days, she'd lie behind one of the chairs on the hardwood under the air conditioning vent, but other days, she'd hop up beside me on the couch and let me pet her for the full fifty-minute session. I hoped those sessions didn't feel like work to her. She got me through the first few weeks when therapy felt useless, like I could talk forever and we'd never get anywhere because the problem was reality, not the way I thought about it.

My shrink didn't see it that way. "You're a pretty classic case," he told me, "of someone whose childhood created a lack of self-worth and everything you're dealing with seems to stem from that." I disagreed. My childhood was great—nearly perfect. If there was a failure, it had to be mine.

"You grew up with a lot of financial privilege. That doesn't mean you grew up with what you needed to develop healthy self-esteem." I worried my shrink was disparaging my parents and I leapt to their defense.

"Parents can be really good, wonderful people who do great work in the world, and that doesn't necessarily mean that a child gets everything he or she needs to build a strong, flexible, healthy sense of self." He said reasonably. He was in his early 70s, bespectacled, but with the build of a former football player. Bearded and bald, he looked a bit like Freud if I squinted and the resemblance gave him gravitas.

The next week, as I was leaving the session, he stopped me on my way out. "Wait, I have something for you." He went to his desk in the corner of the room and retrieved a book. "It's David Richo's *How To Be An Adult In Relationships*. I'm giving it to you because we could talk for years about healthy self-esteem development in childhood and how that shows up in adult relationships, but I think you'd learn faster just reading it."

I went home and devoured half the book overnight. Richo sets out that a child needs five A's from his or her caregivers: Attention, Acceptance, Appreciation, Affection, and Allowing. The first half of the book is all about what we need in childhood to develop healthy, loving relationships in adulthood, and how deficiencies in childhood show up to compromise adult relationships. Fucking mind-blowing. And simple! My parents did nothing *wrong*, they just had gaps in capacity on different A's. For example, "allowing" is about allowing all emotions, helping a kid regulate and normalize difficult feelings. In my dad's childhood, he was praised for always being happy, easygoing, and selfless. There were stiff penalties in his family for being seen as selfish, greedy, or difficult. And he raised me the same way. The penalties weren't physical—I was never beaten or even spanked—but losing his approval felt like a slap. If I expressed feelings that he saw as bad, he rejected them. So, I learned that I wasn't supposed to feel that way. That good people didn't feel bad things. That if I felt an urge to be selfish, or greedy, or petty, that I *was* selfish, greedy, and petty. It literally took me into my 30s to learn that feelings are just feelings, they pass like the weather, and even the best people—Mandela, MLK, Gandhi, Mankiller—feel "negative" emotions and not just about issues of justice.

Both of my parents were deeply, meaningfully engaged in the non-profits. They started doing important work on poverty and reproductive rights when I was still little. I think they were both so concerned that their kids *not* end up spoiled and out of touch that there was never a time I thought I was the most important thing in the world. I always knew I was less important than global poverty and women dying from botched abortions. It made me grow up feeling like love was earned, and most valuable when it was wrenched away from someone focused on more important things. This set me up to fall for anyone who made me feel like I was lucky to have their attention.

It's not like everything fell into place and I immediately understood where all my issues came from after a few months of therapy and a self-help book, but it cleared up a lot. The issues didn't feel so overwhelming or disparate anymore. It felt like fifty minutes of therapy each week got me new, actionable insights that allowed me to change my entrenched grooves of thought and behavior. Just like psychedelics but available locally, legally, and on a weekly basis. Hallelujah.

I had always self-diagnosed as (episodically) depressed. But my shrink saw it differently. "I think you have constant, at least low-lying levels of anxiety and I think that's why you self-medicate with pot. I think that when the anxiety gets too much, it burns you out and you fall into depression."

I didn't know what "anxiety" was and asked him to describe it. I was familiar with the word but what did it mean? He went on to describe the way I felt, all the time, constantly, for as long as I could remember.

"It can feel different in different people, but I think yours shows up as a churning self-doubt, an ever-present worry that you are not okay."

Well fuck. I thought that was, just, life.

"You mean there's another way to be?"

Chapter 21

White Horse

Burlingame, California
April 2016
Substances ingested: probably a toke or two

Still in regular therapy, I was working from home on a bright Wednesday afternoon when my phone rang from an unknown number. I got plenty of unknown calls at my new-ish job so I answered, fully expecting a question about our latest newsletter or communications for the upcoming event.

"Is this Anne?" said a woman who rhymed my name with "can" rather than "canny," which is how people always mispronounce it.

In my most dismissive I-don't-have-time-for-telemarketing voice, I said, "May I ask who's calling?"

"I'm Natalie? from Network Effect Dating? I'm calling because I might have the perfect man for you?" Her voice turned every statement into a question.

It took me a moment to adjust from work mode, but I was all sunshine by the time I said, "Oh hello! So nice to hear from you!"

"Do you have a minute to talk?" When I said yes, she asked to confirm some details: I graduated from Stanford, I was 32, 5'10", and Jewish.

"I mean, Jew-*ish*," I added with a verbal shrug. "I don't go to temple or know any words to prayers or anything, but yes, culturally Jewish with Jewish grandparents and I really like to feed people, so based on Reform laws, yes, I'm Jewish." I said it all in one, rushed sentence.

"That is great." She sounded genuinely thrilled and even a bit relieved. "Our client—let's call him Mo—comes from a powerful family in the Middle East. He collects exotic animals," at this, I imagined a conservation preserve, thousands of wild acres dedicated to the protection of endangered species. I thought how well we might get along if animals and environmental rights meant so much to him.

I retrieved myself from my daydream to hear, "He splits his time between Dubai and Silicon Valley? He is looking for a tall, Jewish, Stanford-educated wife to help him run his businesses and philanthropies?"

I couldn't help but smile at how specific his desires were. But the specificity made me feel chosen. When I was tripping on truffles, imagining all the details of the love of my life, somewhere across the world there was a man describing me, to a tee, as his ultimate dream girl. Fate. Natalie was delivering my perfect man.

I couldn't imagine caring so much about my spouse's alma matter that it would be a prerequisite, and it didn't occur to me that collecting exotic animals could be a Tiger King situation, but the idea that he wanted help "running businesses and philanthropies" made me think he was looking for a real *partner*—a capable adult he could love, trust, and depend upon—and in that way, we were looking for exactly the same thing.

"He's about to be 30, dark hair and eyes, 5'9'—"

"Sorry. Can I ask something? Is he…" I hesitated. I didn't know if I was allowed to ask for information she wasn't volunteering. I certainly didn't want her to think I was some kind of gold digger, but I was also having flashbacks to six months before, in Amsterdam, when I asked the Universe to deliver me up a prince. From my experience in the international MBA, I knew that the level of wealth in the Middle East that Natalie was describing probably meant royal connections. "Out of curiosity," I asked as delicately as I could, "Does he happen to be a member of a royal family?"

"That is correct." She sounded happy I'd picked up her hints, then added, conspiratorially: "He's a crown prince."

I laughed out loud, double-checking the date on my phone to make sure it wasn't April Fool's. It was mid-month. More significantly, I hadn't told anyone about my request for a royal boyfriend, so this couldn't be a prank. I hadn't told anyone about anything that had happened in Amsterdam. Everyone still thought I'd cut my hair just because I hankered for a change. Still, a good part of me was stuck in disbelief. And then it occurred to me, "Wait, is he Muslim?"

I didn't really care about religion, but historically the Middle East cared a *lot*. I couldn't imagine that the family of a crown prince would feel great about him marrying a Jew. I was also taller than he was, and older. How was that not three strikes in his mind? It also seemed like a pretty good thing that neither she nor he knew that I was a decently committed pothead. Surely that would be a disqualifier. Questioning my memory of the conversation, I confirmed: "The man wants a tall, *Jewish*, Stanford-educated woman?"

"That is exactly what he said he's looking for." She sounded as perplexed as I was but proud of herself for having found it for him. I felt proud for being what someone wanted.

And that was all it took for me to begin fantasizing about my future husband: he was clearly a rebel prince who wanted to use his power, and the power of *true love*, to bring peace to the Middle East after thousands of years of conflict and suffering. We were Romeo and Juliet! But with a happy ending and no death! In my tale all of us—the Capulets and Montagues, the Jews and Muslims, the Israelis and Palestinians—would become closer than friends, we became *family*, sitting around a common table, breaking bread peacefully.

I didn't need more information. I was sold. I wanted to meet him and make him love me and end religious warfare as quickly as possible.

I knew that might be a little much to hope for, but if instead I got lasting love, partnership, and mutual desire, that was worth being excited about too.

Natalie requested a few recent pictures with no or natural makeup and—if he liked them—she would connect us via WhatsApp. For the next week, I waited on his determination, keeping myself busy with work (which was easy because work was really busy).

When he finally reached out, I was surprised to see:

"Hey."

On OkCupid or Tinder, a "Hey" would have meant me ending the "relationship" before it started because such a bland first message conveys a lack of thought and effort that presages a lack of thought or effort in relationship. Or at least I thought so. But the man was a prince, so maybe it was a refreshingly low-key approach? Maybe he was shy? There was so much I couldn't know; I assumed the best.

I responded with, "Hey! How are you? Nice to hear from you!" hoping the exclamation points made me sound warm and inviting.

Twelve hours later, he responded. "Good."

I figured he wasn't a texter and that I'd have to wait until we met in person to determine if there was chemistry. People can be very different in person than over text and I wanted to allow space for the possibility of a slow burn.

In our polite back-and-forth, we determined that I was going to be in Europe before he would be in the US, so I suggested we meet in the middle, say: Amsterdam? I had planned a two-day stopover there before my MBA reunion in Barcelona in late May. I hadn't consciously decided on roughly annual visits to consult the Universe in Amsterdam, but it seemed I'd defaulted into that loose pattern. My reunion was a convenient excuse for a pilgrimage.

The prince agreed to the dates I suggested, and we nailed down our plans: dinner at the Ritz Carlton at eight PM the second night I was in town. It was perfect—I'd arrive the night before, go to sleep early, wake up at dawn, take mushrooms, receive some wisdom from the Universe, come down, and float on a cloud of bliss—luminous—into my last first date ever with this man who would be powerless to resist my aura of peace and vitality.

I could barely wait.

Chapter 22

Harvester of Sorrow

Amsterdam, Netherlands
May 2016
Substances ingested: 12.5 grams of magic truffles, and tooooooo much pita

I rose with the Dutch sunrise, intending to start my day with a tiny breakfast of the magic truffles I purchased immediately after arrival in Amsterdam the previous day. My Airbnb was spacious and brightly lit, one side of the apartment overlooking a canal and the other, a courtyard shared with a kindergarten. It was one of the nicer Airbnbs I'd stayed in, with a modern interior and classic exterior, select and tasteful décor designed for guests, not overly furnished... The bedroom had everything necessary for comfort—fluffy pillows and comforter, side tables with reading lights, a clock mounted on the wall opposite the bed.

I slept well and awoke eager. Without changing out of my pajamas, before even brushing my teeth, I went to pop one of the smaller bundles of truffles into my mouth but paused when I noticed what looked like white mold in the crevices of the mottled green and brown skin. I remembered that the tourist information booklet about safe drug use (I'd read it three times) said white mold was fine but double-checked the booklet to make sure. I'd remembered correctly but still decided to google it because I needed more reassurance.

And shit. A lot of people reported getting sick from mushrooms with visible white mold. I didn't know if truffles were any different from mushrooms in this respect. I didn't want to deviate from my planned timeline because it was already pretty tight, so I decided to believe the pamphlet over the internet. I had a date with a prince at eight that night, which was enough time if I started tripping now. If I had to wait for the Smart Shop to open at eleven, that would cut it close. Steeling myself against the taste of mold, I dumped the truffles into my hand and I noticed that the clump didn't separate into smaller bundles when released from the vacuum-sealed plastic. Looking closer, I noticed that the small bundles, each between the size of a pea and an almond, were connected by thousands of thin filaments of a blue, hairy mold. Disgusted, I scraped the clump back into its container before washing my hands. On the corner of the package, stamped beneath printed warnings about keeping children away, was an expiration date from exactly a month earlier.

There was no way I was eating that, so I rationalized. The booklet said trips lasted 3-6 hours; with an hour for coming up and one for coming down, I could still make an eight o'clock dinner if I started my trip slightly after eleven. Ignoring that my past experiences weren't nearly over after six hours, I told myself that the worst-case scenario was I'd roll up to the date a little glassy eyed and over-awed at the world. Maybe it would give me a childlike innocence and fascination with the mundane that the prince would find endearing. I had come to Amsterdam with two goals and wasn't going to let either slip away.

In the four hours to kill before the Smart Shop opened, I watched TV on my computer, checked email, and dozed a bit. I smoked a few tokes off one of the Indica joints I had purchased the night before, figuring its effects would wear off by the time I'd replaced the truffles. I'd gotten in late enough that the grocery stores were closed—no stroopwafels or aged gouda to take the edge off my escalating appetite.

By 10:30 am when I left the Airbnb, I was ravenous. I'd been awake for nearly five hours, high but eating nothing, watching Top Chef. The guy at the Smart Shop swapped out my truffles with no hassle after I showed him the expiration date. On my way home, a vegan fast food pita shop seduced me with the scent of French fries, and I bought a giant falafel, telling myself that I'd wait to eat it until I was on my way down.

Back at the Airbnb I kicked off my shoes while ripping into the stapled brown paper bag from the Smart Shop. There was nothing reverent about this process. I shoved a small handful of the truffles into my mouth and chewed as quickly as possible. The first taste was fine but the second was bitter and the third was . . . *intensely* bitter. I tried to wash the taste away with water, but that only spread the flavor. It was just the excuse I needed to take a cautious bite of the pita, which helped. My incipient nausea faded away. And the pita tasted *good*.

I alternated bites of truffles with bites of falafel. This helped with the taste but by the time I'd finished the truffles, I'd also finished most of the pita.

I started to feel high and full at the same time, the two sensations colliding into intense nausea. I wanted to lie down and stay still, desperately, to quell my nausea, but my high was coming on with its usual insistent current of energy that wanted me up and dancing. I should have known better; I did know better.

I sought the bed, lying on top of the covers where I experienced an epic case of something like restless leg syndrome, except violent. I kicked both legs in the air, fast and with force, trying to shake them as much as possible *while*—this was key to keep me from vomiting—maintaining perfect belly stillness. My legs were screaming to do squats and lunges, high jumps, box jumps, jumping jacks—and the rest of my body wanted nothing more than to never move again.

I focused on my breath—in, out—and every moment was torture. As with ayahuasca, I succeeded in not puking but it took all my attention. Lying on the bedspread of the Airbnb, I wondered, was *that* why I didn't have any good hallucinations during that trip? If I'd just puked, would the insights have come?

This time, I decided not to resist. The next time I felt the urge, I'd give in. Mere seconds passed before I felt pressure rising in my chest. It was only a few long strides to the bathroom but still I worried I wouldn't make it. I half-fell, half-slid into the base of the toilet, vomiting before I landed. I took a breath but did not have time to release it before another stream of bile and acid forced its way out. It was more than just the pita. I vomited uncontrollably. Things I'd eaten and things I swear I hadn't. I choked, then choked more. Tears streamed down my face, gasping, gripping a stranger's toilet bowl with my bare hands, I worried I was going to die this way: a woman alone, choking on her own vomit.

I'd had the thought before. More than once, Lyme Disease had made retch so violently that I nearly passed out from lack of oxygen. Each time it had happened, it happened slowly enough for me to become certain I was going to die that way: scared and alone, choking on my own vomit, face too close to toilet water. Now, it was finally going to happen. Here, in a stranger's Airbnb.

I rested my cheek on the toilet seat to give my neck a break from holding the weight of my head against the explosive stream, but I never stopped puking. The force of my expulsions splashed water onto my face and couldn't do anything to stop it. One hand was holding my hair back, and the other that was holding onto the toilet seat was already flecked with vomit. Powerless and pathetic, a disappointing excuse for a human being, it felt right that I was covered in puke. The misery was intense and all-encompassing, much more powerful than rational thought, but not exclusive of it.

Rationally, I thought "So this is why they say not to eat beforehand." But the thought was barely a whisper compared to the cacophony of self-hating emotions screaming their stories at me: I was a worthless, disgusting, selfish, greedy, gluttonous. Just a shitty, shitty, shitty human being!

I wished I could rewind time and undo every decision that got me here: not eat the pita, not eat the truffles, not buy the truffles, or the plane ticket, or suggest meeting in Amsterdam at all! I had *a date that night.* It flashed through my mind, but I was too concerned with too many other agonizing thoughts—mainly not wanting to die like this—to worry about anything hours in the future.

I vomited and choked and strategized. I was so desperate and scared that I had punched 911 into my phone to save me the time of dialing if I had to call, but the minor comfort of that plan evaporated when it occurred to me that 911 probably wasn't the emergency services number here. Would my phone even work here? I hadn't enabled any sort of international calling plan. I decided I could run outside and make the choking symbol. I had experienced this specific panic enough that running outside was my go-to plan in well-populated areas. But what if I lost consciousness before I made it to the street?

I started to cry. I cried because I was so pathetic. But crying made the choking worse. I tried to relax. I told myself, "Let it up and out. Don't fight it. Relax your throat." Telling myself things I didn't necessarily believe, I comforted myself with, "You're safe. There are tons of people on the street who would save you if anything happened. Everything's okay." I talked myself through the panic until the vomiting subsided.

But I felt no relief because just as my vomiting lifted, depression so heavy it literally pushed me to the ground. I curled into the fetal position around the base of the toilet. Feeling the cold porcelain against my bare stomach where my pajama shirt had ridden up would have caused me to shiver, but I couldn't summon the energy for it. Bleakness invaded my mind, leaching everything—thought, vision, memory—of color. It stripped away meaning and obliterated hope. Even though I was no longer vomiting and not imminently scared of choking, I knew there was no escaping dying alone. It was not fear. It was fact. Either here, now, from puke, or in fifty years of a blood clot. I would—it was a fact—die alone.

Alone, alone, alone, alone, alone...

The word echoed through my head, through my body, deeply through my soul. I lived alone. I worked alone. I grocery shopped alone. I even had sex alone. I did everything alone. I was alone right now, here, in this moment, and I would be every moment going forward. I was always, only, ever alone. Even with other people.

Alone was the only reality.

Eyes closed, a puddle against the cold tile floor, some part of me vaguely understood that *this* was what it felt like to have a "bad trip," but knowing didn't change my experience. I was so entirely, so *completely* alone. I felt myself getting sucked closer and closer to oblivion.

A spark of insight flashed, and I knew what I needed. I needed someone. Someone firmly entrenched in life who could reel me back in. A vague sensation rose in me, almost like a memory, of a category called "friends" and another called "family"—these were the people whose love was supposed to be a lifeline. But I couldn't come up with anyone. There was no one there, no being to tether me, no one to call, no one to reach for, no one who could make me feel *not alone.*

I searched my memory for people I'd thought of as friends and family only hours before, but each face came with other faces: the faces of the other people they loved more than they loved me. I saw my mom and the man she moved to Oklahoma to be with. I saw my sister and my niece, connected and complete in their dyad. I saw my dad going to the movies with his friend of 40+ years. I saw Adelynn and the new best friend, Lia, who'd replaced me. I saw my college friends—then their husbands, kids, in-laws crowded into the picture. No one else was alone. Not one of them. Everyone had someone. I was the only being who had ever been *this* alone.

The pain was so acute, so factual, so *physical,* that I felt its devastation wrack my body. I cried, open-mouthed but silent, wanting the catharsis of tears, of sobs, needing some physical and emotional act to purge me of this loneliness, but nothing came out.

I just wanted, more than anything I'd ever wanted, to be empty. I wanted to *be* as empty as I *felt*. I wanted nothingness. I wanted to fold in on myself again and again and again and again and again until I disappeared into two dimensions, then one, then none. I wanted to disappear if I was going to keep hurting like this. I wanted to die if I had to go on this way: alone, lonely, not good enough, separate from everyone and everything else.

But more than I wanted to die, I wanted to be loved.

I wanted to go home.

Passingly, I wondered if I could cancel my return and book a new flight home *right now,* but I knew that the "home" I had to return to was not the one I was missing. I wanted the home from my childhood, the one that maybe never existed. A home with two observant parents cued to my emotional needs and overflowing with unconditional love beyond anything normal or maybe even possible.

Lying on the black-and-white checkered tile, what I wanted was to be held. I wanted someone to rock me, to hold me, to hold me together with their love. I wrapped my arms around myself, squeezing, but felt only more pitiful for it.

A slideshow played before my closed eyes: I was too difficult, too sensitive, too stubborn, too fat, too hairy, too tall, too messy, my breath stank, I didn't clean up after myself, I was too entitled. The slideshow had only just begun but I was convinced: There were plenty of good reasons no one loved me.

My position on the floor hurt but I didn't move because it was what I deserved. I was cold and uncomfortable, but I was a shitty, sucky, awful human being with no redeeming value so physical discomfort was the *least* I deserved. This feeling, like the fear of choking to death, was not new. This was how I'd felt in middle school when I'd started cutting myself. The internal, emotional pain had been so overwhelming that I needed to create a physical exit for it. There on the floor I briefly considered cutting or burning myself, but I had vowed no self-harm of any sort while on psychedelics. I had also vowed no self-harm in general because therapy had helped me realize self-destruction was the opposite of what I needed when I was hurting.

A quiet part of my psyche, one that I didn't often hear, a part that sounded completely unperturbed by my present chaos, offered up a memory for my consideration. It was a social media post by a life coach I followed, saying how she often found that what she most wanted from someone else was what she was denying to herself. I considered the possibility:

What if I didn't feel loved because I didn't love myself?

What if I *decided* to love myself? What would that even mean? I thought about how it felt to look on the world (including myself!) with love and knew it would mean giving myself everything I needed, unquestioningly and without hesitation or resentment. I experienced the thought like a dare, and it gave me the strength to find a seated position. I sat on my knees, ankles under my butt, eyes closed—and tried to love myself.

It was hard.

Far away. Incomprehensible. Immense and unpracticed. But I hated giving up on any dare, so I decided to start smaller. I asked myself, "What do I need right now?"

"Get up!" my right ankle shouted, throbbing in bright red pain in my mind's eye. The bony protrusions were pressed flat into the tile holding my full bodyweight and it hurt.

With relief, I realized that the pain didn't feel good anymore. I didn't want to hurt myself.

I stood up, slowly. I offered my ankle some slow, gentle circles and I noticed its immediate appreciation. The poor thing already looked bruised. I favored it on the steps back to the bed where I lay on top of the covers, still feeling the grips of nihilism, but proud of myself for finding my way back from the event horizon.

At the corner of my awareness, I understood that it was early afternoon. I realized I might be able to sleep through the remaining high. This was not the time to push my limits by following advice I'd gleaned from the internet about leaning into a bad trip. I knew an Advil

PM would knock me out almost immediately. I was afraid of oversleeping and missing my date, but I was way *more* afraid of losing my mind or my will to live, so I took the tablet.

Hours passed in an eerie grey zone between waking and sleeping. When I heard the whine of an insect that struck my face once, then again, I opened my eyes. The clock on the wall told me it was 4:20, reassuring me that I had plenty of time before my date. I didn't notice or care that it happened to be a stoner's favorite time, "420" being the police code and a common euphemism for getting high, but I was grateful I had more time to sleep

Time passed, until the enormous black fly bounced off my face, again. I opened my eyes and saw him bumping against the bolted-on window screen. I watched him struggle; his pointless life no different from mine. Despite the hours that had passed, my thoughts continued to spiral lower and lower. My chest ached and I realized I'd stopped breathing. Breathing felt like a choice to live and right then, I didn't want to make it.

But that thought required me to correct myself: I was not allowed to die, or kill myself, over a bad trip. This was, I reminded myself, a bad trip. This would pass. It was a matter of time.

The booklet had said exactly that: "Tell people who are having a bad trip that it's only a matter of time."

Somehow, even then, I noticed the irony that my biggest fear on previous trips was the experience not lasting long enough for the Universe to reveal her wisdom, whereas now, I was terrified that this would never end.

"It's only a matter of time," I told myself. I closed my eyes and started counting. To ten, twenty, thirty. I willed myself to keep my eyes closed, trying to pass as much time as possible before checking the clock again. I closed my eyes for what had to have been at least a couple minutes, hopefully five or seven. I squeezed my left eye shut, peeking out of a squinted right, but the clock still seemed to read 4:20. In shock, I opened both eyes to focus better. Still, exactly, 4:20.

Not *one* minute had passed. I stared at the clock, willing it to move, desperate for some sign I was getting closer to the end of this nightmare. It was perfectly, inanimately, still. Not even the second hand moved.

That's when I noticed: not even the *second hand* moved. *Something* should have been moving. I had taken seventeen breaths, which *had* to take more than one literal second.

The clock must be broken. I rose, the relief lifting me off the bed, and pulled it off the wall. Immediately I noticed how light it felt in my hands. The thing didn't even have batteries.

Suddenly the clock being stuck on 4:20 was hysterical, comical, joyous, ironic, a gift. My belly and cheeks hurt from laughing but I did not want to stop. The levity was an antidote to the day's previous gravity. The Universe and I were in on the joke. The Universe and I were together now. I couldn't help but marvel at the elaborate nature of her horrendous-bad-trip-broken-clock prank, and I found myself impressed that the Universe's sense of humor was so overt. There, now, I felt thoroughly entertained. No punchline could work without setup and I felt totally, lovingly, delightfully, set up.

Laughter subsided to manageable giggles, and eventually, I checked my phone for the real time. I'd been through hell and back and it was only 3:48. I felt relieved that I had even more time than I originally thought to make myself fit for a prince. I was still emotionally fragile and wrung out and more than a little unsure of how I would pull this off, but I saw it as a measure of relative sobriety when I acknowledged that I could not cancel. He was here; I was here. I wanted to know if we had chemistry, and the only reason I wanted to cancel—that I was coming off a bad trip—was one I couldn't tell him.

I set three alarms on my phone and settled back onto the bed in a pool of light. I noticed that, with the sun beams on my face, everything was okay. It was the darkness of the bathroom that allowed my nightmares, fears, and demons to take over and become indistinguishable from reality. With my eyes open and the sun's rays kissing my cheeks, misery was distant.

I filed this realization away with my new and visceral understanding of why it was not recommended to eat before taking psychedelics for future use *if* I ever got up the courage to try psychedelics again.

***

When I woke up, needing all three alarms, I felt the shadows of my demons, but no longer their teeth. I was exhausted, but mildly elated for having survived, like I imagine it would feel to complete a marathon. I felt like I'd gotten, in some ways, what I'd wanted from ayahuasca. I had purged myself and come face-to-face with my greatest fears. My throat felt raw, swollen, and bruised—like I'd puked snakes.

I decided to wear two sheer silk nightgowns, layered so they were opaque and looked like a dress. They were the only option I'd packed that didn't require a bra, which was prohibited because my stomach wouldn't allow anything constrictive. I'd added a cropped lambs' wool bolero with mink collar from the 1940s that I'd found at a consignment store to cover my nipples and obscure the fact that I was braless. My makeup was natural in deference to what the matchmaker told me about his preferences, but I stained my lips a deep burgundy in deference to mine. All in all, I thought I'd done a reasonably good job of covering up my escapades from earlier in the day.

The castle—the Amsterdam Ritz-Carlton—was in the middle of the outermost ring of the canals that form the concentric arcs of Amsterdam Central. At eight PM on the dot, I found the basement bar where the prince suggested we meet, but it was empty aside from the bartender. Seated on an eggplant-colored velvet chair at a round table by the door, I tried to look engaged in my Kindle, but it wasn't even on. Even on its lowest setting, the light was too bright. The basement bar felt like an odd choice for a first date—they didn't seem to serve food down here—but I appreciated how dimly lit it was. The silk of my dresses stuck to the velvet of the chairs and I felt Velcro-ed into the seat. I texted to let him know I'd arrived and a few minutes later, a young man walked unhurriedly through the entryway, fitting the description the matchmaker had given me. He had never volunteered pictures and I had never asked.

Though I didn't know what I had imagined, he was different from my expectations. I guess I expected a large personality, likely accompanied by an entourage. Someone who walked into the room and took up a lot of space. But he walked in alone and slouching, as if shy. I expected a loud laugh, bold gestures, aggressive royal entitlement. But he looked more like one of the guys who sold loose beers, can-by-can, in the shadows of Barcelona's Gothic district. He had prominent eyebrows, a strong nose, and wore all black. In a t-shirt, hoodie, and track pants, he looked more dressed to commit robbery than impress a date, but I liked that he was casual. He was quiet and soft, if I read his energy right. Maybe I was just fatigued and projecting. Part of me had expected him to arrive on a palanquin so I appreciated his restraint.

I stood up when he moved closer, prepared to greet him but unclear whether we were shaking hands, hugging, or giving cheek kisses. I went in for an air hug and left-to-right cheek kisses as I'd become accustomed when in Europe, and he...waved. I didn't know that many Muslims don't touch the opposite sex after puberty—not even the most formal of handshakes—outside of marriage. I had chosen not to do any research about him, or to guess at his cultural or religious customs because I wanted to let him reveal himself to me, for him to decide what was important and for me to learn through him. As Zoubair had taught me and I hadn't forgotten since, as many followers as a religion has is as many different ways as it will be practiced, interpreted, and communicated. "Muslim" or "Christian" or "atheist" told you roughly as much about a person as their shoe size.

He pulled out my chair for me, then sat down across from me and picked up the drink menu. I asked him what he was going to get.

"Sprite. I'm not hungry." I wondered if he'd found a food menu I had missed.

I agreed, waving away the idea of an appetite as I thought a princess should, even though I was famished. His Sprite reminded me that he'd told me he didn't drink alcohol in one of our brief text exchanges—which was fine with me, especially now, when my stomach felt so fragile—but it made me wonder what we were doing on a restaurant date if we were going to neither eat nor drink.

Barely moments had passed before a server emerged from seemingly nowhere to take our order. I thought about my usual—a club soda—but that seemed too reserved, so I ordered a ginger ale instead figuring it was the champagne of non-alcoholic drinks.

And there we sat. In silence. Until I began asking the questions I'd been accumulating since we started texting: What's your daily routine like in Dubai? What do you do that brings you to Silicon Valley? What's life like for your sisters at home? What issues do you care about and fund through your philanthropies? What do you hope to build with your legacy?" He gave general answers to the most personal questions, and it made me wonder if he was being intentionally obscure. Thinking about why that might be, I imagined lots of women have pursued him for status, which probably made him guarded.

The chemistry I was hoping to find electric when we met was not there, but also, I couldn't exactly blame that all on him. No matter how many times I'd brushed my teeth, I assumed my breath still smelled of vomit. All I wanted to do was cram my face with Vlamese frites from my favorite stand on my walk home, put on pajamas and sleep until the absolutely last moment before catching my flight to Barcelona the next day.

After our first round—of *soda*—I suggested we call it a night. It had only been maybe 45-minutes, but I'd run out of both questions and steam. He acted mildly surprised and said something about dinner, but my heart was set on a street-bought paper cone of the greasy Flemish fries and a sleeve of stroopwafels if I could find a grocery store still open, so I made excuses about an early flight.

"Then I will walk you home." My heart dropped at the kind offer. I appreciated the chivalry, but I was so tired of *smiling*. "Oh, no no. You're already home. My place is so far away. You don't even have a jacket. I'll be fine."

"No, it's good. I'll grab my jacket and come down."

And it seemed very sweet that he insisted. Maybe, maybe there was a possibility for us? I had felt no heat or attraction but if he had a chivalrous, take-charge side? Maybe we had a future.

With him gallantly on the traffic-side of the sidewalk and my arm threaded through his—again, I didn't think of looping my arm through his elbow as a sexually aggressive move but maybe I should have—he started talking about music. He grew animated, almost passionate talking about what he liked and listened to, and I grew more interested. I couldn't tell song titles from band names or even what genre of music he was explaining, but I was intrigued because I assumed that the man must be some kind of poet if he writes music. I relaxed into his arm, let myself stop asking questions, loosened my smile into something more genuine as we passed under gas streetlights that flickered over quiet canals and sleeping geese. It almost made up for the snacks I'd missed out on when he kissed my cheek—no awkwardness this time—said he had a good time and that he'd like to see me again. If I'd let him see me order, and then hoover to completion, two-and-a-half pounds of fried potato smothered in mayonnaise, I wasn't confident he'd be asking for a second date. I went to bed hungry but proud of myself for pulling it together.

***

The matchmaker called first thing the next morning, then again, a few hours later when she still hadn't heard from me. He wanted me to come spend a few days in Dubai with him. He would pay for my flights, accommodations, and activities. Like a drug dealer or an overly pushy best friend, she asked what I needed to say yes. I could tell she saw a massive commission—a royalty if you will—if this worked out.

I wanted to say yes, for him and for her, and for a girlish version of myself who loved the idea of a romantic pursuit spanning several countries. But it was too much too soon. I was haunted by images from a memoir about a woman abducted into a royal harem. I knew not one other person in *any* of the United Arab Emirates, and I'd heard of a man who was sentenced to two years in jail after airport security detected an invisible amount of cannabis on the bottom of his shoe. I would be coming from Amsterdam. What on earth would airport security detect on me?

When I declined via text to him directly, he upped the ante, "Where would you go if you could go anywhere in the world?"

"The Maldives."

"Then I'll take you to the Maldives." He texted me a picture of what looked like the fanciest airport lounge I'd ever seen—large white leather recliners that looked like they'd give moan-worthy massages, an aquarium large enough for a small shark, room between the chairs spacious enough to do yoga.

When I asked what I was seeing, he wrote: "The plane I'd take you on."

I was stunned. It felt like another fantasy coming true.

When I was in my early twenties, I met a married couple who seemed to have it all—love, beauty, money, great kids, vacation homes in three different countries, and a sexy vibe even though they'd been married for decades. The day after they met, he'd invited her on vacation in the Bahamas for a week. She went and the rest was history. Hearing that story at the time, it seemed like both the height of romance, and that it would never happen to me. She was the type of woman whose body was always ready for a bikini, naturally taut and hairless. That's why he asked and why she was able to say yes, and that's why no one would ever want that with me.

But now I was being asked, and my offer was even better because I think that husband had flown them both commercial. Commercial was better for the environment, but no one flies to the Maldives to be good for the environment and I wasn't thinking about climate change at the moment. Basically, every fantasy I'd ever had about being wooed was coming true, but all I felt was anxious. Each time he raised the stakes, my stomach dropped a bit further. It had been tough to maintain my ideal-girlfriend-and-future-princess performance for a single hour the night before. I couldn't do it for a full weekend, much less a week, trapped on an island with only each other for company. My true self—a deal breaker—would come out. Besides, I didn't want to obligate myself to sex, or whatever weird kinks and fetishes he'd expect in the exchange. Not that I got that vibe off him specifically, but that was basically my expectation of all men who try to woo women by spending gobs of money on them. If I said yes, I would be accepting an unspecified obligation to keep him happy. Even if the awkwardness of the first date magically evaporated and I desperately *wanted* to have sex with him, I worried about giving him the impression that I could be bought.

Somewhat reluctantly, I declined again, and I could tell he didn't understand. I explained that I'd like to see him when he was in San Francisco the following month, that I wanted to move our relationship toward reality, not further into fantasy. I wanted to know what it would feel like to be together in a normal way, just us, chilling and watching TV or eating pizza in cozy clothes. He was confused, but texted "ok."

Chapter 23

Thank U, Next

San Francisco, CA
June 2016
Substances ingested: wine, mussels, and an edible

When the prince was in San Francisco, he stayed in a penthouse at the Four Seasons Embarcadero, but meeting there would have been meeting on his turf again. Instead of a five-star roof-top virgin drink, I invited him to my place to hang out. I barely knew him, and he didn't know me at all, but maybe that was because I hadn't given him a real chance?

In the kitchen of my one-bedroom condo in Hayes Valley, I busied myself pouring him a glass of water after an awkward hello. Coming up from behind, he wrapped me in warm hug, kissing my shoulder. I leaned into him, liking his heat against my back. We stayed like that for a minute, enjoying the closeness. When I eventually pulled away, he broke the silence with, "I like you a lot. I've felt it from the moment I met you."

"Really?" I was genuinely surprised. "That's really nice. I—I feel like you hardly know anything about me."

"But I want to."

His interest felt so good. I handed him his glass, wishing I'd picked up some Sprite, and we made our way into the living room. I told him that I'd had a hard day—minor bullshit on a board of directors' meeting—and that, in my ideal world, I'd smoke a joint, he'd be cool with it, and we'd cuddle together in front of the TV for a bit, seeing where the night went from there.

I had a joint, rolled but unsmoked, sitting in a clean ashtray on the coffee table in front of the couch and gestured to it as I told him my fantasy. I watched his face closely, prepared for disapproval, shock, and revulsion, but all he did was move closer to me on the couch when I said "cuddle."

I asked him explicitly, afraid he hadn't understood. "I want to smoke some marijuana. Pot. Hashish. Are you sure you're okay with it? I'll open a window but you'll still smell it, breathe it in, get it on you... You're *sure* that's okay?" I didn't want to make him uncomfortable, or worse, put him into danger if he didn't wash his clothes and wore them to the airport in Dubai or something.

"Yes. It's fine." He said, moving my hair behind my ear and laying a quick brush of a kiss against the base of my neck.

He wasn't offended, judgmental, or turned off at all. His reaction shocked me.

"Wait, have you done this before? I thought it was massively illegal there."

"Not when I do it," he said. The perks of being royalty, I guessed.

I leaned away from him to give him space, so I wouldn't be blowing smoke on him directly, and asked him what he wanted to know about me.

"What is your job?"

I assumed he wanted to know more than just my title because I'd already told him that. I indulged myself in a long-winded answer because this was the first real question he'd asked about my life. During my preamble, the part where I told him about how I got into education work even though I felt more called to prison reform, before I'd even touched on my current job, I noticed him yawn. Maybe he was just tired from travel and jet lag was catching up with him despite his best efforts to resist.

I let my hands fall into my lap. "Are you interested in this?" I asked, giving him a chance to apologize and explain that it had nothing to do with me.

"No, but you can go on."

I barked a laugh of surprise at his candor. Usually, people at least *pretended* to be interested.

It emboldened me to ask the question I'd been holding onto since the beginning, knowing that how he answered would determine everything. "We don't have to keep talking about my job. But I'm curious: how do you deal with being a prince?" He looked confused and I tried to clarify. "As I understand it," which was decently well after years of exposure to anti-slavery work through my sister's career in the field, "your wealth is built—haha, pun—on the construction industry, which relies on enslaved migrant labor. How do you deal with that? Like, the guilt?" I was sincerely curious. I asked because I struggled with my, albeit much smaller, version of the same thing. My family wealth came from Levi's, which had always been a leader in the garment industry in terms of how they treat their employees and contractors, but the denim industry as a whole has a bad reputation for good reasons. If I felt so much internal conflict and guilt at my privilege, I couldn't imagine what it must be like for him.

He looked at me, uncomprehending. The question must have been too convoluted, and I'd lost him.

I prompted him, "How do you deal with your family's wealth depending on enslaved migrant labor?" I put down my joint and leaned in, ready to receive his thoughts and engage at a deeper level.

"They're migrants," he said. As if that explained anything.

He leaned in for a kiss and I recoiled. All my fantasies crumbled at once.

As the excuses and rationalizations fell away, I understood: He was an exotic animal collector—the kind that put wild beings into cages for the pleasure—and I was an exotic animal to him. He wanted to collect me, trot me out for his purposes and convenience, then forget about me. I did not want to be someone's trophy.

I made an excuse about a headache and showed him to the door, knowing that when we hugged it would be the last time we saw each other. It reminded me of leaving the note for David, knowing it was goodbye. The memory made me notice other similarities.

When David asked me to marry him, I had said yes to the non-royal version of the same offer on the table here: become my wife, become who I want you to be, live your life as an accessory to mine. When David asked, I had said yes but—thanks to psychedelics and good therapy—this time, I knew it was a trap and it held no temptation. I wanted *my* life.

Sitting on the sofa with a box of Cheezits, an oversized knit blanket, and Hulu playing an episode of *Real Housewives of Potomac* in the background, I realized I *liked* my life. It was less glamorous than the life of a crown princess, but it was *mine*. I had chosen every part of it: from the sweatshirt I'd put on the moment the prince left to the blanket warming my legs, to the job causing me stress to the full-fat, extra salty Cheezits that were never purchased in my all-organic home growing up. The realization was an epiphany. I didn't want to be a princess to a prince, a Mrs. to some husband. I didn't want to live for someone else, my life a satellite orbiting around theirs.

Rising to pour myself a rare glass of wine in celebration, I realized that I suddenly felt free. Not just free but oddly *excited*. I could make all my own choices. What did happily ever after look like if it was all mine? If it didn't involve a prince, a partner, or time wasted waiting to be saved? I really wanted to know.

With my hand on the door of the fridge, I found myself closing my eyes and thanking David, silently, for dumping me. I would have married the guy. I would have willingly sacrificed my life in meaningful ways to enable his. I never would have gone to Costa Rica or had my life altered by the practice of yoga. I wouldn't have gone to any business school, much less one in Barcelona, and that had given me friends all over the world. I definitely wouldn't have cut my hair or started wearing red lipstick or recognized my own beauty.

If he hadn't ended it I would still be mired in insecurity, an unhappy marriage, and disordered eating. I would still be striving to mold myself into the two-dimensional ornament he wanted, disavowing everything about myself that didn't fit into his ideal, and he would still be disappointed in my inevitable, persistent failure. I would never—could never—take up as little space as he allowed for me.

Stretching my legs out, I lounged back on the sofa with my organic Chardonnay in one hand and the remote control in the other. Rewinding a particularly shocking set of accusations being flung between two screaming Housewives, I felt proud of myself. I felt like I'd finally learned my lesson, something the Universe had been trying to teach me for a while: I needed to *choose*. Instead of waiting to be chosen and then becoming what was expected of me, I needed to figure out what I wanted, in my life and with a partner, then seek it out. This happened to echo my therapist's repeated advice, but in that moment, I finally got it.

The screen of my phone lit up with a text from Adelynn. "How'd the date go? Am I losing you to Dubai? You know they have strict drug laws. Let the State Department know you're going. And don't get kidnapped!"

"Haha, I'm not going anywhere," I texted back, happy it was true.

Chapter 24
Can't Help Falling In Love

Big Island, Hawaii
August 2017
Substances ingested: none, yet.

In an effort to choose rather than be chosen, I downloaded Bumble and began swiping. Of the half-dozen candidates who caught my interest, only one stood out: Ares, 34 years old, 1.7 miles away. Standing, self-assured in head-to-toe Patagonia, surrounded by forbidding ice but smiling easily—he struck me as someone with a joyful zest for life and adventure. He was 6'3" and rugged in a way that would border on ugly if he didn't have perfect teeth.

We matched, exchanged a few texts, and when I suggested we meet for beers in the park by my condo, he agreed. Sitting on a bench in the grassy dog park, somewhat shielded by a group of tourists, I got to watch him as he strode across the street. He moved confidently, looking agile and comfortable in his body. I was temporarily and pleasantly paralyzed by the combination of thought, feeling, and imagination that created a single word—yes—spoken by my whole body as he approached.

The date only got better from there—lots of easy laughter, interesting and varied conversation, palpable chemistry. We talked in the park until after it got dark, then stayed another couple hours. When he kissed me goodnight, I thought, "So this is what it's supposed to feel like." Effortless.

We planned our second date for 48-hours later. It lasted fourteen hours and by the end of it, I was a good part of the way toward imagining our next forty years together. Of course, just as I was falling for him, I was scheduled to leave town. My family—mom and dad (separate but proving how amicable they could be together), my sister and my niece—were meeting for a weeklong vacation in Hawaii, to which I'd tacked on an additional week, mainly because I could. The timing was less than ideal but I figured the weeks apart would be good to slow down our courtship a bit. If we were going to be together forever, waiting fourteen days for it to start would be pleasurable suspense. When I didn't hear from Ares during the first few days, I was disappointed, but he'd been clear that he was not a texter, so I didn't make much of it.

About a week in, I sent him a picture of endangered sea turtles sunbathing on a nearby beach, *eighteen* of them in one small span of tidal pools. Their massive shells, flecked with barnacles, covered in a slick film of algae, and patterned with shades of brown, black, green, tan and beige, the turtles were indistinguishable from lava rocks at a distance. I wrote "There are 18 sea turtles in this pic," because... well, that's remarkable. He didn't respond that afternoon. Or that evening, or the whole rest of the next day. I was pretty successful at seeing this as yet more evidence that he was, as admitted, not a texter, but I definitely noticed his delay.

Minor dramas, like my parents squabbling over who was being more generous in the divorce settlement, kept me emotionally engaged in family time despite silence out of San Francisco. One evening at dinner I was the one who was entertaining when I asserted that it was so weird how "we" can only wink one eye, not both. Every single person at the table—sister, mom, niece, dad, Jaramie, Gary, and a couple other local friends from the island—immediately demonstrated winking with both eyes, easily. I sat with my elbows on the table, agog. I winked my left eye with no trouble. When I tried to wink my right, it looked like I was making fun of a stroke victim. Efforts throughout the meal only led to laughter and light mockery by all the naturally talented winkers, but I found myself oddly fixated on the fact that I couldn't do it. In front of the mirror and over the next few days, I made no progress. When it dawned on me that I could google the matter, I found that winking was connected with eye dominance and muscle control. Apparently—like wiggling one's ears or arching one eyebrow at a time—if it wasn't learned as a child, it was impossible as an adult.

***

When my family headed home a few days before I did, I reveled in being alone in a house with exactly the right amount of time, sunlight, beauty, and privacy to try acid for the first time. Before my day-long slog through nauseated misery in pre-prince Amsterdam, I preferred the naturalness of mushrooms and truffles. Now, made-in-a-laboratory-ness of LSD was more appealing. Suddenly, good old American manufacturing practices seemed to offer safety. I wanted to "get back on the horse" as they say, but maybe not the exact same horse that had bucked me to the ground so violently.

LSD was far more measurable, and thus (I hoped) controllable, than mushrooms or truffles. Albert Hoffman first synthesized lysergic acid diethylamide, LSD or acid for short, in the late 1930s when he was working for a pharmaceutical company synthesizing alkaloids from the ergot fungus in search of a drug to treat post-partum hemorrhage. His discovery led to the discovery of neurotransmitters and arguably, eventually the entire category of anti-depressants as a class of medicines. I didn't know much about it other than that Jaramie had tried LSD a bunch of times and was a big fan. She was the most "natural" person I knew: made her own toothpaste, grew her own staple crops, raised her own chickens that she hand-fed organic raw coconut discarded from overburdened trees. If she endorsed acid—which she did, heartily—that was enough to convince me to try it.

A few months earlier, I put my desire into the world, telling anyone I trusted and thought might have a good source, that I was interested. Quickly—shockingly quickly—what I can only describe as an Acid Fairy gifted me with a red envelope slipped into my hand with the parting words of "Safe travels." The envelope read "Dear Albert" in elegant script, held a blank notecard and a gridded slip of paper slightly smaller than a postage stamp into which a scientist had soaked approximately 400mcg of LSD. On the slip, a grid demarcated squares about the size of two match heads, each containing a dose of 80 micrograms.

I had been waiting for the right time and environment to try it. Given my new post-Amsterdam understanding of the importance of sunlight in recognizing the passage of time during a bad trip, I figured sun-drenched Hawaiian serenity was the perfect place to experiment. The day after my family left, I set intentions, going down to the ocean and even burying my legs in the sand just in case there were any messages or orgasms waiting for me there. The next morning, I went for a long walk, placing each foot with purpose, allowing my walk to be a moving meditation. Returning home, I was really looking forward to the afternoon's wisdom-revealing encounter with the Universe—until a text came through.

I stood in the living room, my hands suddenly shaking when I read Ares's message: "*Wow, I've never seen that many sea turtles much less on land. Hope you're having a great trip. When you asked if I was seeing anyone else, I said no because it wasn't serious at the time but that's changed recently, so I'm not going to see you when you get back. You seemed really cool, and I wish you the best.*"

Something split inside me. It felt like lightning cracking down the center of my being. The tears were immediate. How could he do this? How could he not choose me? How could he have felt the same thing—*more*—with another woman than what we had experienced together? How was she better than me? What did I do wrong? Why did no one ever love me?

I crumpled to the rug. Everything was ruined. My future was gone. Long-term and short-term. I didn't want to do acid anymore; I figured it would open me up, make me more sensitive, and the last thing I wanted was the ability to feel *more* pain.

I would have to wait until the next day.

It was early afternoon. I had cleared my entire day in preparation for my trip. I had nothing to distract myself from the obsessive self-recriminating thoughts, so I smoked a joint, and then another, and the beginnings of a third before I was able to displace my rage and shame onto *The Real Housewives of Whereverthefuck*. I put the red envelope on my bedside table as a reminder that I had something to look forward to, and so that it would be the first thing I'd see when I woke up.

After a fitful night of stress dreams, I put on yoga pants, a sports bra, and running shoes for what I'd come to think of as my pre-trip ritual shortly after sunrise. I hadn't taken a walk or meditated before my bad trip in Amsterdam, and I wondered if that—together with eating—was what had gone wrong.

Down the driveway and to the left ran the old Ala Kahakai path, a set of trails used by Native Hawaiians that circled the island. The terrain was volcanic and unforgiving. Large swathes of rugged barren land, dusty, the color of cardboard, dotted with gnarled kiawe trees bearing chestnut-colored seedpods stretched to where it met the ocean. The ground was treacherous—broken and steep, with small rocks that rolled out from underfoot on every step.

I felt wind on my belly, hating and loving it at the same time. Always, I had envied how men—no matter their size—were allowed to go shirtless in public. It seemed that the rule for women was you can wear just a sports bra if your boobs are the only part of your torso that jiggles.

That was not true of me. That would never be true of me. I hated the width of my belly, but I was learning to love it, too. More belly was more surface area to feel the sun and caress of the wind. I wanted to feel embraced by Mother Nature, to be connected and a part of her. I needed to feel the sunlight on my body. I wanted to store it for later as an inoculation against future darkness.

Still, though, every time I started to feel light, started to really enjoy the view of the ocean spreading away from me at the top of every hill, I remembered that Ares didn't want me. On some level, I knew it had only been two great dates and I was overreacting to his rejection.

But it was *two great dates!* And it was *two great dates* for the first time in *years*. Why didn't he feel the same way about me?

Rushing, glaring down at the path, putting one foot in front of the other in forced motion, I realized I was obsessing, not meditating.

I wanted to stop feeling bad about Ares. I wanted to feel better about myself. I wanted acid to make everything better. I cut my walk short and returned to the house the quick way, not taking in the views or the wind or the scent of hibiscus.

I opened the front door to the very clear sense that someone had been there. In the laundry room to the left of the door was a heap of sheets. Down the hall in the bathroom sat a small pile of towels. In the kitchen, spray bottles that lived under the sink waited on the counter near a note from Sammy, the housekeeper. She had gotten the date wrong. Once she realized I wasn't gone yet, she left. This was, of course, no problem at all. I put away the spray bottles and moved the towels into the laundry before it occurred to me that she might have cleaned my room.

I sprinted down the hall. The red envelope was gone. The wastebasket: empty. The room was stripped entirely bare. I panicked. I let my head fall back and swore at the ceiling. I needed wisdom now, today, more than ever.

I looked around the room, blinking rapidly like if I wanted that red envelope badly enough, and cleared my vision enough times, the Universe would make it reappear.

I sat down on the floor. I closed my eyes and silently asked, "Why the fuck is everything I look forward to taken away from me?"

I had no sense of perspective, could see no silver lining. Feeling entirely pathetic, I decided to go rummage through the trash. I went out to the bushes behind which we hid the garbage cans and found all three full. Thankfully, the bags at the top of the first two cans were recycling—empty cans and bottles—heavy but not gross. Something scurried away from me as I riffled, but I pretended not to hear it. At the top of the third can I found a small, clear plastic bag that I recognized from the wastebasket by my bed. As I lifted it, I felt a surge of hope at what turned out to be an orange "priority" sticker from my checked luggage tag. Shaking the contents lightly changed the way things were sitting and suddenly, an unmistakable red envelope revealed itself right on top. I retrieved it from the bag, double-checking that it said "Dear Albert" on the outside and still had a notecard within. Walking back to the house, I paused to open it, thanking the acid gods. Cupping my hand around the notecard so that the tab of LSD wouldn't get carried away on an ill-timed gust of wind, I shook the notecard softly. Then harder. Then flapped it like a bird's wings.

Nothing fell into my hand. There was nothing inside the notecard. It was empty.

I felt beaten, wholly devoid of any hope, my moment of relief gone. In a last-ditch effort of ridiculous optimism, I decided to check the bedroom one more time.

The moment I stepped through the door I saw it. There, lying in the middle of the floor as prominently as it could possibly be, was the tab of acid. It was the one single item in the room other than furniture. It had clearly been dropped, left behind by mistake and without notice. Everything that had been conspiring against me moments ago now felt like it was on my side.

The Universe loved me!

I found scissors and cut 115mcgs off the tab—about 15mcgs more than I'd planned to take but after the panic of loss, I was that much more committed. I expected to taste something—lemon or vinegar or chemicals—but all I tasted was paper. I let it sit on the tip of my tongue and then moved it underneath against the base where I hoped it would get absorbed the fastest. I'd been told it can take about 45-minutes to feel anything, so I used the intervening time to get dressed, brush my hair, and do all the other normal morning rituals that I had delayed in favor of dropping acid. I was only really thinking about when I would start to feel something.

Washing dishes at the kitchen sink after an hour of waiting, I was ready to call the experiment a failure. I wasn't seeing shit. Nothing at all was being revealed to me. I felt fine. Good. Happy. But also like I could have done data entry on a spreadsheet or maintained myself on a conference call. I wondered if I should have taken more, but before I could start to second-guess in earnest, a very chill voice inside my head asked, Why worry about it? Why worry about anything? The sun is beautiful, warm, and loving. I have shelter, clothes, and food. My family has a *vacation home in Hawaii*. I should enjoy it. I should enjoy everything. The voice was indistinguishable from my normal internal monologue, except and importantly, it was not anxious. It was the same voice, same source, same volume, except it was *relaxed*.

I decided to listen to its suggestion, to focus on enjoyment. I'd been sitting on a lounge chair, watching small birds delight in bathing on the infinity-edge of the pool, though I didn't remember ever choosing to go outside. I only half-succeeded in getting dressed, wearing bikini bottoms as underwear, a man's button-down shirt that I'd bought for myself, and a denim miniskirt salvaged from Goodwill. The birds looked like they were having so much fun that I decided to join them. I shed the shirt and the skirt and joined the birds in the pool. I didn't care that I was topless; I was *overdressed* compared to the birds.

Stepping into the pool, I felt the water reach my toes to my ankles...calves...knees... thighs. I felt the sensation of being enfolded and embraced, the joy of it making contact with each tiny hair follicle as it climbed. Kissing like a lover, caressing like a massage, cleansing like a bath, the water ascended my body, and I luxuriated in every sensation. I laughed aloud as it reached the sides of my belly. I felt the water flirting with me, and I let it, inviting it to touch the soft curve of the underside of my breasts, the peak of my nipples, the most sensitive part of my neck...

Twisting from the waist, I spread my fingers wide and swirled my hands through the water, feeling like a sea anemone. I dipped slightly farther, holding my breath even before I was submerged, letting it go as slowly as possible in discrete streams of bubbles. Each release sank me a centimeter lower, my hair fanning out in a cloud around me. As I went under, my body merged with—dissolved into—the water around me, into the amniotic sac, into the primordial ooze. I came from water, I was water, my home was the ocean.

A vacuum in my chest called me back into my body, reminding me I still needed to breathe. My fingers were plugged firmly into my ears because ever since childhood I've hated the feeling of water in them. Still, I was myself.

I came up for air. I inhaled as fully as my lungs allowed, then did a dead-man's float, face down, my lungs like a balloon keeping me at the surface. Again, I let out my breath slowly and sunk lower into the water, fingers still in my ears, my body curling into gentle summersaults in time with my breathing. Time disappeared as I floated, at one with the water holding me.

I got out when the pruning on my fingers and toes became interestingly painful, but even out of the water I kept moving with the current. I turned on music I didn't need, just so it wouldn't look quite as strange if a passerby caught me dancing. The rhythms came from inside me, increasingly lively and demanding. I was breathing hard, dripping sweat, smiling like a fool, but it was not fatigue that made me slow. I couldn't keep my balance while moving so vigorously because I'd started having double vision. Not normal see-two-of-the-same-object double vision. My double vision was seeing what was going on inside and outside my head at the same time. I could see what I would normally see if my eyes were open—which they were—but I *also* saw what I would see if they were closed.

Open: I saw the cerulean of an infinity-edged pool overlooking the ocean, edged by grass, and concrete made to look like volcanic rock. I saw a pair of Myna birds, hanging upside-down on limb of a tree, eating bright red seeds out of a spherical fruit. I watched whisps of white clouds being blown towards Maui by unseen breezes.

Closed: I saw my body like an anatomical drawing, muscles exposed. As I danced, the muscles I used most lit up. I could see each distinct muscle group turn from a hazy grey to a beautiful vibrant pink as it activated. I sank into a squat, feeling my legs, hips, and glutes warm while they lit up, cotton-candy pink, in my mind's picture of my body. I made punching gestures with my arms, my biceps and deltoids warming, and I saw my upper body turn rosy. Because my feet, neck and head were still grey, I took time to move each in patient circles until they, too, glowed.

Then I started experimenting. I squatted again, slower and lower, enjoying the exquisite sensation through my thighs. I closed my eyes to concentrate on what I was "seeing." I knew the quadriceps had four parts (hence "quad") but I had no idea where each was located or how it worked until now, watching each segment light up at different times and speeds. Paying yet more delicious attention, I noticed two muscles on the outside of my hips that stayed suspiciously grey while every other muscle around them lit up. I had obviously trained myself—somehow—not to use those muscles. I wanted to retrain myself.

Eyes closed, focus inward to notice even the subtlest sensations as they arose, I squatted. When the surrounding muscles started to light up, I invited the greyed-out ones to join. They were reluctant. When they did respond, they were slow and spasmodic, jerky or else completely immobile. But I kept asking. Eventually, they began to glow and warm. By only the third or fourth squat, they were lighting up in time with the muscles around them. I squatted, slowly, repeatedly, until all the muscles fired together. Squats, it turned out, weren't fast enough. I dropped to the ground and finished off with mountain climbers.

Physically fatigued and emotionally alight, I made my way through the open glass doors from the lanai into the living room. I lay down on the seafoam green sectional facing the Pacific and began to float on stain-resistant clouds. I felt myself smiling for no reason and every reason: The energy flowing through my body. The glint of the sun reflecting off the expanse of the ocean. The trill of a tropical bird. The green streak of a gecko darting across the counter to devour a previously unnoticed drop of honey from yesterday's breakfast. The honey itself, sparkling like a piece of citrine or a canary-colored diamond.

I watched. With an enormous sense of peace and contentment, I watched as every element of the Universe did exactly what it was supposed to. Without friction, with seemingly no effort at all, every piece of the Universe acted its part in harmony and conflict, whether I witnessed it or not.

Dissolving further into appreciation, I watched the pulse in my belly. Every other part of me was perfectly still except for the mound of my stomach that rippled from my belly button outwards with every heartbeat. Jarringly, an inner voice—the one I live with every day—interrupted my peace. The tone was cutting, vicious, a voice reserved only for myself: "Your belly wouldn't move like that if you weren't so fat."

Then, an avalanche of thoughts and images, familiar and sickening:

The woman Ares chose to pursue was skinnier. Shorter. Just generally smaller. Better. She was skinnier, prettier, probably kept a neater house. Why wasn't I good enough? Why did no one ever choose me?

They were all the familiar thoughts that made me feel the *most*, and worst. I knew the slide; I had ridden it since childhood. Not good enough became worthless, worthless became might as well give up, might as well give up became clinical depression at age twelve. Constant anxiety into acute depression.

What was different this time, for the first time ever, was that the feeling of having all the worth drained out of me by a single rejection was accompanied by a visual. I could see my mental landscape before the text from Ares. My mind was green rolling hills, verdant and bucolic, extending as far as I could see. It was peaceful, a more pastoral scene, but equally beautiful to the sparkling ocean stretching before me in real life. I was enjoying both my internal and external landscapes until my familiar, self-critical voice kicked in. Each self-hating thought drilled a crater into the tender, loamy soil of my internal vista. No, not a crater: an abyss. There was no bottom to the holes my mind drilled into my sense of self. "She must be easier, more fun, better in bed" resulted in three new gaping chasms.

What had been placid rolling pasture was now pocked and marred by pits of self-hatred. What used to be postcard-perfect grazing land was now eighty percent abyss, separated only by precarious juts of narrow land.

As I surveyed the damage from a bird's eye view, I simultaneously shrunk to the size of a Lego, and expanded to the size of a deity looking down on my world with omniscience. My Lego self was blindfolded and stumbling, trying to navigate around massive pits. Of course, I fell in. This was the landscape I had been navigating my entire life, attempting to walk over and around fissures so large they had their own gravity. A rush of compassion washed over me. My poor Lego-self had always done the very best she could.

In that moment of compassion, I saw my Lego-self grow spider legs. My body shrank even further, to the size of a pin head, carried aloft on thread-like Daddy Long Legs legs. My front legs grew first, stretching over half the mouth of the pit, then my back legs grew to finish the distance. My spindly but reliable legs held me suspended over the center of the chasm, and I looked down. For the first time, I was able to look in without falling in. I peered into the darkness and darkness was all I saw.

I began to look deeper, leaning forward, my legs straining as I focused harder on the blackness. If I were lovable, I would be loved. Ares didn't love me, therefore I must not be lovable. David proposed but didn't mean it; he didn't love me either. Nor did Lucca, my high school crush I spent four years pining for who never saw me as anything other than a friend. Nor did Sam who had another girlfriend the whole time he was dating me. When I issued an ultimatum, he chose her. My mind kept going, conjuring an endless list of rejections, each adding gravity to the black hole. I felt it pulling me in and I allowed it to, until I heard a stern but gentle voice in my head say, "Don't." It was the same omniscient and vaguely feminine presence I recognized from previous psychedelic experiences. I knew it was the Universe because I only heard her utter one word but I understood so much more. She meant, "You've been there before; you know what that is. Stay above it—staying up here is new and where your challenge lies."

And she was right. I had been down there before. I knew the topography of depression, looped thinking, and self-hatred.

I did not know what staying above it felt like. I didn't know what it was like to resist the pull of all those familiar dark spirals. Until now, there had been no alternative to those thoughts because they'd always seemed objectively true.

But now I saw that there was an alternative. I didn't *have* to fall into those pits. I could grow spider legs and walk over them. But how?

I was confused. If I wasn't supposed to think like I normally did, what was I supposed to do instead?

"Shhhh," the Universe whispered. "It's not about 'should.' You can do whatever you want. Would you like to be shown an alternate and equally true way of processing the same data?"

It sounded so reasonable. I couldn't refuse.

"Perhaps consider: It's not that the woman Ares chose is 'better' than you or that you were wrong about your experiences together; it's possible that he simply wants and expects *less* than what you are; it's possible that a simpler girl is a better fit for him; it's possible he's such a by-the-book guy that after they slept together he felt obliged to make them monogamous and they got there before you two did."

These options didn't hurt like ones my mind instinctively chose. They also didn't seem impossible or absurd. My rational mind could find no obvious reason these explanations *couldn't* be true. They didn't *feel* delusional. I realized I'd once again dismissed valid explanations for events and other people's behavior in favor of whatever belief would hurt me the most. It was another example of me choosing the most negative narrative, whatever made me feel most intensely, even if those feelings were horrible. Just like Jaramie said. I found and clung to explanations that hurt me, not because they were truer than others, but because they were addictive and validated what I felt about myself. My whole life, without knowing it, I'd been choosing to make myself miserable.

But only because I didn't know how to do anything else. "Blame yourself" is society's mantra to women and girls. Keep yourself small. Assume it's your fault and that it's probably because you're too fat.

"What's more," the Universe added, thrilled I was finally recognizing all this, "it's even theoretically possible that Ares was a serial killer, and fate was protecting you or has something better in store." Before I could complete my scoff at "serial killer," she asked me to pause and consider.

"Can you even imagine that? What would 'better' look like?"

Of course, I could *imagine* better, though this time imagining a prince held no appeal. Ares was great, but could he be better? Sure! He could be Ares, except an inch taller and not so lean. Ares, except with a cute, adopted dog or two. Ares, except he loved me…

That last thought was the epiphany. If Ares didn't choose me, want me, love me (as much as he could after two dates), it simply wasn't meant to be. It couldn't be. Love *has* to be mutual. Choosing each other, wanting to commit to each other, seeing something special that makes you want to invest in each other and grow together is foundational to a relationship. If Ares couldn't get to that first step, everything else I imagined about him and our potential together was pure fantasy.

His rejection destroyed the daydream and that was disappointing, but nothing more! It revealed nothing about me. As I realized this, my suffering diminished immediately, from core wound to jammed toe. So, some dude didn't want me. Okay.

At the most basic level, my long-term romantic partner needed to choose me, want me, love me. Like, *a lot*. He needed to think I was really special an be as excited about me as I was about him. Also: he needed to respond when I sent him a picture of *eighteen* sea turtles! Fuck Ares.

So this was what the alternative to falling into the chasms felt like. All I needed to do was grow spider legs, look at the issue from a higher (ha!) perspective, and choose an equally true but more neutral explanation for events if I wanted to lessen my suffering.

I was halfway between angry at Ares and completely over it, but also: hungry?

It had been at least a day since I'd eaten. My stomach gurgled, not for the first time today, but for the first time today, I listened. I wanted an ice cream bar. Pulling open the freezer I realized I couldn't tell whether I hadn't been hungry since Ares' text, or if I hadn't allowed myself to feel it because on some deep level, I believed I didn't deserve to be fed.

Usually, I am a slow eater, almost always the last one to finish my meal at a dinner party. Usually, I take small, constricted bites with a little bit of everything balanced on the fork. Usually, ice cream melts before I can finish it.

Not today. I ripped into the box of tropical melon-flavored ice cream pops, unwrapped the bar with my teeth and finished it in four bites. Without waiting or trying to tell myself I didn't need it, I grabbed another one. This time I savored it. I ate slowly enough that it dripped neon-green sweetness down my fingers. With my tongue, I licked my palms from the base of my wrists to the tips of my middle fingers.

It was not easy, growing spider legs, resisting strong and familiar gravity. It took effort—attention and intention—but I could do it. Any time I felt pulled into a chasm of shame and self-recrimination, I just needed to grow my spider legs.

There at the kitchen sink, standing in a pool of late afternoon light with warm water running through my fingertips, I understood that I needed to practice if I wanted to get stronger. I said aloud: "If Ares didn't see how awesome I am, then he is—by definition—not for me. From now on, loving me is a prerequisite for receiving my love. Loving me is necessary for earning the ability to judge me and to have that judgment matter." It was a vow.

Feeling proud and complete having made that proclamation, I moved to my bedroom to lie down. With the glass doors open, the curtains were dancing a flamenco. Unexpectedly, they began to spin and weave. I felt tension, suspense in their separation: How long would it last? What would be revealed? How would they demonstrate their freedom in the time they were apart?

The curtains were a microcosm of existence, and I was rapt. For hours—I know because the show started in daylight and ended in pitch black—I watched the curtains dance in the waning light. So unpredictable, they never repeated their choreography. Every breeze was an improvisation. Oohing and ahhing, I was an audience of one. I filled my iPhone storage with minutes' long videos of curtains until it couldn't store any more footage.

I managed to pull myself away from the curtains only when it was too dark to see and decided to take myself for a hot tub. As I padded across the remaining warmth of the lanai, I felt myself coming down from the trip I hadn't fully realized I'd gone on. Coming down meant that it was becoming harder to keep myself on spider legs, aloft above the chasms. The neutral or positive truths I was telling myself weren't unassailable anymore, and my habitual mind started telling the same old stories. I could feel myself returning to "normal" and all the self-punishing thoughts that came with it. It was daunting to realize how hard I needed to *try* not to fall into a worthlessness spiral.

It was easier on acid. I felt so GOOD. So good and connected to everything. Happy and loving and at peace. I wanted to stay in this frame of mind forever.

"HOW DO I STAY HERE FOREVER?" I shouted my question at the Universe, loud and urgent in my mind.

I heard nothing besides the palm trees rustling in the wind.

I listened harder.

I ignored the hum of the hot tub pump, the buzz of unidentifiable insects, the watery spray of a distant sprinkler system.

I needed to hear what the Universe had to tell me.

I heard no voices, still only the palm trees rustling. I tried to block them, but they only got louder.

"Shhhhh," they were saying. "Shhhhhhh, shhhhhh," the way you would soothe a worried child.

I was the worried child. Asking how I could stay there forever, clinging to that which was inherently fleeting, scared of coming down and feeling the pain, loss, boredom, and difficulty of normal life... I was trying to escape the human experience rather than love it.

There was no voice that accompanied this realization, it was the natural hum of life that imparted it.

If I had been meant to spend my life at ease, in constant harmony with all that surrounded me, I would have been born a palm tree. Or a rock. Something that didn't feel as much as a human. My soul had incarnated to *feel*. These feelings, even the unpleasant ones, are gifts.

Whenever I got tired of so much feeling, or wanted a break from feeling, all I had to do was pretend to be a palm tree. Or grow spider legs. Or just go to fucking *sleep*.

Somewhat appeased by this answer, I asked the Universe a different version of the same question, except respectfully—not graspingly—this time.

"How can I have access to this wisdom all the time, even when I'm not high on psychedelics?"

Because the Universe understood that I wasn't trying to escape necessary and enriching human experiences, it answered.

Like a giant gong inside my head, I heard "YONI SAYS YESSSSSSSSSSSS." It was loud to the point of being percussive and ended with a resonant echo in my chest. And then the sound disappeared. Almost with a pop. I knew I wouldn't be hearing anything else tonight.

I started laughing. The Universe had a flair for the dramatic. There weren't many euphemisms for "vagina" that I liked but "yoni" was among my most hated. The humor, of course, was intentional. The Universe was hoping humor would make the message more memorable. I'd heard a version of this before—that I was supposed to do what I wanted to, to follow what brought me joy—but never with such booming clarity. With those three words—yoni says YES—the Universe communicated that my "yoni" was a built-in compass for joy. All kinds, not just sexual. It was sensitive, the home of instinct even more than my gut. It was the organ most directly wired to my intrinsic animal sense of desire. Its responses weren't thought out, manipulated by society, or controlled by logic. My puss didn't give a fuck about "should"!

The next time I needed to choose a new fabric for reupholstering my couch, I should ask, "What makes my yoni say yes?" In my next business negotiation, "What terms would make my yoni say yes?" When figuring out what I wanted for lunch, I just needed to ask my yoni!

This was a tool I filed away in my brain for long-term use. It felt far more actionable than "Do what you want." I knew what a visceral "yes" felt like when I thought about it with my sex organs: expansive, warm, enthusiastic. I also knew what a "no" felt like: an immediate closing off in self-protection, a physical recoiling, defensive.

Floating and reflecting on my past, I realized I had pursued nos (PhD program) and denied yeses (MBA) because I thought there was value in misery and martyrdom. There wasn't. There was nothing beautiful about self-sacrifice. If you wouldn't sacrifice someone else's joy, then you shouldn't sacrifice your own. The Universe was telling me that I was meant to make my pussy happy. It struck me as crazy and simple at the same time. There was an undeniable truth to asking and listening to what my yoni wanted.

Right then, it was overheated and wanted to get out of the hot tub.

***

Lying down with plans of going to sleep, my body was exhausted but fulfilled, ready to pass out and allow my consciousness to integrate what I'd learned. My brain, though, was still at work. I lay in bed trying to read a novel, but I couldn't concentrate. My brain felt too full of information, and was grinding faster than ever. Voracious and insatiable, ready to consume and rectify any paradox put in front of its attention, my train of thought had become trains, many trains, running in different directions, on different planes of existence, simultaneously, all demanding to be followed. The trains jumped their tracks, switched directions, sprouted wings, turned into butterflies, and took flight...

I couldn't follow what I was thinking, and I was ready for it to stop, or at least calm down. I wanted to go to sleep but every time I closed my eyes, yellow bolts of lightning shot behind my lids like an electrical storm, waking me up again. If it were truly intolerable, I could take a sleeping pill and knock myself out, but it seemed rude to opt out of what felt like the evening's grand finale.

Succumbing to fatigue, my right eye closed against my will. I fought it, until I realized that fatigue had allowed me to do what my will power hadn't. My left eye was open while my right eye was closed. I was winking my right eye, the one I thought was impossible to wink!

I decided to experiment. Placing my palm over my left eye to keep it closed, I closed my right eye slowly. Then I opened it, slowly. Then I did it again, slower and slower each time, focusing all my attention on how it felt. I tried to watch it—see it—from the inside, my eyelid lighting up like my legs during squats. When I closed my right eye, I noticed the way a tiny muscle at the very outside corner of my eye contracted like it did when I squinted. I felt the activation in my upper cheek and the lowest point of my eyebrow. I felt a sheet of muscle between the bridge of my nose and my cheekbone as it tensed. I saw it like a cosmic teacher was leading me through a PowerPoint lecture on the human eye and the muscles that controlled it. I saw each muscle light up as it engaged and fade back to grey when I released the flex. I didn't know the names of any of the muscles, but I could feel each of them separately, doing what was required to open and close my eyelid.

I thought I'd gotten the hang of it and decided to test myself by removing the palm from my left eye that had been keeping it closed.

I tried to wink, keeping my left eye open and closing my right eye. Instead, I blinked. The habit of closing both eyes when closing my right was too strong. I went back to practicing, pressing my palm to my left eye keeping it closed while winking my right, trying to learn to access those muscles on demand.

I kept at it for maybe five minutes, maybe twenty minutes, maybe an hour, maybe more. I practiced winking. I kept at it until I succeeded once, then repeatedly. I kept at it until I could wink my right eye ten times in a row without blinking. I kept at it until the muscles of my right eye wouldn't flex anymore.

It was depleting to focus so much attention on such a narrow thing, and I wanted go to sleep, but—worse than ever—when I closed my eyes, neon fireworks shaped like electric trees, flared then disappeared on the inky canvas of my eyelids. I tried to fight it—to meditate, to imagine blackness, to clear my mind of all thoughts—but I couldn't get the fireworks to go away. Eventually I gave in and decided to watch them like a Fourth of July extravaganza, except no lingering smoke or chemical smell. It took a while, and my dreams were vivid, but eventually I slept.

***

Early the next morning, I woke up groggy and lethargic. Happy, but no longer euphoric or at one with existence. At the sink, brushing my teeth and expecting nothing, I attempted to wink my right eye. It wasn't pretty, certainly not sexy, and not even very controlled, but my left eye stayed open while my right eye closed. It was a wink. I did it!

Until that morning in Hawaii, I hadn't really wanted to know how psychedelics worked. I had felt like understanding the neurochemical mechanisms might undermine the spiritual nature of the experience, as if understanding how the trick worked would destroy the magic of it. But now, my curiosity was piqued. Something had happened that I believed was impossible, and no amount of scientific explanation felt like it *could* undermine my personal, direct, repeated experience of feeling connected to a greater sense of wholeness, wisdom, and belonging. In fact, a scientific explanation would help satisfy my intellect, make me feel valid and substantiated for believing that psychedelics could impart not only valuable insights but actual (if trivial) abilities. The way my experiences had built on each other and stayed with me over time, feeling ever truer and more trustworthy with each trip, made the magic feel indestructible. An intellectual and physiological understanding would only add to my nascent faith.

I wanted to understand how psychedelics worked, and if taking acid allowed me to wink my right eye or if that had been some combination of weird coincidence and placebo effect. Googling "how does LSD work," what I found was mostly unhelpful. I found: 1) anti-drug propaganda, 2) highly technical, virtually incomprehensible scientific studies, or 3) Wikipedia-type articles of dubious accuracy. I realized I didn't want to understand how LSD worked at the chemical level; I wanted to understand if I was justified in thinking a small dose of acid enabled my brain to create new neurological connections that had allowed me to wink for the first time in my life.

Frustrated, I googled "Can I rewire my brain on acid," and hoped DEA agents weren't tracking my searches. Somewhere just before the very end of the internet, I hit an open-ended but peer-reviewed scientific article about how psychedelics might increase the production of "BDNF," leading to "neurogenesis." BDNF is an acronym for "brain-derived neurotrophic growth factor," a protein that causes new neurons to be produced. Neurons are brain and nerve cells responsible for movement, processing sensory information, and communication between cells, among other things. "Neurogenesis" is the growth and creation of new neurons. In short, if my understanding was correct, it was possible that LSD was directly responsible for my new physical ability.

I continued reading and found a picture that struck me. It was an illustration of a neuron forming a new neural pathway by connecting with other neurons. It looked *exactly* like the fireworks I had seen behind my eyes that had kept me awake the previous night.

Scientists posit that psychedelics can facilitate the creation of new neural pathways. I thought about my greyed-out muscles turning pink when I concentrated on them. Had I created new, lasting, neural connections? None of the articles I found mentioned winking specifically, but it seemed like there might be solid scientific footing for believing that I could rewire my brain, consciously toward positive goals, on psychedelics.

I wished, as I headed to the kitchen for some breakfast, that I'd used the opportunity to teach myself something useful, like how to roll my Spanish Rs. Or whistle. Or twerk.

Chapter 25

SUPERBLOOM

San Francisco, California
January 2018
Substances ingested: pastries, a tangerine La Croix, and ~150 mcg of LSD

I returned home to San Francisco ready to practice my new skills: winking my right eye and NOT leaping to the most devastating explanation for any perceived slight. Each morning, I woke up and practiced winking in the mirror. It was still awkward and effortful, but it got easier every day. Each night, I reflected on the day and how I'd made sense of its happenings. I noticed my tendency to choose old, painful stories about why things did or didn't happen, but flexing the new muscles of my spider legs, I resisted. Now, I acknowledged my habitual response, saw it for what it was, and then—if I had the energy—chose a different story.

Standing in line at the bakery around the corner from my condo, a woman looked me up and down, then whispered something to her friend. I imagined she was making a snarky comment about my body, my outfit, or the combination, and I felt shame bubble in my stomach. I heard my brain start to riff on all the nasty things she could have said: "Like those thighs need a croissant," "Who wears leopard print at that size," "Only in San Francisco would someone think those shoes were cool." Then I remembered: spider legs. That part of me able to hold myself above the chasm whispered that I actually had *no idea* what the woman had said. It could have been complimentary. She could have been saying, "I like her jacket" or "See, I think witch-boots are back in." Spider legs reminded me that even if she *was* making snarky comments about me, it said something more powerful about her own body image insecurities and how trapped *she* was in valuing appearances over substance.

Spider legs reminded me she could have been whispering to her friend about recognizing the barista from a one night stand. The world really didn't revolve around me.

A year ago, I might have left the store empty-handed, obsessing over the imagined criticism, and hating myself for thinking I deserved a pastry. Now, I gently shushed the negative thoughts and redirected my attention to the decadent display. I ordered a blueberry cheesecake Kouign Amann, an almond croissant, a turkey-and-brie croissant for later, and a tangerine La Croix for my immediate thirst. Mouth watering and head untroubled, I left with my bag of delights.

***

It had been nearly six months since my last acid trip, and I was eager to go again. I felt like the last experience was dense with learning that I'd successfully integrated into my daily life. I was ready for more. My previous trips had been heavily planned, but that was mostly because I didn't have access to psychedelics without travel and forethought. I had brought the rest of the LSD home with me though and had at least ~300mg, enough for a few full-sized trips or tons of micro doses.

One Saturday morning, I woke up with nothing on my to-do list and decided—given the sunlight pouring in through my window and the nothingness on my schedule—to drop acid. I didn't go for a walk or meditate or come up with questions for the Universe because I didn't want to this time. I'd learned to trust the Universe and I wanted to see where she would guide me without my attempts to intervene or control. I just turned on music and set my phone on airplane mode.

I cut a square and a half from the grided paper and popped it on the tip of my tongue. I moved it around in my mouth, letting it rest under my tongue, between my lip and my bottom front teeth, then nibbled it until it was equal parts pulp and saliva. After I was sure I'd absorbed all the LSD there was to absorb, I swallow the paper, just to be thorough.

Before I felt any sort of high, I just felt cold. I got under the covers of my bed but that wasn't warm enough. Even with a comforter, top sheet, and duvet cover on me, I was freezing. Shivering, teeth-chattering, fingers turning subtly blue, and yet I tried to stay perfectly still because of the nausea. Shivering made me want to puke. The nausea was my first sign that the acid was potent, and I was on the cusp of taking off.

I slithered out of bed and onto the low-pile olive area rug, right in front of the heater. I had vacuumed yesterday and I was grateful to my earlier self. With one arm, I pulled the faux fur blanket off the foot of my bed and covered myself from toes to shoulders, wishing there was more fabric so I could wrap myself in it completely. Instead, I returned to a rigid corpse pose beneath the blanket, inches from the heater, on the floor, trying to stem my nausea with mindful breathing.

Lying on the ground, unmoving, I felt myself merge with the rug. There was no boundary or separation between me and beneath me. My body was half human, half polyester. I could feel my cells and the cells of the carpet intermingling, trading electrons, indistinguishable at the particle level. Everything that used to appear solid was revealed as an illusion. Objects turned to energy gradients, from grey to orange. My heart was beating, moving fast, had more energy—was more orange—than the dead wooden planks of my floorboards, but they were fundamentally the same thing: atoms, particles, energy, space. So much more space than material. I felt the gaps between my electrons slot around the electrons of the rug. We became one.

A distant part of me found this merger genuinely alarming. But a bigger part of me remained lucid. I reminded myself that I didn't actually need to worry about melting into the rug. If I really needed to, or tried hard enough for some reason, I was sure I could accomplish remarkable physical achievements like standing up, walking, or even getting back into bed, which would prove that I *could* separate my body from the ground and my mind from these sensations.

But I didn't want to. It felt like the Universe was trying to teach me something through these sensations so instead of resisting, I leaned into the feeling of becoming one with the floor.

The only thing moving was my heart. I could feel it beating inside my carpet self. Then I began to notice other movements, subtler systems of respiration, digestion, cognition... My exterior was inanimately still, but everything *inside* me was moving. My heart seemed like it was beating too fast. I tried to count the beats but with no external time reference, all I was doing was counting up and up with no end. I worried my heart would explode if I didn't slow it down. I knew I was being silly because NO ONE has ever died from LSD directly, so I tried to switch my attention to my breathing, hoping that slowing my breaths would slow my racing heart.

Breathing slower and slower, I realize it worked, but then I started to worry that maybe it had worked too well. How slow is too slow? Now, I was just holding my breath. Should I be breathing every ten seconds? Every thirty seconds? Every four seconds? What was normal? Should I set a timer to remind me?

When I focused on my heartbeat, it beat too quickly. When I focused on swallowing, my throat closed, and I couldn't remember which muscles to use to open it again. When I focused on breathing, I either stopped, or hyperventilated.

Panic rising, my already frenzied heart picked up speed again. All my cells vibrated too quickly. I was about to come apart. I couldn't control it all. I felt like I was about to spontaneously combust. If I kept trying to control it all, I knew I would explode.

Just then, in a whisper, "What if you... stopped?"

My internal panic was too loud for me to hear the voice clearly, but the question itself managed to fight its way into my consciousness. I couldn't tell if it was my own voice—my higher self—or the Universe, but the suggestion sounded worthwhile. Trying to control my body wasn't working, so maybe not trying to control it would work.

"Surrender."

I heard the word in my head and my whole body relaxed. My breaths slowed, my pulse lowered, I became one with the floor again. My autonomic nervous system took over, doing its job effortlessly, all systems working in perfect harmony without my oversight. I realized: I am not in control and that is a *good* thing. When I try, it fucks things up. Release, surrender, relax.

For the first time, I was overwhelmed with gratitude for how little I actually control. Thank God.

Under the brown faux fox fur, I realized: being alive is the experience of always being on the verge of coming apart. We just learn to ignore it. Vibrating, expanding, exploding, and imploding at the same time—life is a tremulous dance that all my cells know how to do better than I could ever conduct them.

My body was an infinitely complex symphony of systems that I could never create, control, or even understand, and yet I take it all for granted.

I vowed: Not anymore. Never again.

My entire attitude shifted in an instant, and along with it, my temperature. I kicked off my blanket, my legs brimming with celebration because I couldn't believe how fucking lucky I was to be *born* into a *body*. The kicking felt so good that I kept doing it. Crying with gratitude, my nausea was gone and replaced with the desire—familiar now from other trips—to move. Still on my back, I experimented with different frequencies to kick at the air, trying to find the right speed.

There was a certain vibration my legs wanted to feel, and it was difficult to get right. I shook fast, then faster, then slower, until I felt my whole body shaking in resonance with my legs. I kept it up until I physically couldn't anymore, collapsing back onto the rug in a sheen of sweat, feeling thoroughly shaken in a good way.

"Upbeat Instrumental Study" was playing on Spotify, and I was transported by the music. Each song moved me through different lives, lifetimes, galaxies. Certain songs brought me to tears with their exquisite melancholy, others held me in raptured suspense. I never knew Mozart could sound like this. Every song carried textures and colors and emotions too nuanced to name. I knew:

Words shatter reality.

Music transports.

Music is the language of the Universes. It is the way they communicate with each other. We *get* to listen to it.

Here we are, on Earth, with the opportunity to eavesdrop on the conversation of the Universe and we walk around like music doesn't exist! How could anyone ever be "depressed"?? What the fuck? There is *music* in this world. *Everywhere.* What more could we possibly want???

I sought out my phone because I needed to remember this. With one finger and typing each number on the downbeat of the music, I entered my passcode and clumsily opened the voice memo app. Tears were streaming down my face in a combination of gratitude and shame for not appreciating it more, sooner. Music was medicine—prevention, and cure, all in one. I bet there's a frequency for healing everything. My voice was thick with tears and sincerity, "Anne," I said, using my name to catch my attention because this message was urgent. "You walk around like music doesn't exist! It doesssssssssssssssssss. Never forget that." Feeling proud of myself for successfully operating my phone without forgetting what I meant to do on it, I used that momentum to get myself upright.

Bending my knees, testing my legs, feeling the energy of the earth bounce back when I pushed against it, I started wandering in a small circle in the space between the foot of my bed and my desk. I was walking around, bouncing as I would if I were holding a fussy baby on each hip. It looked stupid but felt *delicious*. I wanted more jiggle in my life.

I changed the Spotify station to something pop-y and began to dance with renewed vigor. I was dancing with vengeance and complete commitment when I caught sight of myself in the mirror. I didn't remember getting naked, but I was now and my fat was flying. Waving and flapping, my excess flesh created its own breeze. My thighs were dimpled and bigger than I thought they should be, but it was the ring around my belly that was new. Or I was seeing it for the first time. I hoped it was some sort of acid-induced delusion and distortion. I'd always had belly fat but not like this. Before, it was evenly spread-out chub, not a concentrated muffin-top that looked like leftovers from carrying twins. I could grab the roll with both hands and still have more spill over. I did it, feeling my gelatinous flesh squish between my fingers. The revulsion and self-condemnation were immediate, obliterating any good feelings that had been there just moments ago.

I was disgusted by my body. All I could see were the puckers and shadows caused by overhead lighting on cellulite that shouldn't be there. Horrified by the lack of will-power that had gotten me here, embarrassed by what everyone else must be thinking when they looked at me, I felt the spiral of self-hatred grow too strong and fast for my spider legs to match.

Then, at the edge of my consciousness, I half felt, half saw, a wave of welcoming blue light. A stream of glowing, sapphire liquid separated from an infinite ocean of it and poured into the center of my body, to be covered with layers of mucus, muscle, and fat.

The glowing ocean was the source of souls.

In front of my bathroom mirror, I was getting a glimpse of how souls incarnate. A little bit of soul pinched off from the mass of Source (God, the Divine, whatever) and imbued a body with a piece of the transcendent.

My soul was the most beautiful thing I'd ever seen. It was prettier than any gemstone, but also not markedly different from a gemstone. If gemstones could flow like liquid or crystalize at will, it would look a lot like this. In awe of the beauty, I was consequently ashamed that my soul had to wear my hideous sack of a body for a lifetime.

Almost as soon as I felt the full weight of my shame that my body wasn't as beautiful as my soul, I started to laugh. Of course bodies are ugly compared to souls! We were all gorgeous, divine, infinite souls wearing funny little human suits. The phrase "funny little human suit" stuck in my head like the melody of a song from childhood, and I started singing it to myself. "Bodiiiiiiiiiiiiies are funnyyyyyyyyy little huuuuuuuman suits. Funny little human soooooots!"

Just like we'd need protective suits to go to outer space, souls need suits to come to Earth. Our souls are too big, too limitless, too energetic, to be contained on earth without a body, so each of us gets to choose a body for this incarnation. The ugly ones are just souls with good senses of humor!

With certainty, I thought: Our bodies are machines that exist to encase and disguise our souls! If we recognized each other as infinite souls from the unified field of divinity, we wouldn't fight each other over parking spaces or want to fuck the ones who remind us of our parents in some deep unresolved way. We need bodies to give us the full experience of being human. Souls don't know anything about human beauty standards, so I actually got pretty lucky in choosing my suit. As far as funny little human suits go, mine works really well. I flexed my hands in front of my face, proving my point.

I knew, and remembered from all the other times the Universe tried to tell me something similar, that I shouldn't worry about what my body looked like. Instead, I should focus on maintaining its health and well-being so it would support me through all the things I wanted to do with it. I was so fucking lucky to have a body—any body—that I should go on and enjoy wiggling, in loads of different ways, no matter how funny looking it was.

I went back to dancing, lighter and filled with gratitude, but still not able to shake the visual of my belly. It was a belly I didn't recognize. Was it really mine?

I asked the Universe about it and received a silent and cryptic visual in response. I saw the slab of my lower belly, painlessly, cut away from my body like a fillet. On the inside of the slab, I saw three rows of glowing, orange orbs, nestled like treasures. They were shiny and a little bit translucent, about the size of golf balls, and most interestingly, they were humming with potential energy. I didn't get a chance to count them before my belly reattached, but I'd guess there were two rows of eight and one row of seven, offset in their placement, so twenty-three in total.

Something about the image reminded me of toro-salmon sashimi, which I hadn't liked until I had it a tiny, upscale sushi restaurant in one of the hipster areas of San Francisco. It was my first realization of what sashimi could be—sweet, silken, delectable. The salmon was brightly colored, tiger-striped with thick lines of melting fat. Never had such a simple taste conveyed such sensuous indulgence. Using the image, I understood that the Universe was trying to tell me: My fat was delicious. My fat was abundance. My fat was stored resource and nourishment. Why would anyone seek to divest themself of this richness? To covet insufficiency? I am a woman who has enough and that is a beautiful thing.

I got it—the message made sense and passed the truth filter of my yoni—but I was still resistant. I was scared to allow myself to unapologetically take up space. I feared giving up the desire to be skinny because what would it cost me in society? The more room I take up, the more of a target I am. I realized I had spent a lifetime making myself small to avoid being attacked.

But I didn't want to be small anymore. I was ebullient with the knowledge that I was an infinitely divine being, temporarily wearing a funny little human suit as disguise, and that my fat made me radiant, nourished, and resourced.

This realization blossomed into the desire to take my funny little human suit out into the world and give her a spin. I wanted the company of other radiant souls. But I also knew I was still tripping and didn't necessarily want anyone else to know it.

I decided to visit the ATM. It felt like the right level of challenge and interaction with humanity. It would only mean a half block of walking in public, no conversation required, so I thought I could manage it. Looking down at my underwear, and the one sock that had managed to remain on throughout my dancing, I realized I would have to get dressed first.

I put on a pair of short, black, lace-up boots that reminded me of Mary Poppins. Naked except for the boots and bikini briefs, I knew I'd made a good choice. I loved the way the leather hugged my feet and made me feel a little bit witchy. I wanted something loose that wouldn't retrigger my nausea, so I chose an extra-large shirt dress that I'd bought from Zara before I knew how bad fast fashion was for the environment. Over my head, I pulled the dress on with the aid of gravity in a single smooth, diving motion. I felt the light cotton barely more than the air before it. After lying on the ground freezing for hours this morning, I didn't want to risk the high middle slit and lightweight fabric making me cold outside, so I asked my soul, my glowing crystal center, to choose a coat for me. Immediately, she chose one I'd never had the courage to wear.

For a few years, I'd had an informal policy of buying underpriced vintage fur coats to give them a final, loving home even though I never planned to wear them. Who wears fur? And in *San Francisco*. But I loved this coat. It was a "vintage, black, opera-length fur from the 1940's," according to the man who sold it to me, though it looked more rock-and-roll than opera to me. The shoulder pads were massive and gave me the outline of a linebacker for the NFL. Fear of PETA and of simply taking up too much attention and *space* had kept me from ever wearing the coat out.

I hesitated, questioning my soul's choice, but then I summoned the courage to surrender. I felt the silk lining as I pulled on one sleeve, then the other, the heaviness of the fur lying like a comforting weight across my shoulders. Looking in the mirror, I felt my soul do a flamenco step that assured me I'd done the right thing.

I walked out the door and around the block listening to Spotify through my earbuds, feeling the breeze on my face, and lengthening my stride just for the fun of it. An acupuncturist who specialized in fertility treatments advertised her services with a discrete sandwich board on the sidewalk that I dodged with a deft hop, then, loving the feeling of lightness, I skipped the rest of the way to the ATM. Standing in line behind an elderly man, I noticed a twenty-something woman who looked like she'd stepped out of a fashion spread for *Rolling Stone* gesturing at me to take my earbuds out. Instantly, I worried that I was trailing toilet paper, or that my dress had somehow unbuttoned itself and I was unaware of my wardrobe malfunction, but her smile assured me nothing was wrong. "I just *had* to tell you... you are EVERYTHING right now. I saw you walking earlier and just thought... Wow."

"Oh my god thank you!" I nearly screamed at her in my unbridled enthusiasm. "Thank you *so much*."

She moved away, grinning, and I marveled: It wasn't even the outfit! I mean, it was the outfit. She was obviously reacting to the outfit because the outfit was awesome. But it was also the *energy*. I knew I was radiating power. I had walked down the street like I loved my body, loved my life, loved the experience of being alive. She felt it. I was magnetic.

When I walked through these streets feeling like a fat, ugly, sack of meat, I felt shitty about myself, and others responded accordingly. When I thought of myself an incomparable *jewel of divine origin* who happened to be wearing a funny human costume, I shined.

I pulled out my phone and texted Adelynn, "OMG do you know how gorgeous you are???????????!" followed by heart-eyes emojis until my thumb got sore.

Cash withdrawn, I walked back toward my home feeling like the Universe had been generous with lessons this trip. Having no intentions had been fruitful. Coming to this trip open had allowed me to receive whatever the Universe wanted to give me. I could tell, as I wandered around the block taking the long way home, enjoying my soul *and* my body, relishing my ability to turn my magnetism off and on, that I would use these revelations when I next felt depressed. As with the large scissors I had used to cut emotional cords, the spider legs I'd learned to conjure to carry me over holes in my self-esteem, the idea that I needed to make decisions not with my brain or my even my gut but with my *yoni*, I understood in that moment that I needed to let go of control when I got overwhelmed, needed to let my soul dress me when I wanted attention, needed to remember there was always *music*. There was no pit of depression that could not be marginally improved by the perfect song.

The orange orbs though? Those were a mystery. As I unlocked my front door and moved into a space that felt like a womb I'd decorated for myself, I wondered again what the Universe meant by those. Content and suddenly sure that nothing would feel so good as a nap, I pulled my faux fur blanket from my bedroom onto the couch and snuggled in.

***

A few days later, headed to an appointment with my therapist in Palo Alto, my mind wandered as I drove. Highway 280 was mostly empty at 1:00 PM on a Thursday, allowing the family of deer grazing the median a surprisingly peaceful meal. I reflected on the weekend's acid trip, wondering what I would tell him about it. I wanted his help understanding how

I could feel so much hatred towards a body that I actually thought was pretty great by any reasonable standard—just not my own. My mind settled on my obsession with my belly, which led to the memory of the cryptic glowing orbs and understanding hit so hard I almost slammed on the brakes: the orbs were eggs! My belly held onto this fat because my body wanted and needed it to feed a child! My body wanted to be pregnant. My body wouldn't let go of this abundance until I had satisfied that need.

Merging toward the right lane to exit, I fought with my body. Maybe *it* wanted to, but *I* didn't. I didn't want to have a baby alone. I did, though, want a child. If important elements—like romantic partnership and hope for the future of the world related to war, disease, and climate change—lined up and fell into place, I really, *really* wanted to be a biological mother. I was turning thirty-five in two months; even if I got pregnant today, mine would be a "geriatric pregnancy." If I wanted the best chance, and longest timeline, I suddenly realized: I needed to freeze my eggs. Immediately.

Arriving at my therapy appointment, I started out hesitant to open up, afraid of how he'd respond to hearing that I was about to plop down thousands of dollars for an invasive medical procedure to prolong my fertility because of a cryptic vision on acid. Talking about my psychedelic use was vulnerable, intimate, and revealing—I blushed so hard and could not make eye contact telling him about what happened on the beach after ayahuasca—but in many ways, it felt the same as discussing my dreams with him. Dream analysis was one of the subjects he taught, a particular area of fascination and expertise for him, and since mine were so vivid, we'd talked about them from the beginning. Dreams, like psychedelic experiences, are often communiques from the subconscious delivered in metaphor and layered meaning.

He listened, nodding, asking occasional shrink-like questions to draw out my feelings about certain details. At the end of the session, knowing his opinion mattered to me, he concluded, "Sounds like you're taking steps toward the future you want. I see no reason to slow down or second guess." It meant a lot that, implicitly, he was giving me his professional-mental-health-provider-seal-of-approval on me, eventually, becoming a mom.

He knew all about my drug use and that didn't change his mind. Since the beginning, we talked—or rather, I talked and he listened deeply, asking uncomfortably few yet incisive questions—about what I learned through my various psychedelic explorations, how often I smoked pot, why and how it helped me. He was shockingly supportive. Shockingly because he was in his early 70s, had been raised by a Southern Baptist dad and devout Mormon mom, and I knew he barely even drank. I expected him to judge and condemn my behavior, pushing me toward abstinence and moral purity, but he never did.

By "supportive," it wasn't that he thought my drug use was *ideal* or even necessary for personal growth, but he didn't see it as a problem, no matter how much I needled him to judge me for it. He said that it didn't seem to detract from my life, that I wasn't in danger nor was I dangerous in my usage, and that it seemed to serve a significant function in my life, namely insulation from loneliness and lifelong anxiety. *That*, he told me—the loneliness, the anxiety, the depression—was the real problem.

I was shocked the first time he said "I don't think your drug use is problematic. I think it's *symptomatic*. Let's work on the issues and relationships that cause anxiety in your life and I bet the pot smoking will decrease naturally." As much as I tried to get him to tell me to quit, he only ever asked, "If it were an anti-anxiety medication I prescribed, a pill instead of pot, would you feel the same guilt and shame about it?" He knew the answer was no.

I made the call to a fertility clinic on my way home from his office and was disappointed to find out the soonest appointment was a full two weeks away. I wanted to act now.

Chapter 26
Sweet Child O' Mine

San Francisco, California
March 2018
Substances in*jected*: Gonal-f, Menapur, Cetrotide and Lupron

Two weeks later, as if I needed more evidence that a benign and loving Universe was guiding every aspect of everything, my brand-new fertility doctor did a quick exam, took some blood, asked a few questions, and called later that afternoon to say that my timing couldn't have been more perfect. I was just about to ovulate. I would start the injections four days later and be done with the entire process within the month. The month before my thirty-fifth birthday.

The clinic—the one with the best reviews in all of San Francisco, which was saying a lot given that fertility services were in almost as much demand as tech in Silicon Valley—was even running a promotion: a money-back guarantee if you froze at least twenty eggs before you turned thirty-five. This meant they would refund the egg freezing costs if IVF did not result in a pregnancy. Instead of seeing this marketing plot as a calculated statistical and commercial gamble on the part of the clinic, I fell for a little magical thinking: this was a guarantee of *motherhood*. If I could grow and freeze twenty healthy eggs, I would have a baby.

I asked my doctor what I could do to maximize the number and quality of eggs retrieved. Dr. Nguyen recommended acupuncture and handed me a pamphlet the clinic had produced with a list of dos and don'ts and frequently asked questions. It looked like a services menu from a syringe-happy spa: DO drink lots of water, follow the drug dosages and schedules precisely, eat healthy foods. DON'T drink alcohol, inject the drugs more than a hand's distance from your belly button, or use nail polish during or before the egg retrieval as fumes can harm the eggs.

Shocked by the specificity and potential dangers of *nail polish*, I left the office committed to doing everything right for my future frozen babies. Walking home, I chose a path that led by the acupuncturist's sandwich board, the one I'd seen a million times but that had seemed particularly unavoidable the afternoon I'd made my way to the ATM on acid. I called the number on the board and made an appointment for later in the week before I even got home.

That Saturday, sitting in the waiting room surrounded by leather-bound books and framed anatomical drawings illustrating subtle energy channels, I felt assured in my choice. The room smelled like incense and was lightly playing what sounded like pink noise. I couldn't find the machine making it and was, once again, reassured by the thoughtfulness and privacy implied by the design of the space. I didn't expect the acupuncturist to be Irish, though I probably should have since her name was Aoife O'Brien. Warranted or not, I had a moment of concern about going to an Irish practitioner of Chinese Medicine. As if accustomed to this reluctance, she started by listing off her credentials, educational lineage, and various accomplishments before we even sat down in the exam room. Though most of the names she listed meant nothing to me, her vibe was trustworthy.

The exam room looked much the same as the one in the fertility clinic, except it was almost completely empty. There was nothing on the counters except one blue, lidded ceramic pot and a portable timer. Somehow, the sparse décor made the room feel restful and sterile rather than just sterile. I had the opportunity to study her red hair, pale face, light wrinkles while she took my pulse. I was a little surprised that her questions focused not on meridians and moksha, but on food.

"Do you eat well?" she asked.

"Mostly." I considered. "Yes. No. I don't know. I eat a lot late at night. Obviously, that's not great. What I eat is healthy." I imagined my Cheezits, late night cereal binges, and French fries with every meal. "Mostly healthy. I mean, a lot of vegetables. Not *a lot* of vegetables actually. Also fried food. I really love fried food. Yeah, I don't know." Wanting her to interject, to save me from talking in circles, I said, "I mean, I eat."

She nodded, acknowledging my ramble, while continuing to take my pulses. In traditional Chinese Medicine, there are three different pulses in three different positions on each wrist.

"But you eat three meals a day, roughly?"

"Oh no. I skip breakfast. It makes me hungrier the rest of the day. I just can't seem to manage to feed myself that often."

Seeming surprised, she told me in no uncertain terms that I was going to have a problem. She said the color of my tongue, my pulses, and my unreliable eating habits indicated that I had a "blood deficiency." With the fertility drugs I was about to pump into my system, more blood would flow to my ovaries. "Blood is an insulator. With so much of it in your womb, you're going to feel raw and unprotected."

"Wait. Sorry. I have a blood deficiency? Like, I don't have enough or there's not enough of something in it?"

"Both." She explained the relationship between my liver and gallbladder, how they were yin and yang organ partners. I was mostly lost in the unfamiliar lexicon, but I'd read enough about ancient healing modalities that have been proven effective in large clinical trials to listen open-mindedly, even if I didn't fully understand. Basically, she explained: I was taking from my body without giving. I was asking too much without also nourishing it. It made me sad because I knew she was right.

When I asked if I could improve the situation, she said, "Yes. Eat things that look like blood."

While I was thinking that sounded a lot like a prescription for red wine, she clarified, "Dark berries, black beans, beets. Foods with rich, dark pigment. They build your blood."

Still sounded like a prescription for red wine.

"Also, nothing too cold. Eat warm, nourishing things."

After thirty minutes of Aoife applying painless but electrified needles to the area around my ovaries, I promised to eat more regularly.

When I made that promise, I meant every word. It was only a few weeks, and I was willing to gain weight if that was the price of growing strong, healthy, cold-resistant eggs. Plus, what could be more welcome after decades of depriving my body because it was larger than the media-sanctioned beauty standard than permission to eat more? It was like a short pregnancy but instead of eating for two, I was eating for twenty.

When I got home, though, I found I couldn't keep my promise. Even with good reasons, professional and personal permission, I still wouldn't let myself eat until I was *really* hungry. At the first twinges of hunger, I resisted, again at the second, on and on, only giving in when—finally—my hunger hurt. I had to hurt to feel justified in eating. I had promised myself I was going to feed myself at the first hint of desire but I couldn't follow through.

When I brought the issue to my shrink, he answered my questions—as was his wont—with more questions: What did "feeding" mean to me? In childhood, how did I relate to food? How did my parents model eating?

It was the last question that made me realize: My mom treated food like something only weak people needed. She ate—little, slowly, half-portions that counted as lunch and dinner—but never like food was a physical need. For her, it was a choice. "I ate yesterday" was a reason she didn't need to eat today. She often "forgot" meals. I think it was honest—that food is relatively unimportant to her and that she can take it or leave it, rather than that she was brainwashed by Weight Watchers—but it landed in really unhealthy place for me. I learned that if I was hungry, it was because I hadn't tried hard enough not to be.

My dad brought a different basket of associations with food. From his Jewish family, I learned that feeding someone was a gesture, an offering you made to someone *else*—someone you loved—not yourself. I learned that, like every indulgence or desire, feeding yourself was self-centered, greedy, and consequently shameful. If someone loved me, they would feed me, and if not, I should live on air.

I knew none of this was rational. These weren't even conscious thoughts until moments prior. But now, feeling on the precipice of becoming a kind of mother myself, I wanted to let go of this dysfunctional relationship with food. I decided to use these weeks of hormones and hibernation as an opportunity to be exquisitely attentive and responsive to my hunger.

Even with this newfound clarity, I had repressed these feelings so completely and for so long that it was difficult to even recognize how these learned behaviors were showing up. Because my first and reflexive response to hunger of all forms was to deny and dismiss it, I had to relearn its signals.

As I got better at not withholding, I realized that I still condemned hunger. I hated myself for being hungry. For having hunger that couldn't be entirely, once-and-for-all satisfied. It scared me to feed the hunger. Feeding hunger would make it grow. I would get bigger and bigger and no matter how much I fed it, the hunger would still be unsatisfied.

I cried and cried over this, and everything else. After ten days of twice-daily injections, I had more than one hundred times my normal level of estrogen. Driving down the freeway, again on my way to therapy, I nearly needed to pull over because I saw a car on the side of the road with a burst tire and was overcome by how much it must have hurt the *tire*.

Hormones raging, I felt *everything*, good and bad, subtle and intense. I tried peaceful, instrumental music to insulate myself from the world. I listened to the same meditative playlist on repeat and watched only Canadian dramas with long pans of pastoral scenes leading to predictable, pleasant endings. I took slow walks around the city with my hands in my pockets protecting my ovaries from ever catching a chill.

And I prayed. I'd never really prayed before and it didn't come easily, but I persevered. Every night, with my hands resting on my ovaries, I said "Please," not knowing or specifying to whom I was making the request, "help my eggs to grow strong and cold tolerant. Help my ovaries grow and release twenty-plus healthy, harvestable eggs." During the egg retrieval process, ovaries could swell to the size of grapefruits, and I could feel mine enlarging almost by the hour. My left ovary complained, hot and aching, and I couldn't help but think it was whining unnecessarily because the ultrasounds revealed that it only had six or seven eggs, compared to the dozen or so that the right ovary was housing without protest. Doctor Nguyen expected to retrieve sixteen to nineteen eggs. If all went well, eighty to ninety percent would survive the freezing process. So, I prayed, imagining each tiny seed of an egg growing into a healthy, well-developed sphere, glowing like salmon roe, filling my belly with the possibility of future children. Eyes closed, hands resting, prayers done, I thanked them—my ovaries—for their service.

I didn't know exactly when my egg retrieval would occur because it depended on a balance of hormone levels that were impossible to predict, but there was a rough 72-hour window for it. I could drop myself off but needed someone to pick me up because of the general anesthetic. My dad was the only family I had in town, the only one I'd told about my acid trip, the two dozen glowing orbs I'd seen, and what I thought they meant. He loved that I wanted to be a mom and changed his flight from San Francisco to DC to visit my sister and her daughter to a day later so he would be available for the full 72-hour window.

When the clinic called to say my levels were optimal and that I needed to report the next morning at eight AM, I felt more resigned than nervous. I'd done everything I could do, including feed myself. My doctors seemed competent, I had a ride home, and the procedure would be pretty straightforward. Despite all that, I was lonely. When I took my waiting room seat next to an adorable married couple—the husband doting, bringing her three different flavors of sparkling water—I felt that loneliness most acutely.

The procedure was easy and quick. I was waking up in a curtained section of a recovery room before I had any sense of being knocked out. Before I was fully conscious, hope welled that I had produced a healthy sixteen eggs, maybe nineteen, the upper end of what the doctor thought. When I asked the nurse how many they'd retrieved, she said, "Twenty-three."

I was sure she was talking to a woman on the other side of the curtain.

"Ma'am? Did you hear? They retrieved twenty-three. Froze twenty-one."

"Sorry. You must have me confused with someone else." I felt so much envy for the woman with those numbers.

"Nope. I double-checked just a minute ago. They successfully froze twenty-one eggs."

Gobsmacked and uncomprehending, "You mean me?" I pointed to my face like it was photo ID. "Anne Kiehl Friedman?"

I had seen twenty-three orbs glowing in my belly on acid. I needed twenty for the money-back guarantee. I had prayed for twenty, plus one for a margin of error.

I was so disbelieving, so awe-struck by the numerical specificity of my vision, not to mention my *luck*. I was also probably more than a little confused by the anesthesia drugs, so I asked her to confirm yet again, this time with my birthdate.

It didn't matter if I was making up symbols and meaning, imagining and manufacturing signs from a high power. I had twenty-one frozen eggs and a money-back guarantee! These were incontrovertible facts.

The nurse brought my dad back and he was just as shocked. "That was more than you were hoping for! Aren't you quite the ovary-achiever!" I caught the pun but wasn't thinking quickly enough to return one.

In the car he asked whether they undercounted on the ultrasound, whether this was unusual, whether I thought my vision was coincidence or... something else?

I didn't know what to think. I had a hard time believing in premonition and no trouble at all believing in coincidence. Regardless, I told him that I felt like I'd had angels or a fairy godmother or just fucking ridiculously good luck through this process. The more I gave up trying to control things, the more I listened to the nudges and whispers of my sapphire essence, the luckier I seemed to get.

After my dad dropped me off, I settled into bed, fragile but victorious. One last time, I put my hands over my ovaries and prayed, thanking them for their eggscellent service. I felt open, intuitive, and grateful. Like maybe life wasn't happening *to* me, but *for* me.

This was the attitude I would take on the birthday trip to Morocco with Adelynn the following month, and maybe much, much longer.

Chapter 27
Umbrella

Sahara Desert, Morocco
April 2018
Substances ingested: mint tea, bad cookies, a little hash

Adelynn's birthday was exactly a week after mine, we both had time off, and had loved spending our sixtieth (30+30=60) together in London and Barcelona, so we decided to continue our birthday tradition of celebrating birthdays divisible by five in a foreign country. We decided on Morocco. I wanted to return to Essaouira for the lobster, and Adelynn wanted to ride camels in the desert. We agreed on an itinerary then divided the labor: she planned the transportation and restaurants; I booked the accommodations and any special sites. While planning our two-week sojourn, I was nervous about being without pot because travel always kicked up my residual, Lyme-induced fears of getting sick in a foreign country and not having cannabis to attenuate the symptoms. In my ideal world, I'd always have it available for the few days when a perfect storm hit: hormones from my menstrual cycle combining with usually latent Lyme symptoms to create a typhoon of nausea, migraine, cramping, and general distress. I packed extra Advil, some prescription anti-nausea medication, and herbal anti-anxiety supplements instead of even considering smuggling illegal drugs. As long as this wasn't a perfect storm month, I'd be fine.

Essaouira was all about eating lobster at a beachfront grill—planned for lunch on the next day—and Adelynn was aggressively onboard. "We're gonna eat so much seafood we'll leave with an allergy," she said, the two of us sealing the commitment with a high five. In the meantime, we strolled arm-in-arm until we stumbled upon a line of cannons—certainly unused in any recent era but probably not purely decorative either. We climbed aboard, taking pictures of each other, until I fell off and skinned my knee, the exact moment of "Oh shit!" memorialized on Adelynn's phone.

We walked along the town wall browsing the selections of rugs, painted canvases, woven bowls, and mounded spices that set the white walls awash in color. We stopped to watch kids play soccer as bellicose seagulls dropped fish bones scavenged off nearby boats and dive-bombed the trays of cookies men carried around for sale in the town square.

We ignored the men when they called offering us cookies that, at a glance, looked dry and unappetizing, until a familiar sound caught my attention.

"Did you say 'hashish'?" I asked, whipping around, making a beeline for the young man wearing an old Barca jersey and cigarette-girl tray.

"Shhhhhhh! Ask for your illegal drugs more quietly!" Adelynn said, wisely, while laughing at my exuberance. She might have had some big job that made her vulnerable to random drug testing and immediate dismissal if caught with anything illegal in her system, but we had been best friends for nearly twenty years and—other than not liking the smell—she thought of my vice as no different from her own. She happened to like red wine, not in excess, never to disability, and saw my use of pot as no more morally suspect, though admittedly I smoked a lot more than she drank. She had a job that required, not just in the rulebooks but because of real-life possibilities and consequences, that she not be high (or drunk, or even away from her phone) or else she risked creating problems. As long as it didn't endanger me, her, her job, or anything else that mattered, she was ok with my indulgence in whatever I wanted, on my birthday especially.

"Oh yes. You want 'ashisha'?" On the wooden tray suspended from his neck, crumbly white and brown cookies looked like the leftovers from a cheap buffet. "Here are space cakes," he said, using the near-universal term for baked goods with cannabis in them, and pointed to what looked like grainy blocks of dark chocolate fudge on the side of his tray. Again, I felt my good luck. My sober holiday didn't have to be quite so sober after all. I didn't have to worry about what I'd do if my Lyme randomly flared up, causing the pain and nausea for which pot was the best cure. I would have an easy, known solution if I suddenly felt anxious. Having a bit of a space cake in my literal back pocket would help keep me grounded.

We negotiated a price, and by that I mean I paid him what he asked. I have never been a good negotiator when it comes to black market purchases, mainly because I want them to be over as quickly as possible. He gave me a gram of hash, the size of a pencil eraser but dark and tar-like and rolled up in a ball of tinfoil and deposited into a plastic bag filled with two space cakes and half a dozen regular cookies. The hash was for smoking and would require a pipe, so I'd have to solve that problem at some point.

The next day, I ate a pinch off one of the space cakes about forty-five minutes before heading to the seafood huts for my birthday lunch figuring the munchies would hit just in time to make the lobster I'd been looking forward to for *years* that much more memorable. My timing was perfect.

Adelynn stood behind me as I pointed to a ridiculous array of seafood, only intervening once to say "No, the big one," when I tried to select a petite lobster. Straight off the grill, one by one, they served us our selection of fish, shellfish, and mollusks, delivering each plate steaming and piled with wedges of fresh lemon. We ate until our hands and faces were red, whether from the sun or impending allergy was unclear, then stumbled back home, fully sated.

"We did it. I never want to eat another piece of fish ever again." Adelynn said. We fist-bumped and then promptly passed out, sleeping off our histamine reactions.

***

For the Sahara Desert portion of the trip Adelynn had hired a professional tour company that came with a combination guide-driver. We had a five-hour ride ahead of us. Adelynn listened to podcasts while I stared out the car window. I pinched off another bit of space cake figuring it would make the passing scenery that much more entrancing. I had read enough to know that the desert was more than just enormous breathtaking sweeps of sand dunes but still, I was shocked by the sporadic explosions of plant and animal life. I had thought an "oasis" was synonymous with "mirage," something hallucinated when in the grips of dehydration. As it turns out, underground rivers actually *do* rise to the surface, producing luscious date palms and apricot trees. Garnet-red pomegranates sprouted from crimson flowers, even magenta and violet bougainvillea climbed the plastered walls of the old casbahs that opened their fortified doors to offer mint tea and guided tours.

Rising from the side of a green, forested foothill of the Rif Mountains was the city of Chefchaoen. With all of its buildings painted variations on the same shade of aqua, it was entirely obvious why it was called The Blue Pearl. Adelynn wanted to come for its postcard-perfect beauty, and I was excited about that too. But it hadn't escaped my notice in our itinerary research that this photogenic town was known—worldwide—for its kief.

Kief is a powder-like substance composed of trichomes, the hair-like fibers that grow on cannabis flowers and contain the highest levels of tetrahydrocannabinol (THC). When kief is heated and pressurized it becomes hashish, or hash, a wax or tar-like substance ideal for smoking in a pipe. Because hash is so concentrated, the bowls of hash pipes are much smaller than tobacco or cannabis pipes.

I hadn't really known this until I saw a hash pipe poking out of a miscellaneous box of tchotchkes. The box was sitting in front of a small blue shop on the narrow, hilly, unbelievably charming street that Adelynn and I had happened upon in our wanders through Chefchaoen. I knew, instinctively, what it was. Nearly a foot long with threads of silver, copper, and brass wound together, it tapered to a delicate opening and stretched out of its box toward me. Later, when I raised it to my lips, it felt like playing a flute.

The proprietor said he wanted the Dirham equivalent of three dollars, and I felt bad that he was undercharging.

Late that night, after a hearty dinner of pastilla and tagine, Adelynn retired to bed while I sat out on the balcony to smoke a bowl. My body felt full, which was always a trigger for wanting to get high, and my mind had started to spin. I was worried about all the emails accumulating in my inbox, the mail piling up at home, whether I'd paid the property tax installment bill that had arrived before I left.

I'd never smoked pure hash before and was nervous but excited to try it. I unwrapped the aluminum foil surrounding the pea-sized ball and pinched off barely more than a fingernail's worth of the sticky brown substance. I placed it in the bowl of the pipe with reverence. With a match, sucking the flame toward the hash until the piece I'd pinched off glowed like an ember, I breathed in slowly—four, five, six seconds—and held it in my lungs. Even on my first exhale, as I slowly released it through my nostrils, the anxious chatter in my mind started to recede. My internal monologue slowed and became more positive. Often, without the sedative and meditative effects of being stoned, my mind felt like a radio caught between frequencies that broadcasted alarming news, self-doubt, the occasional pop song, my to-do list, criticism of past and future conversations, all at the same time. But two tokes of this hash from this pipe on this balcony, and my mind became still and clear. Like a blue pearl.

Thinking that phrase, "blue pearl," I remembered it from a different context. In a study comparing brain scans of Tibetan monks while meditating to those of novice meditators, the neophytes showed activity all over the brain: shifting waves of red, orange, and yellow. The monks' scans showed minimal activity in all but the pineal gland, right at the center of the brain, which glowed steadily like a "blue pearl." There seemed nothing coincidental in the phrase coming back to me while I sat looking out over this nighttime "Blue Pearl" of a city, *renowned* for its kief. The hash gave me a glimpse of what those monks might have felt: equanimity, expansiveness, timelessness. I was in this place and in this moment, aware, peaceful, and reverent. Simply put, it felt like enlightenment.

So, of course, I tried to hold on and, of course, the force with which I grasped increased the speed at which it slipped away. I tried to recapture it with another toke, and succeeded, temporarily. As long as I didn't reach for it, pieces (peace) floated back to me, and I felt contented again. I finished the hash left in the pipe, went inside, and answered the emails I'd been putting off for weeks and months in a couple of hours. Then I slept soundly until the braying of donkeys called me into the next day.

***

I decided to let go of, once and for all, as best I could, my inner conflict around smoking pot. Everyone has a vice, a weakness, a coping mechanism, a chosen outlet, a crutch. Just as some people chose alcohol, others excessive caffeine and exercise, pot was my favorite mood-altering device—no better and no worse than anyone else's. If it ever hurt me or others, I would re-evaluate immediately. But until then: no harm, no foul.

Also, if my shrink and straightest of straight-edge best friend didn't judge me for it, why should I continue to condemn myself?

Adelynn and I spent thirteen days together in each other's constant company. We laughed, developed inside jokes about my inability to correctly identify animal noises (Me: "Wow, those are loud birds." Adelynn: "Those are camels. Did you graduate from kindergarten?"), talked about everything, and rested our heads on each other's shoulders when we fell asleep during long van rides. When she and I were on a tour of Ouarzazate, the "Hollywood of Morocco," everyone assumed we were not-so-closeted lesbians because while we claimed to be friends, we were the only couple walking around holding hands, laughing constantly, completely at ease in each other's company. Adelynn never made me feel undeserving of her love and respect. Never had she made me work for her appreciation and never had she withheld it based on whim or desire for control over me. She loved me when I was irritable, ornery, impatient, and unreasonable. She loved me when I was insecure, emotional, anxious, depressed, and falling apart. Since I was *eighteen*, she had loved me for me, She loved who I was when I wasn't even trying and never made me feel like I owed her anything for it.

Our last night, at a hotel in Casablanca, I marveled over the love I'd found in Morocco. It wasn't romantic, it wasn't new, but it was real and deep. This incredible friend held space for me in the world, space in which I could be wholly myself. She laughed at me when I cried hugging her goodbye before my early morning flight. I'd spent a significant portion of the night scrubbing any trace of hash from the pipe so I could bring it home with me.

"Such a crier!" she teased, giving me a hug. "Text me when you land and let me know how all the argan oil fared in transit," she said, referencing the souvenir bottles we bought before realizing the seals were less than tight.

"I love you." I said, meaning it, and gave her tight squeeze.

Chapter 28

Don't Hurt Yourself

Big Island, Hawaii
September 2018
Substances ingested: coconut water, sunlight, podcasts, an unknown but potent amount of LSD

The argan oil not only leaked, but it turned rancid in transport. It stained a pair of purple-tasseled suede loafers I'd hoped to wear as a signature statement piece. The leather dress I bought in Fez would have to suffice.

Six months after my last acid trip—the one that had revealed the truth that bodies were just disguises for souls and my belly fully of salmon roe—I managed to eke out a week of vacation alone on the Big Island. I had acted on the wisdom received from my previous journeys (with 21 frozen eggs to prove it). I'd read Ayelet Waldman's memoir about micro-dosing LSD and wanted to try it. When my Acid Fairy heard I was interested in micro-dosing but I didn't have enough left to supply me for a month, I once again found a promising envelope—ivory this time, no name—slipped into my hand. No exchange of money or request for compensation; simply the unwavering confidence that I would pay the favor forward.

Inside the envelope, in a tiny plastic bag, was a slip of heavy-weight paper roughly 1/8 the size of a stamp, divided into quarters by perpendicular lines. Unlike the first acid I received, neither the squares nor the whole stamp came with a labeled dosage. I knew I could buy acid testing strips on the internet to quantify the LSD doses, but testing would require waiting. Besides, I trusted the source and any acid I tested could no longer be used so I decided to make some educated guesses.

Based on my last trip, some eyeballing of the little grid, and gut feeling, I estimated that I was taking between 35 mcg and 55 mcg. With that range, I expected light, perhaps even imperceptible effects like those Waldman reported—an amount that might lift my mood but not much more. I didn't expect to feel it. There was an outside and extremely unlikely chance of taking 110 mcg at most, but even then I knew I'd be alright.

With a towel and a book, my hat, and sunglasses, I headed to the beach where I found myself a spot not far from the location of my spontaneous orgasm, close to a couple of adults dozing in beach chairs under umbrellas while a handful of kids played in the low surf. The stretch of sand I'd chosen offered half-sun and half-shade, thanks to a low-growing tree I couldn't name sprouting spongey green leaves and white blossoms that look like sun-bleached coral. I settled onto my stomach, situated perfectly to feel the sun massage my back but with my head in the shade. I sighed. I wiggled my legs apart to allow the sun to kiss the insides of my thighs and sighed again. My feet dug into warm sand, the cleft between each toe became an erogenous zone as sensitive as the inner curve of the elbow—and I moaned quietly. It felt so good that I dug my hands into the sand to feel the same sensation between my fingers. Starfished, face-down on my towel, massaging the sand, I continued moaning quietly until I realized how weird this was. The beach was full. There were children in the surf. I needed to contain my moaning.

This was my first warning that the "micro-dose" was hitting me harder than planned.

I pushed myself up on my forearms and turned onto my back. Above my face, tight white flowers burst forth from the limb of a tree and glistened as if embellished in crystals. Before me the ocean sparkled, adorned with frothy white curls that chased the kids now playing tag with the edge of the water. I wanted to run into the ocean, feel it on my body, and swim to the horizon. Water was like sand only better! It caressed every bit of you, thoroughly, 360 degrees, whereas sand could only manage that if you rolled in it. If you did that, then you'd have sand in all your bits whereas water washed itself away when you were done. Swimming wasn't weird at all. I could swim forever!

With the words "I could swim forever," my rational, self-protective brain sounded a warning bell. I heard my mom's voice, sternly delivering the profound truth: Never be reckless with or around the ocean.

Understanding that I couldn't be safe with the ocean just then, I decided I ought to head back to the house.

***

Next to the driveway, standing in the same place she's been since my mom planted her in honor of my niece's birth, was the most gorgeous palm tree I'd ever seen. She was taller than me when you included her fronds, but her trunk ended just about eye-height. And there, she had produced two of the world's most perfect coconuts. Unblemished, symmetrical, *begging* to be touched, the two spheres gave the palm tree quite an impressive rack. I reached to stroke the one on the left—without permission—but I drew back quickly when a movement caught my eye.

On a frond stretching from the left side of the tree, there was a tiny dinosaur! No more than eight inches from the tip of his nose to the tip of his tail, his body was the color of a green apple except where grey skin peeled from his chin. It made him look rugged. I looked more closely, and he puffed his neck, displaying a drum of stretched skin—like he'd swallowed a two-inch disc—dusty red with bright orange spots, utterly striking against the rest of his green.

"Why, sir," I asked coquettishly. "Are you flirting with me?"

His neck puffed wider, his head bobbing as if in confirmation.

"Oh, really! You are mighty forward," I laughed, feeling a little surprised when he didn't answer in words. Seeing a movement in my peripheral vision, I became aware that these palms were teeming with life. Fauna was tucked into the canvas-like covers of furled baby fronds and into the swaying lengths of green. I relaxed my eyes to take in more and noticed another pair of eyes staring back from the same palm frond as my seductive little friend. When something in my central vision moved, I found a third gecko directly at eye-level, no more than a foot from my face.

I felt compelled to match my breathing to the one in front of me and I discovered that he was scared, but I told him he had nothing to fear from me. We made eye contact and I asked, in my mind this time, for permission to devour him with my eyes. He stayed, implying his consent, his fear seeming to shift toward appreciation at being appreciated.

Life was everywhere I looked! A red bird flitted from a kiawe bush in the distance, investigated the palm, and decided not to land. Mosquitoes bit at me. A couple of ants crawled across my sandaled feet.

How could I have ever thought I was alone?

I could see, but even more, I could *hear* the life that was everywhere. Even the sand talked. It whispered when moved by the wind and chattered like a bowl of Rice Krispies when it engaged with waves. This far from the ocean, I couldn't tell exactly who was talking: the water, rocks, shells, or a combination? But as I focused, the noise grew louder, and I understood. This was not one thing talking. This was a *conversation*. Fronds, flies and mosquitoes, finches, small translucent crabs that skittered—hunting and pecking through the sand—all of them *talking* to each other. Below any register I could hear, an unknown microbial substance that wove a network between all the roots underground had its own song.

The next realization was inescapable and obvious:

I had never been alone. Never. Not for an instant. Not for a fraction of an instant. Not when I was born, not when I eventually die, not for a millisecond in between. How silly. How foolish to ever have believed in the *delusion* of "aloneness." There was no such thing. It was only a matter of distance and identification. I might be the only human for miles (I wasn't), but I would never be the only living being. If I wanted company, all I had to do was not be so species-specific about it.

A brushing at my shoulder startled me from my reverie. I jumped. I turned and looked. I laughed when I realized it was just the wind brushing a frond against me. It had tickled. Like a caress from a playful lover. And yet, I had jumped away at the touch. Reflexively.

I considered that: "I jumped away from a caress. Reflexively."

A wave of sadness washed over me. How many opportunities for love and physical touch had I shied away from, reflexively? Why had I recoiled from the touch of a palm? My brain—my busy, busy brain—populated answers: There could've been something gross or sticky or poisonous on the frond. Because it was not clean. Because this tree was wild and dangerous.

I was rocked by this series of revelations, but they only came faster. I realized I was scared of nature. I considered myself something apart from it. Nature was wild and abundant, an indomitable force always eventually victorious. It was so powerful it was scary.

All this time staring at the tree, and I had not noticed my shadow. The noonday sun distorted my proportions casting a shadow that looked like a rotisserie chicken. I knew it wasn't accurate but also that it couldn't distort what wasn't there. I physically poked at the fat rolls causing the edges my shadow to bulge.

Still poking myself, pushing on my love handles to see if I could lean my outline, I realized: I had the same relationship with nature as I had with my body. It scared me. I did not want my body to be wild, powerful, and abundant. I wanted it to be manicured, domesticated, constrained.

Or did I? Was it me or the patriarchy that told me I wanted that?

Looking at the palm again, I knew the answer. What made the tree breathtakingly beautiful was its wildness, its unkemptness, its vitality. Every part of this tree was alive and thriving, sexy and magnetic, because it was *not* starved of nutrients. When this tree thrived, so did the beings in its ecosystem; it was a source of protection, nourishment, and abundance for all connected to it. At that moment, I committed to thriving by feeding myself, allowing abundance and vitality in my body-sized corner of the planet that was an ecosystem in itself.

Wanting to celebrate my commitment, I stepped deliberately in line with the tips of the frond from which I'd just recoiled and leaned into its touch. This time, I giggled. I shimmied into the tickle of it, feeling it like it was Nature's hand, the sensation sending a gratifying shiver down my back. It would stand there, ready and willing to play with me as long as I wanted. It struck me again: I was never, ever, alone. One of my greatest fears—dying alone—would never, could never, happen.

I was born. Every day that I had absorbed the sun's light, the Earth's produce, the joy of another's company—all of that was a gift for me to delight in. All of it was an expression of my worthiness. All of it was love made manifest, delivered by the Universe for my consumption. No other human was nearby to appreciate the palm, the gecko, or the sun, and yet, they still stood, shone, and preened. The show was there for me if only I stopped to look.

I was awed into stillness. I could have stood forever appreciating the beauty of each creature, each phenomenon, each sensation as it passed through my observation, but my shoulders told me I was getting sunburned.

***

I returned to the house and turned on Beyoncé's *Lemonade: The Album*. Doors open to the lanai, I danced in the living room, singing along with complete abandon and minimal skill. The lyric from "Hold Up" about her feeling "worthless" stopped me dead in my tracks. Mouth agape, I pondered an arresting reality:

Beyoncé—the world's most perfect, productive, smooth-thighed among us—felt badly about herself? Even her unequaled level of success, beauty, and public adoration was not enough to insulate her from feeling worthless? Then what was the fucking point of trying!

Rage shot through me as the realization hit: her perfection didn't keep her from getting cheated on. "Perfection" was bullshit and even if a facsimile of it did exist—tens across every relevant category—it was *still* no defense against the things that hurt worst in life. No amount of perfection could protect me from heartbreak, betrayal, self-doubt, grief, loss, death...

The realizations were maddening and liberating at the same time. I felt a lifetime's worth of mistaken beliefs about what it takes to be loved dissolve in moment. Bouncing up and down on my tippy toes, shaking my arms out like a boxer before a fight, I felt the bamboo floors flex and give beneath my feet.

I could be manicured, pruned, starved, eerily symmetrical—everything society demanded—and it wouldn't guarantee what I truly wanted. I wanted to be seen and loved, as a whole being, inclusive of idiosyncrasies and imperfections. If I kept chasing the pipe dream of perfection, erasing everything about me that was unique and unpalatable to society, no one would ever see and appreciate the real me because I never let her out.

Nope. Not anymore.

I'd been staying away from the glass doors to the lanai because I'd noticed that they reflected my jiggling thighs, but with defiance coursing through me I parked myself directly in front of them, swinging my thigh wings with vigor. Fuck Jay Z. Fuck society. FUCK perfection!

In "i ain't sorry," she sang like an angry goddess and I screamed, hands flailing, flipping off every beauty standard, jumping up and down in a one-person mosh-pit.

The phrase "up and out," Andi's mantra in Costa Rica, occurred to me. I heard Andi's voice, "Let the emotions come, feel them, let them go, and don't grab ahold of them after they're out." I nodded, understanding and agreeing with her invisible voice.

Up and out. Singing, screaming, and dancing jostled my long-stored emotional baggage. Ancient sorrows, vintage regrets, primordial wounds surfaced, and I let them go with sound and movement. I thought I was moist from all the sweating, but I realized I was crying too.

I moved toward the bathroom feeling sick, thinking I was nauseated from all the jumping and bouncing. As I got farther from the speaker and the noise didn't get quieter, I realized it was coming from me.

Full, body-wracking sobs issued out of me.

Up and out. Let it all out.

I knelt in front of the toilet, convulsed over it, uncertain whether I would vomit or just cry.

When I was a child, we had a pet red-tailed Boa Constrictor that could unhook its jaw to swallow prey whole.

I hadn't thought about him in decades until I heard my jaw pop, unhinging itself to allow grief to flow unimpeded. The feeling was acute misery, as if generations of grief had concentrated themselves into the howls unleashed by my throat, my tongue giving voice to thousands of years of silenced cries.

I felt out of control. I *was* out of control. Out of habit, I began to stifle myself. I started to hold my breath, to suppress the emotions, to dig my fingernails into my palms.

But then I remembered the shrink I saw after college who noticed that I would hold my breath in times of intense emotion. His profound advice? To keep breathing.

I'd told him that I was afraid I'd cry.

I was afraid that if I started crying, that I'd never stop crying, that I'd waste all my expensive time with him and be worse off than when I started. I was afraid that ancient rivers of sadness—my own, my ancestors, humanity's, I didn't know—would pull me away into an ocean of misery from which I would never emerge.

But it occurred to me while I was kneeling on the fuzzy bath mat striped with baby-shower pastels and browns—who the fuck chose this color scheme?—that it was not reasonable to worry about crying forever. How long can someone cry without needing to eat? Or sleep? Or check email? It can't last *forever*. What if I gave myself permission to feel it all, now?

I decided to try.

My sobbing became a little louder, uglier, more attention-seeking. I had never allowed myself to make these sounds. My body was tentatively testing its limits, used to being shut down and not wanting to commit to any sound or behavior if I was going to take it away. Instead of shutting down, I opened my mouth even wider to see how ugly my ugly cry could get. I wasn't looking in the mirror but the amount of tears, snot, and saliva hitting the bathmat told me I wasn't holding back.

I sobbed and sobbed. I sobbed for an eternity, waves of emotion coming up and out. Misery, grief, loss, fear, feelings I couldn't identify flowed through me so quickly I couldn't name them or their sources. At some point, it felt so awful that it tipped over into feeling a little bit good. Cathartic.

And then, right in the middle of a particularly operatic sob, I had the urge to pee.

Sitting on the toilet, I realized I couldn't cry violently and urinate at the same time. My body wouldn't let me. It couldn't contract and release simultaneously. Letting it decide which was more important, the sobs subsided, and I peed for a solid forty-five seconds. By the time I'd finished, I no longer felt the urge to cry.

Huh. Up and out only took like ... eight minutes? It occurred to me that if I would have allowed myself to cry in front of that shrink when I was twenty-three, we probably would have had most of the hour left afterwards. Maybe, I realized, sitting contentedly, tiredly, on the toilet, my depths of grief weren't quite as unplumbable as I had imagined.

Looking in the mirror and straightening my top where all the sobbing had caused me to pop a nipple, I returned to Beyoncé with my shoulders back and lowered.

***

Sooner than seemed possible, but also with the feeling that lifetimes had passed, the sun set. In a lounge chair on the patio with a large cup of water by my side, I watched it reverently. The palm trees rustled against themselves in the gentle wind, reminding me of their inherent peace. If I needed a break from all the feelings, I could let myself be hypnotized by their serenity. But I didn't. I wanted to take it all in. Watching the Myna birds launch themselves from the branches of a plumeria tree, aiming to land on the disappearing edge of the pool, I noticed that they kept missing. I realized flying is more like swimming than it is walking, in that currents at least partially determine destination. Feeling the final rays of sun against my exposed body, I wondered what it would feel like to be a bird. As soon as I wondered, my skin answered with a sensation from lifetimes ago. It knew. I shivered in pleasure as the breeze ruffled my hair follicles, knowing what it felt like when I had quills there instead.

The moment the top edge of the sun touched the horizon, the tradewinds kicked up and I felt enough of a chill to want to sit in the hot tub. Still wearing the same mismatched bikini from the morning, I tied a sarong around my chest and headed to the jacuzzi. Dropping the towel by the edge and lowering myself in, I held my sarong higher and higher to keep it out of the water, until I shed it and my bikini top in one fluid motion. It felt rebellious and delightful to be topless under stars.

I knew I was coming down from my unintendedly high high, but I didn't know where the ground was in terms of sobriety. Moments, minutes, went by when I thought I was back to "normal" again. I'd start planning my to do list, remembering emails I needed to send and texts requiring response, until right in the middle of reciting the list I burst into tears because of how *good* the water felt on the back of my knees.

One way I could tell that my high was ebbing was that my internal monologue started to get more anxious. Using my fingertips to paint abstract shapes on top of the water, I began to worry if I'd made "enough" of this trip. I hadn't come into it with an agenda. I wasn't looking for a quick fix or essential wisdom. I just wanted my mind to work a little bit better. Instead of being reverent and disciplined, I sang and danced and sobbed and puked, as if psychedelics weren't a sacrament.

Was that okay?

"Who are you asking?" Jaramie's voice, gentle and speaking on behalf of the Universe, popped into my head.

"I don't know who I'm asking." I said, in my thoughts. "You? Whomever you represent? God, the Universe, a higher power...that sort of thing?" I answered, trailing off and wondering briefly how I was any different from the people I had always judged as crazy for believing that God was talking to them.

"What's the question again?" Jaramie interrupted my wondering. She sounded distracted.

"Did I do enough?" I asked. "Was I productive enough? Are you proud of me?" I said, sounding needy even to my own ear.

"Huh?" I could hear the muffled sounds of conversation behind her, like she covered her end of the phone with a hand while consulting a group of people with her in the room. "We don't understand your question," she said, reporting back and sounding bored.

Something about her tone imparted the understanding that she was willing to sit here with me and answer all the questions I wanted, but that my obsession with "productivity," being "enough," other people's approval, all of it, was nonsensical to her and the voices with whom she consulted. They simply didn't understand my angst.

I realized that while I could try to explain it, their confusion was an answer in itself. They didn't understand the question because they didn't care about it. They, whoever "they" were, didn't care about productivity. "Productivity" was—literally—meaningless. There was no word for it in the language of souls.

I heard all this like I was eavesdropping on a debate in which the participants agreed. I couldn't make out any individual voices, but they seemed to speak in consensus like a hive mind. They agreed that "doingness" was the closest translation of "productivity" in soul language—some people expended more energy than others on doing, making them high on the "doingness" scale—but it was a morally-neutral scale. Those high in doingness were no better than those low in doingness.

Now, Jaramie's voice returned clearly and with a message. "You have to be careful with your doingness. Doing can be harmful. Think of all the destruction that has taken place because of the need to do." I saw mountains beheaded for their coal, underground rivers fracked for natural gas, Arctic plains drilled for oil reserves. Environmental devastation was a result of our obsession with productivity. "There's nothing wrong with not doing," she said. It was the first time I considered the idea, but it grew on me quickly. I liked the idea of *not* doing.

She didn't say anything, but I could tell I was starting to get it.

I was not being graded, cosmically, on my ability to do more, or do anything. Joy, self-love, healing, living authentically, accepting myself, recognizing my unique incarnation of the divine and all its holy gifts... that was all I was "supposed" to do with my life. That was all the eternal wanted from me. We are loved. We are love. We are incarnations of divine love encased in funny little human suits and the only thing we're "supposed" to do in this human lifetime is to learn to love ourselves as such.

The jacuzzi water splashed around my shoulders making my head weightless as I dunked under, no longer caring about keeping my hair dry. I giggled at the joy of my own liberation. A shooting star in the periphery of my vision felt like confirmation that I was on the right track. I thought about taking it as a sign that I should get out of the hot tub and go to sleep, but I could tell that the revelation was unfinished.

There was something else the Universe wanted me to understand. I could feel the pinched silence of a crowd waiting in suspense, but I didn't hear anything. No words, no hive-mind murmuring, no voices, familiar or otherwise.

Then, as if she were reading slowly from a textbook, giving me time to take notes or memorize it, Jaramie said: "Love is predicated on knowledge. You cannot love that which you don't know." Then, in answer to questions I didn't know I was asking: "All that you seek to heal can be healed."

Listening, I felt a craving emerge. As physical as hunger after days of fasting, I felt myself overcome by need; I yearned to be healed. Desperately.

Dropping to my knees at the deepest point of the hot tub, water up to my neck, hands together in prayer, I begged. Out loud, I begged of the Universe "Heal all that remains broken within me."

"Ha!" I heard her snort. "Not our job," she said with dismissive finality.

Politely, deferentially, not wanting to piss her off, I probed her answer. I was willing to accept that it was my job, but I didn't know how to do it.

"Self-love. All you need to be healed is to apply self-love. All wounds are directions for where love needs to be applied."

It was simple but impossible. How was I supposed to love what I found unlovable? "Try," she said.

Wow, she seemed impatient today. I guessed she was no longer charmed by my self-flagellation. Then I saw it: she never was. It was painful for her, all of them up there, to watch me hurt myself.

Out of respect and gratitude for their fortitude, I told myself to try.

No bullshitting; what did I hate about myself? My thighs. No one could love them. They were gelatinous, massive, and dimpled. Basically, just overfilled sausages with a three-to-one fat-to-meat ratio. Who could love that?

Okay, try. Who *could* love that?

I rested my head on the edge of the jacuzzi, allowing the rest of my body to float, hoping it would help me think.

What would someone have to know or believe about my thighs to love them? What would someone who loved them say about them?

It felt impossible to answer. I was tempted to give up, but I heard her voice, louder, and encouraging. "Try."

"I love my thighs." I said, but it sounded sarcastic.

Impatient with my shenanigans: "Pretend."

The word pretend clicked and I knew that the path forward was to *pretend* to be someone else. To *pretend* that I was in love with myself. I used to love tangling my fingers into my college boyfriend's back hair. I found it sexy, rugged, manly. It didn't matter that society told me to find it unattractive. There was nothing inherently worse about cellulite than back hair. It was conceivable that someone could find my cellulite soft, feminine, sexy.

It was possible, but oddly terrifying too. I couldn't say it out loud.

What if I came to accept all these shitty parts of myself, but I was the only one who could? What if I really was *not* okay? It would be way worse to love myself when I didn't deserve it than to not love myself when I did.

"What? How does that make *any* sense?" The Universe asked, then continued when it was clear I had no answer. "It's not just you. You're not special. You're just like everyone else: perfect. And perfectly lovable." A pause, then with slight annoyance, "Quit trying to convince yourself you're not."

I couldn't stop myself. I saw myself drilling pits into my internal landscape. What if I convinced myself I was loveable and then I didn't change something I needed to change? What if I convinced myself I was okay, walked around like there was nothing wrong with me, only to meet the love of my life and have him not like me because I wasn't skinny enough?

I didn't hear an answer, but it sounded like the geckos were laughing at me. The love of my life wouldn't love me because my thighs were too big? It was the first time I realized the absurdity of that worry. First of all, if the love of my life didn't love me, he was not the love of my life. Duh. Fucking tautological. Also, if his love were contingent on my body being modelesque, what would happen as we aged? If I got pregnant? If I got depressed, disabled, or developed a thyroid condition? I wanted a man who loved my body as it was and as it changed.

Again, my anxious mind had questions: But what if natural was not good enough? What if I wasn't good enough to attract the love of my life?

"You sound dumb." Again, not unkind, she was just pointing out facts. She could tell I was avoiding the real question.

"Ask for what you really want," she prodded me.

What did I want so badly I was afraid to ask for it? The answer came instantly.

"When will I meet the love of my life?" I asked.

"What do you mean?"

Frustrated that she didn't just say, "Tomorrow," or "Next week," or "You already have," and not understanding how the question could confound her, I said, "I mean, when will I meet my life partner, soulmate, the love of my life..." Running out of other words for it, I continued, "You totally know what I mean; why are you being difficult?" I didn't intend to be rude but thought she was being deliberately dense.

"Would it count if you met the world's most perfect partner the day before he died?" She asked, sounding sincere in her confusion.

"No, absolutely not!" Of course it didn't count if we only got a day together. It didn't count unless we stood the test of time.

"What if you had forty years together?"

"Yes." Then it would count, obviously.

"What about ten? Fifteen? Twenty-five? What number of years counts? Are you only counting the good years?" She lobbed the questions rapidly but not harshly.

"No, that wouldn't be fair—hard years can be growth years. Hard times are necessary for deepening the relationship and proving commitment." I responded, expecting praise for my reasonable and mature response.

"Okay, so if you met someone next year, had ten good years together, thirty bad years, and then divorced when you were in your 70s, that would count." She stated it like she was reviewing a checklist and found a solution that met all the requirements.

"Of course not! If it ended badly then the bad years don't count."

"So, if you two had the best day of your lives together after thirty years of crap and then he died on you instead of divorcing, that would count?"

"No! I don't know. I guess so? No. Maybe?" Now she had me legitimately confused.

"Also, why," she interrupted my thoughts, "is forty years with one person inherently better or more valuable than ten good years with four different partners in sequence?"

I didn't know. "Because a long time spent with one person is deeper than shorter relationships?" I thought. But even as I thought it, I wondered if it really mattered? "I don't know, I don't care, I just want someone to love me for the rest of my life, is that so wrong?" I whined.

"That's it!" She jumped on the end of my sentence and declared triumphantly: "That is what you want."

"I know! That's where we started! I said I wanted to find the love of my life!" She was making a distinction without a difference.

"No, I'm not." She said, responding to my internal comment. "You want somebody to love you for the rest of your life. You already have that."

"No," I refuted with exasperation, "I don't."

"Yes, you do."

"No, I don't!" I wailed inside my head, "If I had someone who loved me, I would be okay. I wouldn't feel shitty and anxious all the time. I wouldn't worry about not being good enough, or if I should be doing more, or if my thighs shouldn't touch! I wouldn't have to worry about any of that!!"

"You don't have to now," she said, matter-of-factly.

"Yes I do! I... have to." I trailed off because I didn't actually know why she was wrong. I definitely *felt* like I had to, but I couldn't come up with a single good reason why.

"You don't have to worry. You're fine. You're great. You're perfect. You're okay. You're loveable. You're all good, babe." She said it sincerely but quickly, like a bathroom pep talk from a best friend. "You want somebody to love you, now, and for the rest of your life..." she trailed off.

"Yes?" I affirmed, in suspense.

"You are the only one who can do that." She said it gently.

"Like, because no one else could love me forever?" I asked in panic.

"No," she hushed. "Because you are the only one who is here, now, and forever. You are your only constant company. You are the only one you can be certain won't be hit by a truck and die before you. You are the only one you can *always* depend on."

All I could hear, over and over again, was "only" and "one." It felt like she was doubling down on my loneliness rather than alleviating it. Mired in sadness, I thought, "I have to do all this work on my own, forever... I don't get a love of my life."

"I never said that," she said, correcting me. "You absolutely get a love of your life."

"I do?" My hopes soared.

"Yes."

"Who is it?" I had to ask.

"You."

"Me what?"

"You are the love of your life."

Was she fucking serious? The Universe was a bitch. A stone-cold fucking bitch for getting my hopes up like that only to crush them. I almost began to cry in disappointment, but I was too angry.

"Why are you disappointed?"

It was obvious and overwhelming. "Because I'm not enough!"

I felt her rolling her eyes. "If that's what you're committed to believing, then yes, this will be a miserable lifetime partnership." I felt like she was ready to tap out of the conversation and I really didn't want her to leave on this note.

"No, no, no! Okay, I'll try. I'm willing to try. I just don't understand. I don't know what I'm supposed to do."

"Be the love of your life. You are the love of your life. *Be* the love of your life."

It was all facts to her. And she was right. I was the only partner I would have for eternity. I needed to befriend myself. Love myself. I was the love of my life.

How do I learn to love myself?

With infinite patience this time, she said, "Try."

***

The water lapped at my ribs, moonlight kissing my nipples as I floated in the disappearing-edge hot tub overlooking the ocean.

I tested my voice.

"I love you."

I didn't believe it.

I heard her voice echo in my head, *Try. Pretend.* I tried again.

"I love you." This time, I imagined myself competing for an Oscar in the category of Declarations of Love to a Stranger. I conjured the image of the first time I saw my niece as a newborn wrapped in a hospital blanket, when I knew I would do anything for that tiny human:

"I love you."

That time, it sounded downright believable.

I tried it again, imagining my own face this time.

"I love you." My voice sounded rigid and tight, just a little too high to be trusted.

How could anyone love these thighs, and hips, and general fatness?

"Okay, I'll begin with the physical." I said out loud, accepting the challenge my internal resistance posed.

"I love the way my hands can grab your hips. I like being able to hold you. And take a hold of you." I put my hands on my hips, gripping them firmly but gently, and realized I was not lying. "I love that you're substantial." I noticed the way my flesh yielded to my hands, and instead of resenting its softness, I felt a slight electric thrill at the femininity and generosity of my frame. I reveled in my abundance.

I caught sight of my feet resting on the faux-lava wall that formed the barrier between hot tub and pool. "I love your ankles, narrow and sculpted." My gaze traveled to the hydrangea-shaped birthmark the size of a silver dollar and the color of milky coffee that a stranger once suggested I get removed but I secretly thought was pretty. "I love your birthmark." No secret anymore. "It is unique and immediately identifiable. Just like you."

I was on a roll now. "I love that you're strong, and powerful, and opinionated."

I gasped at that. I didn't realize I'd been withholding my own love for those qualities until I heard myself state otherwise. I had always thought my strength made me too difficult, too loud, too much. I had no idea how much I needed to hear that it made me *more* lovable, not less. Part of me issued perfunctory objections, but they didn't slow me down because "strong," "powerful," and "opinionated" were qualities I *wanted* in a life-partner.

Thinking about my natural hourglass figure and meaning it, I said, "I love the shape of your body."

"Which shape?" my snarky and disbelieving brain interrupted out of habit.

Out loud—indignant—I said, "I love *every* shape of your body. I love all the curves. Every single one, because you and your body are the same." When I love someone, I love the body they come in. I love their scars because each one tells a story of something they survived.

I said out loud, "I love your scars. Every single one of them, internal and external, physical, psychic, and spiritual." I was grateful for everything that got me here, even if it wasn't fun going through whatever battle had given me those scars to begin with. "I love your heart." I put both hands on my chest. Slowly, and with more feeling this time, "I love your heart so much. I love all the scars on it. I love the way the scars have made it stronger, and bigger, and more welcoming than ever."

I couldn't believe it, but I was making myself cry with my own love. For the first time, I felt like I was seeing myself for all that was *right* with me. I was looking on myself in love.

"I love the way you feel, your empathy, as well as your keen awareness, introspection, and self-knowledge." My tongue was loose now, not searching distant reaches for things to love but choosing from a feast of options before me. I didn't hesitate in elaborating, "I love that when you feel something, you take the time to inquire into what it is: why you're feeling it, what happened, what part of it is yours and what part was dropped into your lap that has nothing to do with you." I'd suffered plenty of people who didn't have awareness or take accountability for how their feelings showed up to affect unrelated situations, so this was worth appreciating.

"I love that you're witty, quick with word play and double entendres." I said. I'd love a life-partner who punned as well and readily as I did.

"I love… how loving, generous, and soft you are. That you are immediately and intuitively empathetic. That your first instinct is kindness. That you ALWAYS want to help."

I felt it now—warmth and pressure in my chest, like my heart was physically expanding to accommodate this swelling of love. My tummy felt loose, my legs weightless, and my head, like just another part of my body rather than a machine. I was breathing deeply, slowly, and evenly without even trying.

"I love your complexity," I said it to myself and heard its truth. If I was going to spend the rest of my life with someone, "easy" wasn't a selling point. I wanted subtlety, depth, challenge. My complexity allowed me to learn to love myself in new and deeper ways every day. This was a love affair that could grow and blossom over a lifetime.

"I love that there is always something new to learn about you. You are not the same person from day to day." I said this loudly, surprising myself with my volume, then laughing at myself with delight. I loved that I was unpredictable, even—and perhaps especially—to myself. It kept me interested. I wasn't "spoiled" or a "dilettante" or "unable to commit" or any of the other pejorative labels I'd often affixed to that set of characteristics. The truth was, I was constantly evolving, allowing myself to grow into and out of passions, jobs, and relationships.

My voice was quieter now. "I don't want you simpler or different." I paused for a moment out of habit, waiting to hear my brain interrupt with an objection or exception, but all I heard was the soft pulse of my heart. "I love you—completely and forever—and will spend the rest of my life learning how to do that better." It was a solemn promise.

Epilogue

The Long Way Around

January 22, 2023
Washington, DC
Substances ingested: none

I'm writing this from my bedroom in Washington, DC. Adelynn and I bought a house here. We moved in together during COVID when it only made sense to merge our bubbles, then realized we were happier that way than in separate one-bedroom condos a country apart. Now, I'm stepmom to her rescue hound and we take family walks in the park every weekend. We bicker about the right way to load a dishwasher, but I've mostly given up, never vocally conceding that she's right, but no longer arguing that I am. It's not the domestic bliss I imagined when I was little, but it's pretty great. I'm happy—not all the time, not as a rule—but as a general trend line. I have an emergency contact, best friend, travel partner, and am only half responsible for mortgage payments and home improvement costs. No complaints!

Professionally, I've never felt more purposeful, authentic, or fulfilled, though I still feel like I'm making it up as I go along. I'm just okay with that now. In October of 2020, I was ordained as a Reverend and Interfaith Minister. It took me—as you know—a long time to recognize and accept my spirituality. It took even longer to feel my calling to ministry. But it was the keystone that brought the rest of my work, and life, into alignment. My theological statement at ordination read, "I am Interfaith. Drawing from many faith traditions and especially the mystical threads within each, my spirituality sums up to what I found to be true even when I identified as an atheist: that we exist to love and serve one another in ways that are joyful to the soul. I believe all life is imbued with a sacred, infinite, interconnected God-force that is our source and destination."

My work is a combination of writing, ministry, social justice investing, and advocacy. It's not an option any of the vocational assessments I took in high school or college led me to think was possible, but it suits me. I can do most of my work in pajamas from bed. I never thought I could have a career I love *and* not have to wear pants.

I still don't know if I want kid(s). I think I don't. Bringing a child into the world feels like betting on the future I'm hoping exists, and I've never been much of a gambler. Climate change, pandemics, school shootings, social media bullying, not to mention sleep deprivation, hemorrhoids, and the possibility of giving birth to a sociopath are all strong reasons on my "cons" list. Besides, I'm going to be forty this year and I already feel tired. Do I want to be playing imaginary dinosaurs while going through menopause? I think I will be a mother someday. Right now, the leading contender for how is through adoption. Infants aren't my favorite, but I love teenagers. Adelynn and I have discussed, if we're still living together in a decade, maybe we'll consider adopting older kids who are about to age out of the foster system. If I fell in love with a man who wanted and was capable of having his own kids, I'd probably be really happy if I got knocked up in the next few years. But overall, it's not an area of life where I'm *trying* in any direction. I believe I can be happy any way it works out and I'm leaning toward being grateful that I likely missed my chance.

I'd love to find a romantic life partner, but I no longer believe that will make my life complete or that I need someone else to make me feel worthwhile.

I still use psychedelics once, maybe twice a year, only when I feel like I've had plenty of time to integrate my last experience, I'm mentally strong and physically nourished, and I make sacred space for the journey. I don't feel like I *need* it—I'm much more in touch with my intuition and spirituality and self on a daily basis now—and I feel like my journey with psychedelics would be complete if I never tripped again. But I'm insatiably curious and will never feel like I've learned everything that interests me. I can see myself dropping acid on my death bed. I still smoke pot and enjoy it.

From a public health perspective, psychedelics may be the most effective, cheap, and scalable treatment for some of society's most intractable diseases including addiction, depression, suicidality, PTSD, and many more. The way forward is pretty clear. We need to 1) decriminalize psychedelics in a way that honors *and compensates* Indigenous intellectual property; 2) fund research toward the therapeutic use of psychedelic substances; 3) reschedule all drugs based upon harm rather than propensity for recreational use, and 4) transform our retributive "justice" system into a restorative justice system based in equity. I commit myself and a meaningful percentage of any profits from this book toward that work. I have deep fears and reservations about the direction of the modern psychedelic movement that are not easily assuaged. In as much as psychedelics are tools for healing, spiritual growth, and ultimately for the benefit of humanity and all beings, I'm wildly supportive. To the degree to which they get commodified and coopted into systems that maintain the status quo which traumatizes and dehumanizes the majority of the world, I'm rabidly against greater access. There are a lot of really complicated questions and few simple answers, but my advice to anyone thinking about trying psychedelics is to be really, really careful. Take a small dose. Make sure you have people you trust who are competent to deal with the situation if you become panicked. Don't get sucked in by the hype that psychedelics will *cure* anything. The most important part of my psychedelic journey has been integration: the time between trips when I've practiced and operationalized what I learned while high. That I've done the work, on a daily basis, to change my experience of and relationship with reality is what has changed my life, not the drugs.

I wish I could say that I learned how to love myself and never ever struggled again with mean thoughts about my thighs or unnecessarily harsh self-talk, but that wouldn't be human. It's an example of my growth that I no longer desire or strive for perfection. I know it's going to be a lifelong effort and I'm up for it. What's fun and exciting is that I'm finally enjoying the process.

I wish the same, or better, for you.

You deserve it.

You were born.

You are loved.

Love,

Anne

Resources

General Information and Research

- UC Berkeley Center for the Science of Psychedelics
- Multidisciplinary Association for Psychedelic Study
- Johns Hopkins Center for Psychedelic & Consciousness Research

Support/Apps

- Zendo Project
- Fireside Project
- Field Trip: Psychedelic Guide
- MAPS' Psychedelic Integration List of Mental Health Support Practitioners by Location
- Tripsitter
- Third Wave
- DanceSafe
- The International Center for Ethnobotanical Education, Research, and Service

Books

- The Psychedelic Explorer's Guide: Safe, Therapeutic, and Sacred Journeys by James Fadiman

- The Way of the Psychonaut: Encyclopedia for Inner Journeys by Stanislav Grof

- Chasing the Scream: The First and Last Days of the War on Drugs by Johan Hari

- Spiritual Emergency: When Personal Transformation Becomes a Crisis by Stanislav and Christina Grof

- Psychedelic Integration: Psychotherapy for Non-Ordinary States of Consciousness by Marc Aixalà

Advocacy/Solidarity

- Indigenous Medicine Conservation Fund

- National Harm Reduction Coalition

- The Drug Policy Alliance

- The Chacruna Institute

Links available at https://www.annekiehlfriedman.com/

Risk Awareness and Harm Reduction
Use of Psychedelics

1. **<u>Psychedelics are NOT for everyone</u>.** Knowledgeable clinicians caution that some people should not take psychedelic plants or fungi, including people with a personal or family history of schizophrenia or bipolar disorder or who are taking certain medications.

2. **<u>If someone has a serious condition like major depression or PTSD, they would do well to get serious, professional help</u>** before using a psychedelic and may fare better in a clinical environment with more robust support. Some counselors and therapists are glad to work with a client before and after a psychedelic journey.

3. It's best to **<u>start with the minimum viable dose</u>**, using more only after you become familiar with the substance and experience.

4. **<u>Don't go solo</u>**. Have at least one trusted friend (called a sitter, guide, or facilitator) be with you, sober, during the entire journey. Commit in advance to honor that person's instructions if they tell you NOT to do something. Psychedelics can amplify the whole range of human emotions, including anxiety which can sometimes lead to panic. Having a sitter gives more comfort and support.

5. **<u>Reverence reduces risks</u>** and can help lead to positive outcomes. In cultures that have long used psychedelic substances, that use is approached with utmost respect.

6. Think in terms of: **<u>set, setting, safety, and support</u>**. Seek out trustworthy sources to understand these terms and develop a plan for your experience that includes appropriate guardrails. Remember that integrating and processing the psychedelic experience may take much longer than the experience itself (days, months, or even years). Don't operate heavy machinery or make irreversible decisions until the experience has settled.

Acknowledgements

First, my family, for giving me permission to tell my truth and telling me I didn't need to ask for it to begin with. Mom, when I think about my resilience, I know it came from you. You gave me the strength and "fuck you for doubting me" confidence that has fortified me through times softness didn't. Dad, thank you for the softness, joy at minutia, and endless punnery. I get my ability to laugh at myself from you and would be insufferable without it. Alison, you've led all my life, and most of the time shown me the path I want to follow. Being able to watch your example and benefit from the grooves you forged made my life immeasurably easier and I'm so grateful for it. You've grown our family to include some of my favorite members. Olivia, thank you for teaching me so much about the person I want to be. Mark and Charlie, thank you for loving and caring for the women who take care of the world.

Sandor Iron Rope and Roberto Lovato—thank you for your leadership, sacrifice, persistence, courage, moral clarity, and resounding voice of truth. "You shall know them by their solidarity;" that is my North Star.

Tatiana and Carlyn—friends but also editors, cheerleaders, and confidantes. I literally can't thank you enough for your support and engagement with this book; it went beyond the normal obligations of friendship and into midwifery. I owe you, forever.

Donna, Lizzie, Jolene, Marjorie, the Slutes—you loved me through it all. Helped me choose covers, read beta versions, and sent fantastic care packages. How could I have ever felt alone?

Everyone at the Dutchess reading (specifically Chid, Rodney, Asmeret and family)—you made me believe in my work and that it was worth putting out into the world. What an immeasurable gift.

Kat—wow, do I have a great eye for quality people. So glad I targeted you for friendship from day one. Thank you for guiding me and holding my hand. Not only are you funny and wonderful and trustworthy, you're also competent AF. If a stranger is reading this, it's probably because Kat's strategy, and the people she brought in to help me get this book out into the world, succeeded.

Seema and Amanda—best new old friends ever. Rarely are people so admirable and inspiring also so much fun. Thank you for everything wonderful you've brought into my life.

Marianne Wellman—I want to work with you forever. The way you're able to translate emotions, metaphors, and big ideas into coherent design that is both beautiful and deceptively simple is miraculous.

Linda Sivertsen, Margaret Riley King, Sophie Cudd, Greg Shaw—in different but enormous ways, your confidence in this book was what made it exist. You took me seriously as a writer and I used that as scaffolding. This might still be a forgotten doc on my computer if not for your encouragement.

Kimberly Chisholm, Susanna Sonnenberg, Cassidy Sacks, Carol Allen—you contributed to this book in ways too broad name. If my endorsement ever means anything, you've got it in spades and specifics!

Bob Jesse and Sandy Samberg, thank you for the content of the risk awareness and harm reduction advisory, as well as your continued and considered leadership. There are so many organizations and individuals in the psychedelics field I'd like to thank. I've learned and benefitted from the advocacy of MAPS, ICEERS, Chacruna, Fireside Project, Horizons, PSFC, RALLY, Land of Verse, NPA, PHEI, IMC, Decriminalize Nature, and nearly innumerable others. Robyn, Sage, Gen, Joe, Michael, Dick, David, Dan, Miriam, and so many others I'd like to name individually but I'm not sure they'd prefer that so I will instead say, if you think I should be thanking you: I agree!

If I forgot you, please blame a faulty memory rather than a lack of appreciation. As you know by this point, I've smoked a lot of pot.

Thank you for reading. I appreciate it deeply.

xoxo,

Anne

About the author

Anne Kiehl Friedman is a multifaceted scholar, author, and entrepreneur. Graduating with honors from Stanford University, she obtained her MBA from ESADE University in Spain, and was ordained as an Interfaith Minister and Reverend after attending seminary at the Berkeley Chaplaincy Institute. Anne's professional journey has been marked by innovation and advocacy. In 2022, Anne co-founded the Psychedelic Communications Hub, a pioneering initiative aimed at educating the public about the therapeutic potential and risks associated with psychedelic use. Anne is a passionate advocate for holistic well-being and spiritual growth. Her commitment to fostering understanding and empathy shines through in her work, making her a trusted voice in both academic and public spheres. This is her first book.

If you enjoyed this book, please leave a review on Amazon and/or Goodreads!

www.ingramcontent.com/pod-product-compliance
Lightning Source LLC
Chambersburg PA
CBHW022027050526
44107CB00096B/59